ALL ABOUT INTELLIGENCE

ALL ABOUT INTELLIGENCE

HUMAN, ANIMAL, AND ARTIFICIAL

ROBERT W. HOWARD

Published by
NEW SOUTH WALES UNIVERSITY PRESS
PO Box 1 Kensington NSW Australia
Ph: (02) 398 8900   Fax: (02) 398 3408
ACN 000 382 669

First published 1991

National Library of Australia
Cataloguing-in-Publication entry:

Howard, Robert W. (Robert Wayne), 1953–
    All about intelligence: human, animal and artificial.

    Bibliography.
    Includes index.
    ISBN 0 86840 252 4.

    1. Intellect.   2. Artificial intelligence.   3. Life
    on other planets.   I. Title.

    153.9

Available in North America through:
International Specialized Book Services
5602 N.E. Hassalo Street
Portland Oregon 9721 3640
United States of America
Tel: (503) 287 3093
Fax: (503) 284 885

Printed by Southwood Press Pty Limited
80–92 Chapel Street, Marrickville, NSW 2204

CONTENTS

PREFACE

This book provides an easy-to-read, broad overview of the whole field of intelligence. It brings the entire expanse of topics about intelligence into a single place, and covers all the major issues. These include questions about animal and artificial intelligence and how they compare with human intelligence, questions about the nature of genius and retardation, new developments in intelligence testing, how average population intelligence is changing, and how human intelligence alters with ageing. Although it is mainly intended for a general audience, this book should also be useful for all those concerned with intelligence, including educators, social planners, and parents.

All About Intelligence has three major aims. The first is to demystify this important area. Few books really do so. This book starts right at the very beginning of each topic, and shows how all the topics about intelligence interrelate. No previous study of the field is assumed.

The second aim is to bring a general audience up-to-date in the area, the study of which has altered dramatically in the last decade or so. Not long ago, popular books were mostly about IQ tests and general and specific abilities, but research in artificial intelligence and cognitive psychology has transformed the landscape completely. Indeed, the field virtually has been turned upside down. Researchers now study learning disabilities, idiot savantes, animal intellectual capacities, computer simulations of human intelligence, strategy training to raise intelligence, expert knowledge, and a host of other new topics. However, little of this work has filtered through to a general audience and no current book brings it all together into a coherent framework that anyone can understand. This book fills this gap.

The final aim is to bring a popular readership up-to-date on many traditional questions about intelligence. These include whether intelligence can be raised, the effects of educational practices such as ability grouping and grade acceleration, and so on.

1

THE MYSTERY OF INTELLIGENCE

Human beings are not particularly impressive creatures when one considers size, speed, and natural weapons. We are not very large or strong, we can be outrun or outswum by many species, and we have no sharp raking claws or massive teeth. We are dwarfed by the whale, rhinoceros, tiger shark, and lion. Indeed, a prehistoric human on the African plain was no match for some of its predators and needed to stay near trees and companions for some measure of safety.

Yet this unimpressive hairless creature now is the undisputed master of life on Earth, and one of the most successful species ever. Humans have organised plant and animal species and even have altered many of them by using selective breeding and genetic engineering. We have decimated or hunted to extinction predators that once terrorised us, ranging from the fearsome sabre-tooth tiger to the smallpox virus. Humans for their convenience have altered the physical environment dramatically, creating lakes, waterways, sprawling cities, and even land where once there was sea. Humans range over the entire planet and can survive in desolate Antarctica, in the rarefied air of mountain tops, in deserts, in ocean depths, and even in outer space. Soon the species may begin colonising other worlds.

Homo sapiens is so successful because of an all-important trait that sets this creature leagues apart from the rest of the animal kingdom: intelligence. Most animals have some degree of intelligence, but humans have it in abundance. It is our species' attribute *par excellence*. It has enabled our great success on this planet, our lives of relative ease, abundance, and freedom from predators. Human intelligence has made us victorious in our struggle with other species.

Intelligence is important. Most governments recognise its value, knowing that a nation's intelligence and knowledge resources give it a great competitive advantage over other nations. Similarly, an individual's intelligence is a big plus when competing against others in society.

Because of the topic's importance and intrinsic interest, it is a media favourite. Reports range from serious discussions of new scientific findings to breathless Sunday-supplement pieces on subjects like a new drug or herb that could make everyone a lot brighter. Most reports are in between and usually fall into one of a few categories. Exceptional ability is a favourite. Newspapers often feature a child prodigy performing great mental feats — a seven-year-old beating established chess masters, a thirteen-year-old graduating from a famous university; a six-year-old with exceptional musical talent is hailed as a young Mozart. Mensa, the society for those who score in the top 2 per cent of the population in IQ tests, is another favourite with the media. Though few who qualify actually join, the organisation has about 90,000 members (see Chapter 4). Another favourite category is the raising of intelligence. Because intelligence is an ingredient of success, most parents want their children's intelligence maximised. Countless courses, programs, books, and even vitamin regimes offer to help.

Then there is the 'controversial' category. Because intelligence is such a value- and emotion-laden subject, new findings or statements can launch a flood of heated arguments. For example, consider the old question of whether intelligence is largely (or even partly) inherited or acquired through upbringing. In 1969 educational psychologist Arthur Jensen argued that differences are mainly genetic and that, as a consequence, social programs to improve the intelligence of the underprivileged had largely failed. This fact had to be faced, implied Jensen, no matter how much it hurt egalitarian ideals. In 1971 Harvard psychologist Richard Herrnstein agreed with Jensen that intelligence is mostly inherited and that social class differences in a meritocracy like the United States therefore were partly genetic. Social status is partly due to education, which is in turn related to intelligence. Thus social class differences are partly innate, and not just due to environmental influence. The views of both psychologists were widely reported and stirred up a hornet's nest the likes of which had never been seen before—their lectures were boycotted or disrupted, they were physically attacked, and the counterattacks by their critics were intense and heated.

Another very controversial topic is IQ testing, controversial because test scores are used to make important decisions about people. In the 1970s and early 1980s the field that constructs IQ tests and studies intelligence was fiercely attacked. For instance, palaeontologist Stephen Jay Gould (1981) accused the field of quackery, of being a pseudoscience on a par with astrology and numerology. Gould's book was widely reviewed and praised, and even won a major award. Many believe that he demolished the entire testing field, but not all psychologists thought so. Gould's own arguments were in some cases selective, almost as though he was a prosecutor determined to prove a case. Gould had argued that because of IQ testing the US Immigration Act of 1924 led to restricted immigration of certain races and nationalities. However, Snyderman and Herrnstein (1983) showed that testing had little or no influence. Gould's arguments really pertain to how tests have been used (see Chapter 3) rather than the accuracy of the tests themselves. To this day, IQ testing continues largely unabated.

A final example of controversy is the effort of financier Robert Graham to breed geniuses. The idea itself is not original, but few have really tried it. In 1979, Graham set up a sperm bank for Nobel Prize winners, used to impregnate highly intelligent volunteer women. No female Prize winners were chosen, evidently because there were too few, they were past reproductive age, or they were unwilling to devote nine months to such a dubious project. Several children have been born already from the program. Graham says that his aim is not to create a super-race but to enrich society with more very able people. The scheme drew much media attention and much flak on ethical and other grounds. But as is shown in Chapter 4, such an approach is fundamentally flawed from the start. Genius depends largely on a reasonable talent level coupled with certain personality traits, and no one really knows how to breed for these characteristics.

A final media favourite is nonhuman intelligence. We share this planet with countless species of animals, all of widely varying intellectual ability. People often wonder just what their dogs, cats and birds can do, and what goes on in their heads. A lot of reports deal with dolphin and whale intelligence, which many people and even a few scientists believe may equal or surpass our own. Some scientists are trying to communicate with them, perhaps hoping to hit upon a Rosetta Stone to understand their communication systems, and some are trying to teach them simple, artificial languages. Newspaper reports also try to rank different animals by their intelligence. Foxes are supposed to be bright and cattle dull, at least in newspaperland. One recent newspaper report discussed the relative prowess of different birds. Apparently the smartest are parrots, crows, and ravens, which learn quickly. Owls, on the other hand, look bright but are quite dull. If an owl is in a cage and the perch is removed, the bird will repeatedly try to land where the perch once was, falling to the ground up to thirty times before catching on. At the bottom of the ladder are true birdbrains: large flightless birds like the emu and the now-extinct dodo, still a synonym for dumbness. Extraterrestrial intelligence is also a topic of occasional media concern. Though it is very unlikely that our planet actually has been visited by aliens, many scientists believe that intelligent life exists elsewhere in the universe. Reports often speculate about what it would be like — could we understand and communicate with it, or to adapt the famous statement by the biologist J.B.S. Haldane, may it not only be stranger than we imagine but stranger than we *can* imagine?

Another form of nonhuman intelligence is evolving before our very eyes: artificial. Though computers have only been around since the 1940s they have since that time dramatically altered human life and work. Some enthusiasts say that they ultimately will become so intelligent that they will be masters of Earth, displacing humans as we have displaced other species. Indeed, Moravec (1988) believes that our replacement is imminent and we may be kept around as pets if we are lucky. Indeed, some artificial intelligence (AI) accomplishments are impressive. Computers are beating humans at many intellectual games — the world backgammon champion lost a match to a computer in 1979, seven games to one; a computer is indisputable world champion in the game Othello; the chess computer Deep Thought can beat all but the very best human players, and in another decade or so may topple the world champion. AI programs called 'expert systems' are outperforming human experts in some narrow tasks. For example, they can diagnose bacterial diseases better than many human doctors, find oil deposits from satellite photos, and analyse mass spectrographs. A program called AM discovered many known and some new mathematical concepts, such as prime number and empty set. One called BACON was fed data about astronomical body movements and from them derived several basic physical laws. The next wave in AI is neurocomputing, the building of AI systems that copy the human brain.

At present, AI remains real Sunday supplement-type material. Many researchers are enthusiastic but some doubters believe that it has been oversold. They point to the relative failure of the much-publicised Japanese 'Fifth Generation' project, which set out to create machines that can easily converse with humans and do all sorts of interesting things. The project's goals were too ambitious for the given time frame, and it was scaled back. The debate between sceptics and enthusiasts fills much media space, as do reports of new AI programs that conduct psychotherapy, predict trends, and replace human experts.

AI has raised another Sunday supplement-type topic that until very recently was restricted to the realm of science fiction. Moravec (1988) develops the idea that the human mind itself is no more than an unbelievably complex computer program, a pattern run on hardware. Our minds are the software and our physical bodies are like the hardware of a computer. Indeed, our programs might run on other equipment. Moravec argues that we may eventually become virtually immortal by recording our individual mental programs and implementing them on more durable hardware. This would mean that we could save our Einsteins, Picassos, and Beethovens for future generations. The general idea has been around for a while, and Frederik Pohl's *Gateway* series of novels explores it. Chapter 9 looks at the idea in detail.

The interest of individuals and governments in intelligence is not misplaced. Intelligence is important, though of course many other human traits are as well. Topics surrounding intelligence affect us all, be they social policy issues which affect, for example, tax-payers, parents, and recipients of social services; decisions about people based on IQ test results; or possible displacement of people by AI.

Let us now look at a major reason for all the fuss about human intelligence and the special fascination that it holds. Intelligence, whatever it may be, is like money. It is distributed unequally and unfairly. Some people have a lot, and others less, and this basic fact of life has many consequences. The following section looks at this unfair distribution, and what it means for human society. The section after that looks briefly at the history of the study of intelligence, and the final section examines the major questions about intelligence that scientists are trying to answer.

THE DISTRIBUTION OF INTELLIGENCE

All persons are not created equal, a point well-summed up in J.B.S. Haldane's famous phrase 'the inequality of man'. Humans differ greatly in many traits. These include physical characteristics such as height, weight, running speed, agility, muscular strength and physical health, and psychological ones such as extroversion, anxiety-proneness and intelligence. Consider the variation in height between people. A few people are very tall, a few are very short, and people have a range of heights between the extremes. The variation between people in many such traits is usually due both to their genes and to environmental factors such as diet and experiences.

Such differences between individuals in a species are universal. Every species of animal and plant has some variation between its members, and for an excellent evolutionary reason. Keeping some variation helps a species to adapt and survive when the environment changes radically. The greater the variation, the better the chances that some members will cope with the change and survive. To illustrate this point, consider two hypothetical bacteria species that live in an environment which previously never rose above 30°C. All survive at that temperature, but species A has little variation in tolerance: If the temperature hits 31°, species A dies. Species B has some variation in tolerance: Some individuals of species B survive at 31°, others at 32°, and a few at 35°. Then things change; a greenhouse effect sends the maximum temperature soaring up to 34°. Species A is wiped out, but species B with some variation has a few members that survive and which happily reproduce and continue the breed. Having variation promoted the species' survival, which is why humans vary a great deal as well. This is also why our wars on nuisance species like insects, viruses, and bacteria never quite wipe them all out, with the single exception of smallpox. The creatures have some variation in tolerance to new insecticides or antibiotics. Most may get wiped out but the few members with inborn resistance survive and breed, and eventually the chemical stops working. Chemical and drug companies know this all too well. They can predict the approximate useful lifetime of a new chemical and so they keep developing new chemicals to keep a species under control. The usual analogy is to the Red Queen's race in *Alice in Wonderland*. Just to stand still, one must move very fast indeed. To keep nuisance species just under control, one must work very hard.

Scientists like to plot the distribution of a particular trait of a species on a graph called a 'frequency distribution'. This makes the pattern easy to see.

Say we take 100,000 adult males and graph their heights. We then graph the number of male adults 1.60 metres tall, the number 1.61 metres tall, and so on. The graph reveals the distribution's shape at a glance. The distributions of many traits have been plotted, and tend to fall into one of a few types. A common one has a peak at the lowest value and a steadily declining frequency as values get more extreme. Consider the number of books written by each adult. It has a peak at 0 books, a much lower frequency at one book, and steadily diminishing values down to 600 or so. Another very common shape is the venerable 'normal curve', which has a peak and steadily declining frequencies at higher and lower values. Many traits such as adult male or female height and extroversion seem to be distributed this way. Most psychologists assume that intelligence is too, though a few say it is not. But that assumption is so ingrained that IQ tests are constructed to give normal distributions of scores.

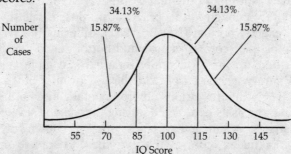

Fig. 1.1 The 'normal' distribution of intelligence, as measured by IQ. Most cases fall around the average of 100, and cases get progressively less frequent as distance from 100 increases. A certain number of people will score between various points, as shown. For example, about 34 per cent of cases fall between 100 and 115 and about 16 per cent fall above 115.

Figure 1.1 presents an IQ distribution. Although IQ is a poor and much criticised measure of general intelligence, we will assume here that it is a reasonable one for the sake of exposition. The curve is 'bell-shaped', with a peak at the arbitrary average of 100. Most cases are clustered around the average; most people have roughly average intelligence, just as most people have roughly average height. There are relatively few very bright or very dull persons, just

as there are few very short or very tall ones. As one gets further
from the average, the number of cases dwindles, but it declines at a
slower rate outside the interval between 85 and 115.

Mathematics tells us how many cases will fall between any two
scores. Indeed, this fact is what gives an IQ score its meaning; it
shows how an individual compares with everyone else. Half the
population score above 100 and the other half score below it. About
34 per cent score between 100 and 115 and another 34 per cent
between 100 and 85. About 16 per cent score above 115 and only
about 2½ per cent above 130. Hence an IQ score of 100 simply
means that an individual is right on the average. A score of 130
indicates a person in the top 2½ per cent of the population. Unlike
height and weight measures, the IQ scale has no real zero point. It is
an *interval* scale, which means that the interval between, say, 115
and 120 is the same as the interval between 100 and 105. Thus, an
IQ score of 120 does not signify twice as much intelligence as an IQ
score of 60. However, what it really means is uncertain. Some say
that IQ is not even an interval scale, but merely a ranking of persons
like runners in a race; for example, first, second, third. The point is
moot.

And now to some complications. A normal curve is a mathematical idea. Nothing in the real world ever fits it exactly, but data
often fit closely enough for all practical purposes. The IQ distribution is not exactly normal (Jensen, 1981), differing in several ways.
First, more people score at the top and bottom ends than would be
expected; there are more mentally retarded and more very bright.
No one is sure why the surplus at the top occurs, but that at the
bottom is partly due to various environmental causes of retardation
(e.g., German measles contracted during pregnancy, severe environmental restriction) and genetic ones (such as Down's syndrome).
Second, more males score at the extremes. There are more male
mentally retarded and more male 'geniuses'. This finding accords
with experience. History has had few female geniuses. Some argue
that this sex difference is due to discrimination against women, and
they could be right. One cause of the male preponderance at the low
end is clear: Some genetic disorders are carried on the Y chromosome, the one which determines a male. This fact has led some
scientists to speculate that sex differences may have evolved. Males
are more expendable organisms, and nature can afford to experiment with them.

Various IQ score cut-offs are used to make decisions about
people. However, a score is rarely used alone. Usually interviews
and other data are used, but IQ scores give a rough guide. The

cut-offs also tend to differ from locality to locality. A score of 50 is a common cut-off for schooling. Anyone scoring below that usually cannot do the work in a school. The cut-off for mental retardation is either 70 or 75, and usually covers about 5 per cent of the population. About one-fifth of that 5 per cent are retarded for specific, known reasons, such as genetic disorders, severely restricted environments, and German measles (Jensen, 1981). The rest simply represent the tail-end of the distribution, just as very short people represent the tail-end of the height distribution. The most common 'gifted child' cut-off is 130, but some school systems use 120 or even 140. There is no specific cut-off for 'genius', but a threshold score of about 120 seems an approximate minimum, some say.

Jensen (1981) also gives some averages for various educational achievements. Again, these are only approximate. The average score of those finishing high school and entering a tertiary institution is about 105, and of those taking bachelor's degrees about 115. An advanced postgraduate degree average is about 120. A study of Cambridge University dons found an average IQ score of 125, but that used a test with a low ceiling, which does not discriminate very well among people at the upper end. Hollingworth (1942) argued that there is an optimum IQ score between 130 and 150. One is bright enough to understand the world and find work easy, but those scoring beyond 150 are apt to have problems with their fellows (see Chapter 4).

An individual's success in life depends in part on his or her place in this distribution. To be sure, many other things are important: motivation, personality, personal connections, looks, inherited wealth, luck, and so on. But intelligence is up there, too. It largely determines how much we can understand and learn and thus how far we go in the education system. Society, by and large, pays the most money for and gives most status to jobs that require the most education and intelligence, though of course there are exceptions, such as film acting. Table 1.1 gives a simple illustration, showing average IQ score in a variety of different occupations. As the job gets more complex, its status and pay increase, and so does the average IQ score of its members. Otherwise, many fewer people would bother to study for years to gain qualifications. Nonetheless, there are distortions. Some jobs that require little training and contribute little to society (e.g., foreign currency trading) have enormous salaries. But the relation holds in general. How could it be otherwise? As mentioned, Herrnstein (1973) argued that this fact means that social class differences partly are genetic.

Table 1.1 Mean IQ Score of Persons in Various Occupations, Taken From
a Variety of Studies

Occupation	Mean IQ score
Professors and researchers	134
Professors and researchers	131
Physicians and surgeons	128
Lawyers	128
Engineers (civil and mechanical)	125
School teachers	123
School teachers	123
School teachers	121
General managers in business	122
Educational administrators	122
Pharmacists	120
Accountants	119
Accountants	128
Nurses	119
Stenographers	118
Stenographers	121
Efficiency (time engineer) specialists	118
Senior clerks	118
Managers, production	118
Managers, miscellaneous	116
Cashiers	116
Airmen (USAF)	115
Foremen (industry)	114
Foremen	109
Telephone operators	112
Clerks	112
Clerks (general)	118
Salesmen (travelling)	112
Salesmen (door to door)	108
Salesmen	114
Psychiatric aides	111
Electricians	109
Policemen	108
Fitters (precision)	108
Fitters	98
Mechanics	106
Machine operators	105
Store managers	103
Shopkeepers	103
Upholsterers	103
Butchers	103
Welders	102
Sheet metal workers	100

Sheet metal workers	108
Sheet metal workers	76
Warehouse men	98
Carpenters and cabinet makers	97
Carpenters, construction	102
Machine operators	97
Cooks and bakers	97
Small farmers	96
Farmers	93
Drivers, truck and van	97
Truck drivers	96
Labourers	96
Unskilled labourers	90
Gardeners	95
Upholsterers	92
Farmhands	91
Miners	91
Factory packers and sorters	85

Note. Two or more averages for an occupation refer to estimates from different studies.
Source. From Cattell (1987). Copyright Elsevier Science Publishers. Reprinted by permission.

At the other end of the distribution are the mentally handicapped. In a nontechnological society, many may have few problems. In a complex technological one, the situation is different. Many cannot acquire the knowledge and skills to hold jobs, go far in the school system, or even live independently. They may need to be cared for by parents, sheltered workshops, or purely custodial institutions. Indeed, some societies spend huge sums to try to solve the retardation problem altogether (Spitz, 1986), and there is a long history of efforts to 'cure' retardation or at least minimise it. A good example is the Head Start program, which began in the United States in the 1960s. The aim was to take preschool children at risk of being retarded as adults because of impoverished environments. Workers visit them periodically and give them a lot of mental stimulation in the hope that it will improve their intelligence and give them a 'head start' on their fellows by school age. In 1990, nearly half a billion dollars was spent on the project, which has had some effects. But studies suggest the improvements disappear after a few years of schooling.

The distribution of intelligence exists, and as with differences in height and agility, it exists for sound evolutionary reasons. This distribution has consequences, and these have to be faced. However,

many controversies surrounding issues of intelligence arise because
people do not want to face them. A major reason is ideological. It
offends egalitarian ideas, notions of social fairness and justice that
these differences occur. This is especially true in the United States,
where the idea that all are equal at birth and failure to do well in
society is the individual's fault is deep rooted.

Inequality is a given, and indeed, the species would be less
adaptive and the world would be dull and gray if all were equal.
Much talent would be squandered by insisting on all being average.
One cannot legislate equality in all things, and trying to do so can
lead to absurdity. Indeed, the efforts of some to do this were brilliantly satirised in Kurt Vonnegut's short story 'Harrison Bergeron'.
The setting was a future America which so prized equality that a
Handicapper-General made sure that no one was superior to anyone
else in any way. The beautiful had to wear ugly masks. The strong
were burdened with enormous weights. Ballerinas were loaded up in
various ways so that they could not move more gracefully than
average. The highly intelligent had a blast of loud noise every few
seconds to disrupt their superior thinking.

Important things such as intelligence are studied in depth. Let
us examine the long history of efforts to understand it.

HISTORY OF THE STUDY OF HUMAN INTELLIGENCE

To understand something — be it a person or a nation or an idea —
one must understand its history. So it is with the study of intelligence, which has a long, long history. Human beings in prehistoric
times must have noticed that some individuals learned most things
quickly and easily, and tended to make sensible decisions, while
others did not. The ancient Greek and Roman philosophers discussed intelligence at length. The word itself was coined by Cicero,
the Roman statesman of the first century BC. Earlier, Plato made the
fundamental distinction between emotion and rationality and classified people by ability into men of bronze, silver and gold. There
have been many philosophical studies and speculations about what
intelligence is and about its highest expression — genius. As well,
laypersons and teachers have developed their own ideas about intelligence from time immemorial.

But science has only studied intelligence for a century or so. A
major early figure was Francis Galton (1822–1911), a Victorian
Englishman who fits the Renaissance ideal of a 'universal man'.
Galton had a wide range of interests and contributed greatly to such
varied fields as genetics and statistics. A very precocious child, one

study (of somewhat dubious validity, however) estimated he would have scored an astronomical 200 on an IQ test. At the tender age of four, he wrote this immodest letter to his sister Adele:

> My Dear Adele,
> I am four years old and can read any English book. I can say all the Latin substantives and adjectives and active verbs besides 52 lines of Latin poetry. I can cast up any sum in addition and can multiply by 2, 3, 4, 5, 6, 7, 8, 9, 10, 11. I can also say the pence table. I read French a little and I know the clock.

Galton conducted an influential study on the backgrounds of 400 very eminent persons in history, asking whether genius is due to genes or upbringing. He looked at their relatives, found that eminence tends to run in families (Galton was himself a cousin of Charles Darwin), and argued that this showed that intelligence is inherited. But his study does not separate out the effect of genes and environment. Wealthy and brilliant parents usually provide their children with an especially stimulating environment and may be producing very bright children in this way. Galton also was the father of intelligence testing. In fact he was obsessed with measuring all sorts of things, and in one study on the 'power of prayer' he tested whether bishops lived longer on average. (They did not, but the measure is questionable.) Galton reasoned that knowledge comes through the senses, and that the more intelligent may have sharper sensory acuity. Other possible measures were speed of reaction and sheer physical energy. In 1884 he set up a stand at a London exhibition which tested these factors in thousands of interested passers-by, measuring skin sensitivity, judgments of pitches, and reaction-times. But later researchers found that these are poor measures of intelligence, with a low correlation. However, Galton's influence on the field remains.

Another major influence began in 1904 when the French minister of education, facing limited resources for schooling, sought a way to separate the unable from the merely lazy. Until then, selection for special classes largely rested on the unreliable, hazardous judgment of an interviewer. Alfred Binet got the job of devising selection principles and his brilliant solution put a stamp on the study of intelligence and was the forerunner of intelligence tests still used today. He developed a thirty-problem test which tapped several abilities related to intellect, such as judgment and reasoning. The test determined a given child's 'mental age'. The test previously established a norm for children of a given physical age. (For example, five-year-olds on average get ten items correct.) Therefore, a child with a mental age of five should score 10, which would mean that he or she was functioning pretty much as others of that age.

The child's mental age was then compared to his physical age. A large disparity in the wrong direction (e.g., a child of nine with a mental age of four) might suggest inability rather than laziness and mean that he or she was earmarked for special schooling. The first version came out in 1905 and a more sophisticated test followed in 1908. Binet, however, denied that the test was measuring intelligence. Its purpose was simply diagnostic, for selection only. This message was lost, and caused many problems later.

The test was popular. But it was still a bit inconvenient to deal with a variety of physical and mental ages. So in 1912 Wilhelm Stern suggested simplifying interpretation by reducing the two to a single number. He expressed mental and physical age as a quotient, with the mental age on the top, and multiplied the result by 100 to give a 'mental quotient'.

$$\frac{\text{Mental age}}{\text{Physical age}} \times 100 = \text{Mental quotient}$$

For example, say a child of five has a mental age of four:

$$\frac{4}{5} \times 100 = 80$$

An average child would score an MQ of 100. A number much lower than 100 would suggest the need for help, and one much higher would suggest a child well ahead of his or her peers.

Stern's idea soon led to a term that now is in everyone's lexicon; IQ. The term itself was coined by Lewis Terman of Stanford University in 1916. He had constructed an enormously influential revision of Binet's test, called the Stanford-Binet, versions of which are still given extensively. The first version used Stern's formula to produce an 'intelligence quotient', or IQ — a term now used interchangeably with intelligence in popular jargon. We think of bright people as having high IQs, while a very dull person has a 'room-temperature IQ'. In the early 1980s, New Zealand prime minister Robert Muldoon commented acidly on the large numbers of his countrymen seeking better economic conditions in Australia: 'The average IQ of both countries will be raised'.

But using IQ to measure intelligence soon met with a major problem. The mental/physical age formula only works up until late adolescence. Mental prowess grows by leaps and bounds until fifteen or sixteen, but only slowly afterward, if indeed at all. There is an enormous difference in ability between an average six- and twelve-year-old, but hardly the same sort of difference between a twenty- and a forty-year-old. The problem is that physical age will keep increasing inexorably, while mental age will not, and IQ score will start to plummet alarmingly. However, it took some time to realise that the formula was suspect for adults. There was an occasional scholarly tome bewailing the 'decline of genius' after childhood, and wondering where it went. Commonsense should suggest that it was not going anywhere; the formula was limited. Later IQ tests got around this problem by scrapping the mental age idea for adults and using an IQ score only to show how a person performed in relation to others.

Another enormously influential early figure in the study of intelligence was Charles Spearman (1863–1945). An English engineer and army officer who served in India, Spearman took up psychology relatively late in life. He developed mathematical techniques for analysing human abilities, notably factor analysis, and also began a debate which still rages. In two major works (Spearman, 1904, 1927) he argued that there is a general factor of intelligence, a superability which aids performance of virtually any mental task. He called it g, for general ability. It is distributed unequally in humans, he argued, and partly accounts for individual differences in prowess. Much of the history of the study of intelligence has involved debate over whether g exists, and if so exactly what and how important it is. This is discussed in Chapter 2.

Sir Cyril Burt (1883–1971) was a student of Spearman who contributed much to the field but nowadays is believed to have fabricated a lot of his data. He had an *idée fixe*, an obsession that intelligence is largely genetic, and apparently made up twin studies which supported this idea, at the same time inventing two co-workers who were supposed to have gathered the results. Burt was also a firm advocate of intelligence testing. His ideas fitted in well with English cultural ideas of elitism, and in part led to a dramatic restructuring of that nation's education system. A government committee which reported in 1943 used some of Burt's ideas in devising a rather primitive typology which labelled children as 'abstract', 'technical', or 'concrete' thinkers. The abstract thinkers were the elite, capable of understanding complex ideas, and were creamed off in special schools and prepared for the few university places available. All were given the eleven-plus test at age eleven. The top 15 or 20 per cent went to grammar schools with good teachers and a fast pace of work. The other children attended lesser secondary or technical schools and faced the prospect of eventual educational oblivion.

The Committee's intentions were good. A lot of very bright

working-class children, who otherwise never would have, made it to grammar schools and universities. But the system for the rest was often disastrous. They felt like dumb failures, officially labelled as such by science. Each had 'failed' the eleven-plus. Motivation to study tended to plummet. Entrance to university was extremely difficult, and many left the education system as soon as they were old enough. Parents who could afford to sent their children to private schools. The public education system was finally reformed by the Labour government elected in 1974.

The field studying intelligence and developing tests eventually coalesced into a subfield of psychology called *psychometrics*: psycho for 'mind' and metrics for 'measurements'. Psychometricians measured the mind. The field was very heavily tied up with intelligence (and other) testing, with tests the usual starting point of studies of human mental abilities. In fact some regarded intelligence as what the tests measured! The tests even tended to direct what was studied. The kinds of questions tackled were ones such as whether intelligence is a single ability or a cluster of abilities, for instance. The mathematics involved in constructing tests became very impressive indeed, but psychometrics became isolated from the rest of psychology. Indeed, Cronbach (1957) pointed out they had virtually become different disciplines, with little contact. Psychometricians built and used their tests. Other psychologists hunted for general principles of the mind.

The practical side of psychometrics — the development and use of tests — became widespread quite early. Indeed, virtually everyone in Western society has taken some such test and has been affected by someone else's interpretation of the score. It all started with Binet and within twelve years, in 1917, mass-scale testing was in use. When the United States entered World War I the military had to build up an army very quickly. It had nearly two million inductees to sort out. Where to place them? Who would become officers and who enlisted men? Psychometricians developed two intelligence tests that helped sort all these people out, at least to some extent. The Army Alpha was used for literates and the Beta for nonliterates. Gould (1981) criticises this as the first major use of testing to decide who lived and who died, as officers were a lot safer on the battlefield. But it is not clear how much the army actually used the test results.

The tests themselves were given under horrendously bad conditions, and the examiners seemed to lack commonsense. Picture a mountain man from impoverished Appalacia filing into a large hall with hundreds of other men. He is handed a pencil and some sheets with strange drawings on them while, on a stage far in the distance, a demonstrator mumbles what to do and sets a timer going. The inductee looks at some of the pictures, tries to figure out how to hold the pencil, and soon is told to lay it down. The tests are collected and out he files. A lot of recruits simply had no idea what to do and in several sessions most inductees scored zero! The examiners also came up with the quite astounding conclusion from the testing that the average American adult's intelligence was equal to that of a thirteen-year-old! A little thought will show how absurd that conclusion is.

The tests also were used to screen immigrants in the United States. Before the 1920s, American immigration rules were very relaxed and the nation became a haven for those fleeing from tired Europe. But in 1924 laws restricting immigration were passed. Gould (1981) argued that psychometricians wielding their pseudoscientific tests were a major spur to the legislators. Apparently, testers manned booths in New York and gave new arrivals strange tests supposed to tap their intelligence. The results confirmed existing prejudices: Northern Europeans were the brightest and should be let in; Southern Europeans and Jews tended to be 'feeble-minded' and should be excluded. The tests themselves again tended to show the examiners' poor commonsense, as the migrants might be asked questions about baseball or other bits of American culture. But, as mentioned, it is not clear if this testing really influenced the legislators.

Nonetheless, the problem of test bias has plagued psychometrics for most of its history. It became a major issue in the 1970s, when court cases were launched to stop anyone using IQ tests for important decisions. The main criticism is that current tests don't really measure intelligence. They measure knowledge and skills of white, middle-class American culture; they are biased toward such persons and discriminate against others. A good example is an item from the widely used WISC test that asks what a child should do if any other boy hits him. The white middle-class answer (scored as correct) is to walk away. But black American children raised in a different subculture are explicitly taught to hit back. Walking away would be social suicide, so they are likely to get the item scored 'wrong'. Undoubtedly tests are culture-specific to some extent, and should just be used for members of that culture.

This point was made strongly by Williams (1974), who wanted to show just what it might be like for blacks to take white IQ tests. Imagine for a moment that you belong to a subculture in a society where the dominant culture is black American. Black leaders run the government, school and industry, and construct the IQ tests to decide who does well in them. You have to take a test that may determine your future and it asks: What is an alley apple? A blood is a . . . ? Running a game is . . . ? Cop an attitude means . . . ? Black draught means . . . ? and so on. How would you do? Williams argues that blacks would be more likely that whites to know these terms and that blacks currently face the reverse situation with white IQ tests. He developed a test called the BITCH (Black Intelligence Test of Cultural Homogenity), from which the above items come, to emphasise the point. His argument has some merit, but the BITCH is an extreme example of a biased test. However, the debate over test bias still rages (see Chapter 3).

One response to such criticism has been to try to develop 'culture-free' or 'culture-fair' tests. These just use pictures and diagrams and try to be as free of cultural bias as possible, hoping just to tap *g*. The best known is Ravens Progressive Matrices, published in 1938. Figure 1.2 gives some examples of questions from 'culture-fair' tests.

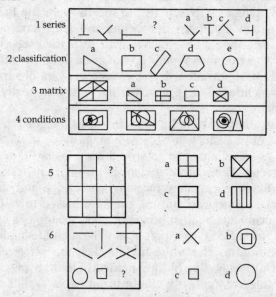

Fig 1.2   Some examples of the type of item in nonverbal intelligence tests such as the IPAT Culture-Fair Test and Raven's Progressive Matrices. The items are thought to be good measures of *g*. The series problem task is to select the figure that continues the series. The classification problem task is to pick the odd one out. The matrix problem task is to complete the matrix. The conditions problem task is to place a dot in an alternative that matches the conditions in the sample (e.g., within the intersection of the circles but outside the triangle). The task in the two matrices problems is to complete the matrix. Answers are 1c, 2e, 3d, 4 (as shown), 5a, and 6b.

By the end of the 1960s, psychometrics was firmly entrenched. It had developed a lot of tests, many impressive mathematical techniques, and tests of all sorts were used for major decisions in education, industry, the armed forces, and government. But psychometrics' attempts to understand intelligence had pretty much come to a grinding halt. Little real progress was being made and the whole field's test-based approach had become stale and arid.

Then something happened that would change the whole tack. Psychometrics' parent field began to take a serious interest in its wayward child. Mainstream psychologists got interested in intelligence. They brought with them lots of new ideas and methods, all to fertilise the parched soil that psychometrics had left. The parent had some criticisms. The first was that the intelligence tests developed were not good measures of intelligence. The developers had picked tasks and questions that seemed to require intelligence to do (e.g., solve analogies, define words) but had little real rationale for choosing them except appearance. Most test designers say the test is measuring g but say little more. What exactly is intelligence, however? Do we need to know this before picking tasks to measure it? The second criticism was that psychometrics did little to analyse what an ability really was. What exactly did a highly intelligent person have that allowed him or her to score well on a test? Smith did well because he has high ability and Jones did badly because he has low. But what did that ability really boil down to? It was a bit like the character in a satirical Molière play who pleased an examining committee as follows. When asked why opiates put people to sleep, he answered 'Because it has in it a dormitive principle'. This statement explains nothing.

In the early 1970s a few cognitive psychologists tackled such questions. Earl Hunt (e.g., Hunt, 1978) began to try to find out the differences between people with high and low verbal ability, with prowess at using words. What exactly made high verbals different? Experiments turned up some major findings. For instance, high verbals are faster at retrieving information quickly from memory and in moving from physical stimuli to articulation. Other work has examined how people solve analogies (A is to B as ____is to D) and what underlies spatial ability (see Chapter 2).

The field also was greatly enriched by input from a subfield of computer science. The study of artificial intelligence (AI) began in the 1950s but only began to make real progress in the 1970s, bringing with it a lot of new ideas and some useful methods for studying intelligence. The best example is computer simulation, that allows ideas to be tested out and forces the people who have the ideas to be specific about them. Vagueness is punished by the program simply not running, as anyone trying to program a computer to do anything knows. Every step must be spelled out, else it will not work. Here are two examples of how simulation works. Say one wanted to know how humans carry out a certain task. One conducts experiments with people and develops some theory, then writes a computer program that embodies all the steps. When the program is run the first question is 'Does it run at all?' If not, then one can examine it to find out why, which is often a humbling experience with gaps in one's theory becoming all too apparent. If it does run, computer and human performances are compared to see if the machine makes much the same kind of errors as people. If not, one must either tinker with the theory some more or return to the drawing board.

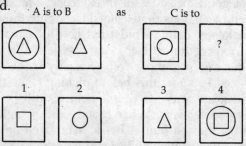

Fig 1.3 The sort of nonverbal analogy problem that IQ test designers like and the AI program ANALOGY can solve. The task is to find the alternative that relates to C as A relates to B. The answer is 2.

Figure 1.3 shows an example. Nonverbal analogy problems are well-liked by IQ test designers because they are supposed to be good indices of *g*. How do people solve them? One proposed theory is that we first figure out the rule that turns A into B and then each rule that turns C into 1, 2, and so on. Then we match the A to B rule to each of the C to 1 and C to 2, etc. rules, and pick the most similar. An AI program called ANALOGY carries out these steps in order. It runs quite well, and solves geometric analogy problems quite adeptly, suggesting that people may solve them the same way.

A second example is from Norris (1990), who was interested in an astounding phenomenon called the 'idiot savante syndrome'. Savantes (who are discussed in Chapter 4) are mentally retarded persons who develop extreme competence in one or two very narrow areas — who become geniuses at one or two things. A common instance is skill with dates. For example, give such idiot savantes a date like 4 June 1453 and they will instantly tell you what day of the week it fell on. How do they do it? No one is sure.

But, at least some seem not to learn a set of rules regarding dates, like the rules of arithmetic. In fact they cannot themselves say how they do it. Norris postulated that perhaps savantes learn at a very low 'connectionist' level, just from being fed information about dates. To see if this were even possible, he wrote a program which simulates calendar calculation acquired by this method. The program did indeed run and perform quite well.

AI research has shed much light on human intelligence. It has shown how versatile and impressive it is, and how heavily it depends on knowledge. Some apparently simple tasks that humans perform with ease turn out to be frighteningly complex when one tries to get a computer to do them. The versatility of an average six-year-old child is far beyond that of today's supercomputers. As M. M. Waldrop put it: 'If two and a half decades of AI research has done nothing else, it has given researchers a sense of awe in the face of the ordinary'.

And so to the present.

SOME MAJOR QUESTIONS ABOUT INTELLIGENCE

Science begins with questions — questions about nature. Physicists ask broad ones such as how and when the universe came into being, what its ultimate fate will be, and what the basic constituents of matter are. Biologists ask what life is, how it started, how the genes spell out a complete organism, and what the nuts and bolts of evolution are. Most scientific research tries to answer big questions such as these, or more modest ones which shed light on the big ones. These questions may be asked out of pure curiosity and/or because the answers may have practical applications.

Scientists have some big questions about intelligence as well. Some have been around for a long time, while others have arisen from new work in AI and cognitive psychology. Here are some major ones. The rest of the book will look at the possible answers to these and a few other important questions.

What is Intelligence?

We talk about it, think about it, speculate about its nature, judge that of other people, and try to measure it with IQ tests. But just what is this elusive quality called intelligence? Most of us have some intuitive idea but find it difficult to put into words. Scientists also have a number of ideas. Psychometrics typically has a fairly narrow view, but new research and approaches have greatly broadened the concept.

How Can Intelligence be Measured?

Measurement is fundamental to science and technology, and to measure something means to assign it numbers or names according to a
rule. Thus, measuring a plank's length means assigning a number
such as 'one metre' to it, while measuring the weight of a cat means
assigning a number such as 'three kilograms'. Scientists try to measure such things as distances to a star or a galaxy or across an
atom's nucleus, and temperatures, immune system responses, ten-
sile strengths, and gravitational forces. Science often advances in
leaps and bounds when measurement devices improve.

Psychometrics has long tried to develop ways to gauge psychological qualities such as intelligence and more specific abilities,
anxiety, extroversion, emotional stability, compatibility with marriage partner, and so on. Millions of tests of all sorts are administered every year and the scores are often given enormous weight. A
single IQ measurement can take on a life of its own if teachers and
educational administrators see it as definitive.

However, whether intelligence can be measured at all is controversial. Some say it cannot. Others say that IQ tests are
psychology's greatest accomplishment. Chapter 3 will look at how
psychometricians try to measure intelligence and at some new tests
based on cognitive psychology.

Is Intelligence in Part Genetic?

This is a very old and much debated question, on which just about
everyone has a view. The answer has many implications for education and for social policy. A question that derives from it concerns
the changes in average population level in the last fifty years, and
future trends. For example, the eugenics movement of the last century was greatly worried that human 'quality' would decline
because, on average, duller people tend to have more children. Many
very bright persons nowadays have few children or none at all,
forsaking reproduction for a career. Now, as family size increases,
average IQ score of the children decreases, but only on the average.
If intelligence is partly genetic, over time the average population IQ
level may decline because dullness is being selected for.

Cyril Kornbluth showed the possible horrors of a dull future in
a satirical story called 'The Marching Morons'. A few hundred years
from now virtually everyone was a 'moron', while the few remaining
intelligent people held society together. The 'morons' were concerned with little more than endless mindless parties, TV quiz
shows, and cars with speedometers rigged to make them appear

faster than they were. They treated any 'wise guys' very harshly, and the society was disaster-prone. There were countless car accidents and passenger rockets kept crashing from the sky, but no one was much bothered. Kornbluth in part was parodying our own society, of course.

Others have worried about the trend. Lee Kuan Yew, when prime minister of Singapore, was concerned about average intelligence level dropping in his nation. Apparently female university graduates there were having trouble finding husbands because many Chinese men prefer non-intellectual wives. All that breeding potential was going to waste. Lee's solution was to arrange free holidays, dances, and moonlight cruises for male and female graduates to promote romance, marriage, and lots of bright children.

A lot of studies have examined what has been happening to average population IQ and we shall see whether anyone was right to be worried.

How Does Intelligence Grow and Age?

Human intelligence never stands still for long. It grows until late adolescence. We acquire a lot of knowledge and skills and our power to understand the world and deal with it gets better and better. Such growth raises some questions. The first is what we know and can do at birth. Many a mother has wondered just what is going on in her infant's head. The second is exactly how growth proceeds and when abilities such as language appear.

Human intelligence also ages. The decline actually starts pretty early, around age twenty, and by forty is quite pronounced. We can ask exactly what does decline and why. Quite a lot is known about these questions.

What is Genius and Retardation?

Extremes of intelligence raise lots of questions. At the upper end are the highly gifted and the 'genius'. We owe our understanding of the universe and the great ease of our lives to many of history's geniuses, such as Isaac Newton, Albert Einstein, and Thomas Edison. In the arts, such geniuses as Ludwig van Beethoven, William Shakespeare, and Pablo Picasso have greatly enriched our lives. Geniuses come in many fields: Napoleon in warfare, Renoir in art, Morphy and Steinitz in chess, and Whitman in poetry.

What is genius? A dictionary definition is 'great originality in thought'. George Bernard Shaw called it 'the ability to see deeper and further'. A traditional view is that geniuses are virtually a different species. But recent work and analysis of such phenomena as the savante syndrome suggest otherwise.

At the opposite end of the distribution is retardation. We can ask about its causes and what deficits the retarded actually have that make them such poor learners and thinkers. A lot of research has examined this question, and has turned up some very interesting findings.

We can also ask what the limits to human intelligence are, and how much these can be overcome by computers.

Can Intelligence be Raised?

Lots of people want to improve intelligence; to make people actually smarter, so their nation can compete better in the world and the individual may compete better in society. Until 1984, Venezuela actually had a minister of intelligence, whose mission was to raise the average intelligence level of the entire population. Other governments have tried to improve intelligence with projects like Head Start or through the entire education system. As well, there are numerous popular books, programs, and courses that promise immense gains; some even recommend starting before a child is born. Many worried parents have been encouraged to buy vitamin supplements, personal computers, encyclopedia sets, and educational toys to improve their children's ability. How well do such efforts work?

Questions About Other Intelligences

We share this planet with animals of greatly varying intelligence, with developing artificial intelligence, and we may share the universe with extraterrestrial intelligences. People often ask what is going on in the minds of various animals, what their capabilities are, and if they can be ranked along a single intelligence scale. A lot of work has been done recently on animal intelligence, and some things are becoming clear. There has also been much speculation about extraterrestrial intelligence. Some argue that, should it exist, it may be so alien that we could not communicate with it at all, or that we might not even recognise it as intelligent life. Others counter that intelligent life anywhere would have some fundamental similarities. Final questions concern artificial intelligence, how it compares to human intelligence, and what its likely future is.

2

WHAT IS INTELLIGENCE?

Here is an interesting classroom exercise. I ask university students how they tell how intelligent a person they have just met is. We often make such judgments about new acquaintances (though sometimes revising them drastically later), but what cues reveal that he or she is bright, average, or dull? After some thought the students give a long and varied list of 'signs' of 'brightness'. Some seem trivial: 'wear glasses' (from reading too much?), 'dress well', 'dress badly because they do not care what others think', and 'have bright eyes'. Some seem more telling: 'have certain facial expressions', 'grasp complex ideas quickly', 'can speak and read well', 'can understand what you say to them', and 'hold themselves in certain ways'. The cues keep on coming, and soon fill up the blackboard.

The exercise shows some important points. First, people have some intuitive idea of what intelligence is and how to estimate it in a given person. Second, their ideas and cues overlap but are not the same. Some stress social and practical ability. Others go for skill with words and mental speed. Some use posture and facial expressions. If the exercise was repeated with people in a quite different

25

culture, the range of cues might be different or greater. Western ideas tend to favour mental speed and verbal prowess, but some African cultures may see the bright as slow, wise, and reflective (Gardner, 1983).

The classroom exercise — or straw poll — is borrowed from Sternberg et al. (1981), who asked a similar question of laypersons collared in shopping centres and railway stations and also of some experts in the study of intelligence. The resulting listing of indicators was long, but it showed some agreement between expert and layperson. Most cues fell into three categories which, together, give some notion of the everyday idea of an intelligent person. The first category is verbal ability; the power to speak fluently and well, to easily read and understand written work. The second is social competence; adeptness in dealing with other persons. The third category is practical ability; being able to solve everyday problems easily, such as fixing a roof, car, or television set. An archetypal intelligent person is seen as being adept with words, socially adroit, and practical.

The list of cues also makes a third point: Intelligence is not something tangible. We cannot point to something and say 'that is intelligence', as we could point to a tree or a rock. Intelligence cannot be isolated on a laboratory slide or in a test tube and pulled apart to see what makes it tick. Intelligence is an *idea*, a concept that exists only in people's minds. We abstract it out by observing people behave. If we see someone repeatedly behave intelligently, investing time and money wisely, adeptly solving his or her problems, and behaving appropriately in social situations, we infer that he or she is bright. If we see a person repeatedly making errors, showing poor judgment, and never seeming to learn from experience, we infer that he or she is dull. We learn to pick up cues to help quickly see who is bright and dull and we then build up an idea of intelligence from watching dull, average, and bright people in action. It is like the concept of *happiness*. We cannot point to something and say 'that is happiness', but we can usually identify happy and unhappy persons. We use cues such as posture, gait, and facial expressions to judge and we build up a concept of happiness from repeatedly watching people.

People's ideas about intelligence usually involve some notion of *ability*. An ability is a power to do something; to jump three metres, run a mile in less than four minutes, pilot a jet plane, or write a novel. Bright people are *able*; they can do things. A *disability*, as mental retardation is sometimes called, is a lack of power to do things.

It must be noted, however, that we are not always rational creatures and that human behaviour is related to more than just ability. People sometimes behave stupidly for reasons that have nothing to do with ability. For instance, we may behave foolishly under great stress. Army trainers know this well and train recruits to repeat certain actions and obey orders automatically, so that in the stress of combat they still fight well. People may also behave foolishly when in love. Hence the old espionage ploy of the 'honey-trap', in which an individual is helped to fall in love with an enemy agent to induce him or her to gather information. People may also behave stupidly through poor motivation or impulsiveness (Eysenck, 1979).

Eysenck (1988) points out that intelligence is a concept and, along with lots of other scientific concepts, it is just an idea in scientists' heads. Examples include *energy*, *gravity*, *time*, and *heat*. What is time? We cannot point to it, and although we have some intuitive idea of its meaning, physicists say they don't really know what time is. Eysenck says that scientists still do not know exactly what intelligence is, just as for a long time they did not know exactly what temperature was; only this century was it discovered that temperature is the speed at which molecules whiz about. It will be some time before scientists do know for certain what intelligence is, argues Eysenck.

Here is a rather dramatic illustration of lack of agreement. In 1921, the editor of the scholarly *Journal of Educational Psychology* asked several experts what they thought intelligence was. All gave different answers, with not much overlap. Here are two examples: (1) the ability to carry on abstract thinking; and (2) the capacity to acquire capacity (which really needs thinking about).

Sixty-five years later Sternberg and Detterman (1986) repeated the exercise with twenty-four experts, to find that progress toward agreement had been unimpressive. There were twenty-four replies with little overlap. Here are four: (1) differential ability to solve problems; (2) proficiency in cognitive performance; (3) repertoire of knowledge and skills available at a single time; and (4) a set of independent abilities operating as a complex system.

Does this make things sound complicated? It gets even more so. The word 'intelligence' itself has so many meanings and applications that many researchers would like to scrap the term altogether. Adding to current confusion is the fact that the various usages overlap. One sense of 'intelligence' is being able to adapt to the environment. An intelligent animal is one that responds to

changes. Using 'intelligence' in this sense refers to the set of functions that make something adaptive; abilities such as the power to
sense the world, build and use knowledge about it, and control
movements. A robot becomes more 'intelligent' when it gets more
mobile and manipulative, gains more senses, and when its ability to
learn improves. This sense of the word relates to the others, and in
many places in this book these other elements of intelligence are
examined as well.

A second major sense of the word 'intelligence' is as a kind of
superability like g, a *general* ability (Howe, 1988a, 1988b; Lohman,
1989). According to this notion, people differ in this general ability,
and this results in differences in intelligent behaviour. Others
counter that there is no superability; that people have a lot of
separate, largely unrelated abilities, such as spatial relations or
verbal prowess; and that the term 'intelligence' should be banished
(Howe, 1988a; Mackintosh, 1987). Accordingly to this belief there is
really an anarchy of abilities, with no central control, rather than a
dictator with his hand in everything. However, the separate abilities
idea is not necessarily incompatible with the idea of intelligence.
People may differ in their adeptness at using all their separate
abilities, thereby producing an apparent distribution of a general
factor. Using the word 'intelligence' is a kind of helpful way to
think, even if it is not very accurate. It is like thinking about people
differing in 'efficiency' (Howe, 1989). Efficiency may be made up
from many separate abilities and propensities, but it may be useful
— and even efficient — to think about people this way.

Nonetheless, these problems of definition are unresolved, and
this book will take a broad approach, considering the two major
senses separately for exposition's sake. Sometimes intelligence will
be examined as a sort of superability, while at other times it is
useful to look at its components; senses, memory, and so on. Clearly
the two approaches are related, in that the superability ultimately
derives from all these others.

This chapter is organised as follows. First it examines the seat
of intelligence; the brain, and what it does. Understanding a few
things about how it works is needed to understand extremes of
ability, human growth and ageing, and new developments in artificial intelligence. We also look at some of the brain's major functions;
memory, attention, and so on, the elements of intelligence. Then
follows a section on scientific ideas about what intelligence actually
is, and finally some traits that are related to intelligence. This chapter is by far the book's most difficult. I suggest reading it twice.

NEURONS AND BRAINS

Plato believed the seat of human intelligence to be the heart, perhaps because it is physically central. Nowadays, of course, we know that the brain is. The human brain weighs about 1,400 grams on average and floats in a fluid, encased in protecting bone of varying thickness. However, brain size varies in humans and *The Guinness Book of Records* gives a range from 2,019 grams down to the unquestionably intelligent Anatole France's 1,017 grams. Cattell (1987) records 1,820 to 794 grams. Brain size across different species does correlate with intelligence. Very roughly, the bigger the brain in proportion to body size, the more intelligent the animal. Humans can do many more things than ants or pigeons partly because our brains are proportionally much larger. This principle does not seem to apply between people, though a few psychologists argue it does (Cattell, 1987).

The Units of Intelligence

The brain of every animal has two major types of unit; cells called *glial* and cells called *neurons*. Apparently the glial cells simply support the ones that do the work — the neurons — holding them in place, supplying nutrients, and removing wastes. They are a bit like support staff. However, a few scientists believe that glial cells may do more than that. Einstein's brain had many more than average in critical areas. But neurons do the real work, and all intelligence in animals with any brain at all is based on neurons. The human brain has an estimated 10 billion, each of which has up to 100,000 connections with other neurons, and on average about 1,000. Figure 2.1 shows a typical neuron. It has a body, called the *soma*, and a long appendage called the *axon*, which splits into numerous appendages at the end, like fingers on an arm. These connect to the somas of other neurons. There is a tiny gap between one neuron's soma and another's axon, called the *synapse*.

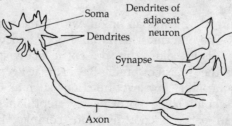

Fig 2.1 A 'typical' neuron. It has a body and an appendage called the axon which connects to the dendrites of adjoining neurons.

A typical neuron works as follows. An electric current is set up, which travels down to the axon's end. There a chemical is released which flows across the synapse to the next neuron or two and triggers off an electric current. In this way a pulse may travel through a long chain of neurons, just as a telegram can be sent though a series of relays. For example, the eye picks up a scene and transmits the image to the brain along chains of firing neurons; or a muscle is ordered to contract by an impulse sent from the brain along a neuronal pathway. It is much more complex than this, however. Some neurons when fired stop neighbours from firing, or raise or lower a given cell's threshold for firing. But the basic principle in action is that, somehow, this system of interconnected units that fire or do not fire produces human intelligence.

Scientists are starting to work out how the neurons manage impressive tricks, such as learning and remembering, which for decades was as deeply mysterious as what lay on the dark side of the moon. Karl Lashley investigated the question for most of his life, and in frustration said that the only conclusion he could come to was that learning is just not possible! But of course it is possible. Learning is related to neurons altering the strengths of connections with their fellows. A simple example is learning not to react to a repeatedly presented stimulus. There is a large sea slug called Aplysia, with a tiny brain of about 18,000 neurons. It cannot do a great deal with so little equipment. If stimulated in a certain way, it withdraws an appendage, but if it is repeatedly stimulated harmlessly it stops withdrawal. This learning occurs because some synapses controlling the chain of neurons alter their connections' strength. They get less willing to fire, so to speak. Some efforts to create artificial intelligence use computers that work the same way: Units like neurons are connected to other units which can alter the strength of their connections. They can also learn and do other interesting things, as we see in Chapter 9.

Brain Structure

The human brain is a bit like an onion, with three major parts laid over each other. The outermost parts have been added during evolution. At the core is the oldest bit, present in many species, which Carl Sagan calls the 'reptilian brain'. Basically, it keeps us alive by automatically controlling low-level functions such as breathing and sleeping. The second layer, covering the reptilian brain, is the 'paleomammalian part'. It controls more complex functions like body temperature, hormone levels, and behaviours such as eating, fighting, and sex. The third part is the cerebrum, where our complex thinking and learning takes place. It is very well developed in humans, but less so in less bright creatures like rats and pigeons. The cerebrum is divided into two hemispheres, connected by a band of fibres. The right hemisphere in most humans is concerned with intuitive thinking and spatial-relations ability. The left controls language and logical thinking. In a few surgical patients, the link was cut to control epilepsy, and the two halves then seem to operate alone. Though the patients say they feel no different, tests show that two minds are present in the same body.

The Brain at Work

The brain is like a busy newspaper office—constantly active. It never shuts down, even when we are asleep or in a deep coma. The electrical activity of chains of neurons can be recorded with electrodes clamped to the skull, or inserted directly into animal brains. Such recording shows different waves of electrical activity that are linked to certain mental states. For instance, someone in a drowsy, relaxed mental state typically shows an 'alpha rhythm', a slow, large-amplitude brain wave. A few companies sell devices which indicate this pattern for people who want to learn to relax. A fast, low-amplitude wave correlates with alertness, as if one is to deal with a sabre-tooth tiger.

There is a brain wave of special interest in the study of intelligence — the evoked potential — and it occurs after some stimulus is presented. If, say, a bright light is flashed, a bell rung, or an arm touched, electrodes show a wave being produced in response. The waveforms are complex and variable, and one needs a computer to process them, but they appear to show the brain's evaluation of a stimulus. Some recent research suggests quite striking differences in evoked potential forms between the bright and less bright (Eysenck, 1988). The very bright, as measured by IQ, seem to show more complex waveforms. Perhaps this is a physiological index of g. Eysenck suggests that raw intelligence has something to do with the noisiness of the brain. The very bright have less noisy brains because they make fewer errors in neuronal transmission: Messages get through more easily and memories can be stored much more readily. Further research may tie intelligence differences down to some clear property of the brain, and if this happens it could even lead to physiological intelligence tests.

Other recent research has suggested similar things. One technique measures blood flow in brain areas at work. If a given area uses more blood when a person is performing a particular task, that area may be involved in that task. The technique may help pinpoint what areas in the brain do what. Work with this technique suggests that the brains of the highly intelligent work more efficiently. It takes a lot more brain activity for the less bright to do a certain task (e.g., matching shapes), and this may mean that their neural circuits do not work as well. This and the evoked potential work support Spearman's idea of g, but research is still in a preliminary stage.

Some Things the Brain Does

Machines have functions and do things — wash clothes, keep food cool, play music. Body organs also have functions. The heart pumps blood, the kidneys clean it, and the liver gets rid of toxic substances. The brain has many functions, some of which have already been mentioned. Some other major ones, that are components of intelligence, will be referred to in a number of places in this book.

The first of these is some power to take in information about the world outside. The brain itself is cocooned from the world and must gather data about it before it can make decisions. A lot of the brain's mass is devoted to making sense of such data. We usually think of having five senses, with vision by far the most important, but when one includes others, such as temperature sense and balance, the real number is probably closer to eleven. Other animals have senses that we do not have at all (see Chapter 8). For example, pigeons can detect magnetic fields to navigate, sharks can detect electrical fields, and bats have a sonar sense.

Another important function is attention. We are continually bombarded with all sorts of stimulation; voices, traffic noises, sights, smells, colours, thoughts, and so on. To be effective, to behave intelligently, we need to select out and pay attention to just a tiny fraction of all that. We select what is important at a given time; for example, a hungry lion coming down the jungle path rather than beautiful flowers or birdsong. We have a brain mechanism to allow us to select out from the smorgasbord, which is well-illustrated by the famed 'cocktail party phenomenon'. One is at a party and involved in a deep, fascinating conversation. A buzz of distractions occur all around; other conversations, glasses clanking and being refilled, music playing, the roar of traffic going past on the street outside. Somehow we can exclude all this from our mind and just concentrate on what we want to. We can do so within limits, at any rate. Indeed, this is a useful practical device recommended for pain management. In the Lamaze childbirth preparation method the mother-to-be is taught to focus her attention on something other than the pain, to 'gate' the pain out. We can get so good at gating things out that we become disturbed only when they are absent. During long-term wartime bombing, people get so used to the noise that they only wake up when it stops. Once in Chicago, the police began to get strange phone calls in the early hours. People would complain that 'something funny was going on', but were not more specific. Eventually the problem was solved. Railway timetables had been changed and very noisy trains were no longer going through. The importance of the selection mechanism is best illustrated by what happens when it breaks down, as it apparently does in schizophrenia. A schizophrenic cannot gate and select. He or she is continually bombarded with more sensations and stimuli than can be coped with, both from without and within.

Our attention mechanism does more than just select. We can also divide it, being able to focus on two or more things if we have to. For example, we can drive a car, chew gum, listen to the radio, talk to a passenger, and think original thoughts all at once. We do this in two major ways. One is just by automating our attention. Once a task like driving is practised a lot, the ability to pay attention becomes nearly automatic and frees up our consciousness for other things. Second, we can rapidly switch our attention back and forth. A person can read a book, watch television, and listen to music by rapidly switching from one thing to another, just as people can watch two television programs by switching between channels.

Attention has a lot to do with consciousness. We use our awareness for a variety of things; to make choices, to understand the intentions of others, and so on. But a great deal of what goes on in the mind is unconscious.

Another function is the ability to learn and remember, which humans have to a greater extent than any other species. If we could not learn, we would not be able to bring past experiences to bear in dealing with a new situation. A lot of the brain mass deals with memory, storing up new information and retrieving it when needed. We actually have several memory systems. The most important are *working* and *long-term* memory. Working memory is one's immediate consciousness: It holds whatever one is currently thinking about. An illustration is looking up and dialling a telephone number. Once the number has been dialled, it disappears from consciousness. Another example is a waiter remembering orders only until they are relayed to the chef. We do much of our thinking with our working memory; mental arithmetic, planning, and so on.

The capacity of working memory is tiny — only about seven items — and is a major bottleneck in human intelligence. But we have a good trick to partially overcome it. The limit may be about seven items, but what is an item? A letter, a word, a sentence? We improve capacity by grouping items into larger ones called *chunks*. Consider this series of digits: 3–6–5–3–6–5–5–2–5–2. It is ten digits long, which is beyond normal capacity if one tries to remember it as ten items. But they can be grouped into 365 365 52 52, the number of days and weeks in the year, and if we do so the number of items is well within capacity.

Chunking is a fundamental principle of learning. If we could not chunk, we would be very unintelligent creatures indeed. And as expertise in an area grows, we form larger and larger chunks and get more adept at using them. Consider Morse code. Initially one's items are individual dots and dashes, but then one learns to group them into larger units, making letters, and then words and phrases. Speed of receiving or transmitting code increases as these chunks get larger. Similarly, one starts at the individual note and chord level in music, but learns to group them into phrases, passages, and whole compositions.

Someone once tried to find out how far chunking could improve memory for digits, and a heroic subject spent a couple of hours a day for two years being read digits quickly and repeating them back. By chunking, he soon got beyond the usual seven to an astronomical eighty.

The long-term memory system holds information for as long as a lifetime. It holds everything we have learned, and as far as anyone knows, its capacity is for all practical purposes infinite. No one has ever gone to a doctor complaining that his or her long-term memory capacity has been exceeded. In another heroic experiment, subjects viewed 10,000 pictures for a few seconds each, one after the other. Then they were shown pairs — one already seen and the other not — and had to say which was which. Subjects were about 90 per cent accurate, showing they were remembering something about most of the 10,000 pictures. Human memory is pretty good.

These functions — senses, attention, learning and memory, and also the ability to move — allow us to behave intelligently. They also enable us to build up our knowledge base, which is of fundamental importance in intelligent behaviour.

The Knowledge Base

A few decades ago, scientists began to try to build computers with general intelligence. They wanted a machine that could solve problems from lots of different areas. An early example was Newell and Simon's 'General Problem Solver', which knew a lot of general tricks for problems of many types. But these general machines never worked all that well and designers eventually realised why. To solve problems intelligently in an area, the machines needed a lot of specialised knowledge about that domain. The more that is known, the better the problem-solving. General rules of thumb were not enough.

The lesson was clear. Behaving intelligently often depends on knowing a lot. A person with much relevant knowledge is apt to behave more intelligently. Indeed, everyday language suggests as much. The word 'intelligence' also means knowledge, as in military intelligence (concerning which there are many jokes). We often say an inept person is 'naive', lacking sufficient knowledge to behave intelligently. Doing well in daily life usually involves having a lot of practical information and knowing when to use it. Consider avoiding being conned. Losing money to a con-artist is unintelligent. Avoiding being trapped depends on being aware of a few general principles (e.g., 'you don't get something for nothing') but also on having a lot of specific information. Confidence tricksters rely on a set number of standard ploys with just minor variations. An example is 'two brothers and a stranger'. Two apparent strangers have a dispute and the actual stranger is induced to bet on a contest to settle it. In reality, the strangers are in league, and fix it so that the stranger loses his money. Another con is sending a company a bill for an ad or directory entry it never ordered. It may pay simply because the accounts clerk believes someone actually ordered it. The trick to behaving intelligently is to know the standard cons and identify one being perpetrated on yourself. A lot of our knowledge gives automatic, intelligent responses to situations. For example, managers learn preset solutions to practical problems such as 'cut inventory in certain circumstances'. Many problems in most areas have standard solutions or standard ways to attack them. People just learn them and recognise one when they see one.

A good way to illustrate the importance of knowledge is to compare people at extremes. Experts in an area generally behave much more intelligently in it than do novices. A high-ranking chess player shuffles pieces about much more intelligently than a novice 'wood-pusher'. The expert knows all the tricks, finding quick paths to victory, rapidly exploiting errors, and placing pieces in powerful positions. The expert computer programmer solves programming problems with concise, neat lines of code most likely unknown to the novice, just as the expert automobile mechanic diagnoses faults and fixes them more adeptly than an apprentice.

Studies show that experts organise what they know into larger useful chunks which allow great feats of problem-solving and memory. Composer Richard Wagner had Beethoven's nine symphonies memorised, and conducted them without notes. Mozart could hear any musical piece once and then play it from memory. Some chess masters can play not just one game without sight of the board, but up to forty-five at the same time. Then when the exhibition is over, they can repeat all the game moves accurately. They do it by chunks. Having a lot of relevant knowledge also means a person can learn more about the area more easily than a novice who scores a lot higher on an IQ test. A study by Schneider et al. (1989) looked at how easily people could learn information about soccer. His subjects' general intelligence did not much affect how much was learned, but prior knowledge of soccer did. Again, this idea accords with experience. Everyone knows people who are not particularly bright but who may be good at chess, bridge, tennis, or billiards. They know a lot and because they do they outperform the bright but less knowledgeable.

But being an expert is not always optimal. Sometimes we can know too much. Thinking can become so automatic that experts dismiss new considerations. The history of science is full of cases of the experts ignoring new findings that did not tally with what they already knew; X-rays, radioactivity, the expanding universe. When experts have to reorganise and rethink what they know, they may lose out to people who know less. Physicist Niels Bohr once said that a new scientific idea only really takes hold when the older generation of scientists dies out and is replaced with one that has grown up with the new idea. Frensch and Sternberg (1989) say that the typical decline in ability to deal with novelty with age may be due to our knowledge solidifying.

The link between intelligent behaviour and knowledge is not news. All human societies have known about it. They give children lots of education, and excuse their occasional misdeeds because of their lack of knowledge.

Knowledge is the raw material for intelligence to use. But there is much more to intelligence than the accumulation of knowledge. Here are some scientific ideas about what intelligence is, beginning with psychometric views.

PSYCHOMETRIC IDEAS ABOUT INTELLIGENCE

Studies of human mental abilities have produced a very impressive finding; virtually all such abilities correlate. Say one gives a large group of people a lot of mental tasks to do; crossword puzzles and analogies to solve, shapes to match up, words to define, and digits to remember. On average, people who do well on one task tend to do well on all the others. Those who do badly on one tend to do badly on the others. That is only on average, however, and performance on some pairs of tasks correlates better than on others (the range is about 0.3 to 0.7; see Chapter 3 for a discussion of correlation). Such a finding ties in with memories of school days. Students typically do well in most subjects, badly in most, or about average in most. Nature seems to dole out the ability to succeed unequally.

What this finding means still is controversial (Kail & Pellegrino, 1985). Spearman (1904, 1927) took the view that it shows something very important indeed — the existence of a superability that aids performance in virtually every mental task. He called it g, innate, inborn intelligence, an efficiency of the brain. Performance on all tasks correlates because all need g to some extent. Some tasks need more g than others and are more 'g-loaded'. Examples are analogies, series, and vocabulary problems. Crossword puzzles and memory for digits are less g-loaded. Most IQ tests purport to measure g, and so use analogies and vocabulary problems lavishly.

Spearman said that g is the ability to reason and to 'educe correlates'. To educe is to draw out, to abstract out parts from a whole, to extrapolate trends, and to tell how things are similar and different. Nonverbal tests like the Ravens purport to be good measures of g, and can illustrate the ability. Look at the problems in Figure 1.2. To solve them, one must pick out similarities, abstract out what is important, and extrapolate trends. It also is easy to see how this power would help in many other tasks. Virtually any task requires abstracting, picking out similarities, and so on. Schoolwork certainly involves lots of it.

There is so much evidence for g that Jensen (1988) argued that intelligence researchers should focus on it, and what he believes is a major aspect of it; mental speed. The physiological studies mentioned above also support the idea of g, distributed unequally in people, while a study by Reuning (1988) provides a yet more striking example. Reuning studied African Bushmen in the Kalahari Desert, a society as different from Western society as one can imagine. They live in a harsh land, and have few possessions. Yet he found that they believed in some sort of general intelligence, much like g. A nineteen-year-old there was teased because he was considered dull, and indeed performed badly on a lot of ability tests that

Reuning gave. Another who did well on the tests was considered bright by the others, who were not surprised at his high scores. Some Bushmen consistently did well on the tests, grasping quickly what was required and making few mistakes. Others struggled to do even the easy problems. Our culture may affect what abilities we develop, but the evidence is good for a general ability as well.

Belief in g has had enormous consequences. Many educators believe in it, or at least in some innate general ability, while the rationale behind most IQ tests·is that they measure g. The belief justifies streaming students by ability, and was one reason for England's eleven-plus system.

Splitting g Up

Horn and Cattell (1966) split g into two types; fluid and crystallised. The distinction is very useful, especially for looking at ways to improve intelligence and to study its ageing. Fluid intelligence is one's native, biologically endowed ability. It is the power to take in information, to perceive things, and indeed is quite close to Spearman's idea of g. It seems to peak early, around age twenty, and thereafter decline slowly. Crystallised intelligence is the sum total of what one's education and environment have done. It is the ability to see relationships, to solve problems in specific domains, to make sound judgments, and it depends heavily on a good knowledge base. A good index of crystallised ability is verbal skill, which depends a great deal on learning. Crystallised ability may increase until one's sixties.

The two types of g are related. A person with high fluid intelligence is better able to learn and use knowledge adeptly. However, people with a mediocre ration of fluid may still acquire good crystallised ability through much study.

Expanding Intelligence Further

Some later theorists constructed 'models' of intelligence which use g and a few others of Spearman's and their own ideas. Perhaps the best known is Vernon's (1969) hierarchical model (see Figure 2.2), which is based on Spearman's statistical technique of factor analysis. Just a brief account of the method of factor analysis is given here, but Gould (1981) gives a clear and more detailed description.

To use factor analysis to study human abilities, one gives many tasks to a large group and then puts together a table of correlations between them, as in Table 2.1 The table shows how closely performance on one task correlates with that on another. One then derives 'factors' or 'clusters' of correlations. An example from Kail and

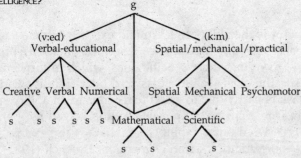

Fig 2.2   Vernon's model of intelligence. Abilities become more specific as one descends the hierarchy. At the top is g, a general ability that 'flows' into all the others. The Ss are very specific abilities. Adapted from P. Vernon, *Intelligence and Cultural Environment*. Copyright 1969 by Methuen & Co. Reprinted by permission.

Pellegrino (1985) is performance on a number of athletic tasks; say the discus, javelin, marathon, and 100-metre sprint. If many people did these tasks and their performances on them were correlated, various factors might emerge — a general running factor, for example, in which performance on the sprint and marathon correlated; or a throwing factor, in which performance on the discus and javelin correlated. One might also find a general factor of athletic ability which flowed into all tasks, with performance on all correlating to some extent. Someone high on this general factor would be a good general athlete. If one applies the same technique to mental abilities, evidence for a general intellectual ability (g) and also for more specific abilities may emerge.

Table 2.1   A Hypothetical Table of Correlations Between Scores on Various Tests

	Analogies	Digit span	Crossword puzzles
Analogies	—	0.4	0.2
Digit span	0.4	—	0.3
Crossword puzzles	0.2	0.3	—

Vernon (1969) put together a model based on this idea. G is at the top, being like a source of energy flowing into all abilities below it. G breaks down into two broad abilities. V:ed is mostly verbal ability, the kind of talent needed for school success; academic intelligence. The second cluster is spatial/mechanical/practical, abilities useful in more practical tasks. Spatial is described in more detail later. Mechanical ability is the power to deal well with machines, to understand how they work, and to build and repair them.

Psychomotor is the ability to learn and execute deft movements and corresponds to bodily-kinesthetic, described later. The broad abilities break down into more specific ones, which in turn break down to very specific ones such as crossword puzzle ability. Performance on any task is partly due to g and partly due to an ability specific to that task. Doing crossword puzzles well is helped by g and a very specific crossword puzzle ability.

One more addition deserves mention. Eysenck (1987) took the analysis a bit further and argued for three sorts of intelligence: A, B, and C. Intelligence A is like fluid ability, one's physiological endowment. B is intelligence A in action; it is much like crystallised intelligence, what a person's environment and knowledge base have combined to do. Related to A and B but not identical with them, intelligence C is what IQ tests measure. We cannot measure A and B directly, so we must make do with the imperfect measure that C provides.

Some recent work has tried to integrate all this with cognitive research. For example, Sternberg (1985) sees his task as filling in the gaps left by psychometrics. This involves figuring out exactly what abilities consist of. But before looking at Sternberg's complicated theory of what intelligence is, we will look at a theory that really straddles psychometric and cognitive views. As well, some human abilities, such as spatial relations, will be described in more detail.

INTELLIGENCE AS MANY UNRELATED ABILITIES

Gardner (1983) put forward some intriguing new ideas about the nature of intelligence. His theory of 'multiple intelligences' borrows from Vernon, puts a new slant on his work, and also uses new research on the brain. He says that there is no single intelligence at all, no superability like g. Instead, there are several relatively independent intelligences which have little to do with each other, which develop at different rates, and which are distributed differently in individuals.

General intelligence is sometimes defined as the ability to solve problems, and Gardner defines each intelligence as a set of problem-solving skills in a given domain. He lists seven 'intelligences', most of which are drawn from psychometrics but without the g.

First, a preliminary. There are numerous human abilities, from language skill down to anagram solving prowess. How do we decide if a given ability is important enough to be called an intelligence?

Gardner gives eight 'signs' that he believes allows us to spot one when we see it. Just a few need mention. One is localisation in a specific brain area. An ability has to be sited somewhere and for most humans verbal ability, for example, is controlled by the brain's left hemisphere. Damage to it affects language while damage to the right hemisphere does not. A second sign is the existence of persons with exceptional talent in that domain, an individual exceptionally good in that area but not necessarily in others. Such talent develops early and with little apparent effort, as was the case with Mozart and music or T. S. Eliot and language. A third sign is a clearcut developmental pattern. The ability must develop in a quite fixed way, although different people may progress at quite different paces. Language is a good example. Children the world over learn to speak in pretty much the same pattern.

When such signs are applied to human abilities, seven intelligences remain. Gardner says there is room for more, but these are the most clearcut at present. Three are tapped by traditional IQ tests and are part of academic intelligence. The rest are more of a surprise but have been included in past works on intelligence. Each is described below, along with some new research which casts more light on their nature.

Linguistic. This is familiar verbal ability, facility in dealing with words and their meanings. A person high in it reads and speaks well and fluently, can easily learn new verbal concepts, and in extreme cases may become a great poet or writer. Language is basic to many mental activities. Much of our thinking and learning involves language and its possession is one reason why our mental capabilities outstrip those of animals. Verbal ability correlates more than any other with school performance, largely because so much teaching and evaluation involves words. Most IQ tests are heavily verbally based.

However, it is not essential to be high verbal to succeed in many academic fields. Many scientists and engineers do not score all that high, Einstein being a classic example. His first word appeared at age four and he himself said he was never much good with words. He thought in images, as many theoretical physicists appear to do (cosmologist Stephen Hawking says the same thing). Einstein had great ideas in images, but difficulty in translating them into words and mathematics.

Spatial. This intelligence is very interesting and much recent cognitive research has tried to pry out its secrets. It seems to peak in adolescence and thereafter decline, perhaps because Western society values verbal skills more highly. Men are better at spatial skills on average, and it seems to be localised in the brain's right hemisphere in most people.

Spatial intelligence is the ability to visualise spatial arrangements and to manipulate the resulting images. According to Lohman (1988), it has several components. One is visualisation vividness; how well one can conjure up mental images and how vivid these are. Some people report no mental images while for others an image is as vivid as looking at something (Kosslyn, 1980). Luria (1968) reported a man whose imagery was so intense that he could not forget anything, and he sometimes slept late because his image of the alarm clock showing an early time was more vivid than the sight of the actual clock. A second aspect is manipulation, which seems to be unrelated to vividness. It is the power to do things with mental images, to rotate them, to determine how they 'look' from another perspective, to alter them in various ways. Figure 2.3 gives some examples of tasks that tap this ability. A third aspect is orientation; being able to see how an object or scene looks from another perspective (see Figure 2.4).

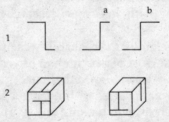

Fig 2.3 Examples of the type of test problems that measure spatial relations ability: the power to visualise objects and manipulate the images. In problem 1, the task is to decide which alternative is the figure on the left at a different angle and/or inversion. In problem 2, the task is to determine whether the blocks could be the same. The answers are 1a, and 2—Yes.

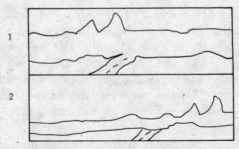

Fig 2.4 An example of a test item that measures spatial orientation ability. The panels show scenes depicted at different times. The task is to decide how one's position has changed. Here one has moved to the left and to higher ground.

We appear to use spatial intelligence for many tasks, the most obvious being to find our way around environments. To navigate around a city, one needs a mental map which shows the relative locations of places and the best routes between them. We also use it in painting and sculpture, in architecture, interior decorating, and engineering. For example, an architect needs to visualise different building types and designs, rotate the images, and add or subtract from them. Spatial intelligence also seems useful in chess: A chess-player needs to visualise how a board position will look some moves ahead.

This ability seems necessary for such occupations, but computer graphics may allow people poor at it to compensate for their lack. Programs are becoming so good that architects can use them to design buildings, rather than having to rely largely on their imagery and on drawings. Here again computers are amplifying our mental powers or making up for their absence.

Logical-mathematical. This intelligence, which is also tapped by many IQ tests, is very important in education systems and in many occupations. Gardner says that Western technology largely derives from the exercise of this intelligence, which has been crucial to the history of Western civilisation. The logical part is the ability to think logically, to abstract from experience, to think hypothetically, to see the implications of various situations or proposals, and to construct analogies between things. Not everyone is high in it. People are sometimes quite illogical, quite commonly committing certain types of logical errors (Anderson, 1990). One method of improving this intelligence is to teach people some rules of logic and how to apply them (see Chapter 7).

Mathematical ability is related but quite specialised, great skill at mathematics being a rare gift. As the philosopher Alfred Whitehead put it: 'Almost no one is capable of doing significant mathematics ... each generation has its few great mathematicians and mathematics would not even notice the absence of the others ... those with true genius are discovered virtually immediately.' Gardner says that this ability involves both a love of dealing with ideas and the power to follow very long chains of mathematical reasoning.

Musical. This ability and those that follow are non-traditional ones that many might dispute as parts of human intelligence. In fact, musical ability is often seen as a gift from the gods: While some excel at music early, others struggle for years and never achieve proficiency. For Gardner, however, musical intelligence involves the power to understand the music of others, to reproduce it, and to compose one's own. Music has three major elements: pitch, timbre (the quality of a sound; e.g., a trumpet vs. a violin), and rhythm. Those high in musical ability can integrate these well.

The most impressive exercise of this intelligence is composition. It seems mysterious to most people, but Gardner says that to composers it is as natural as an apple tree making apples and may occur with little conscious thought. Paul McCartney reports waking up in the morning with wonderful new tunes in his head. Richard Wagner got the idea for his famous Rheingold theme which begins the opera *Das Rheingold* while dozing on a riverboat. Much of the work of composing is quite conscious, however. Many composers use a piano but others use mental imagery. Beethoven, for example, composed some of his very best work while stone deaf.

Interpersonal. A slight variant of social skills, or the 'social intelligence' that a few tests purport to measure, interpersonal intelligence is the ability to understand and deal well with people from a wide range of different backgrounds and with different characters and motivations. People so skilled have an intuitive understanding of others, of what they are thinking and feeling, and how they are likely to react. Gardner adds that it is the power to notice and make distinctions between individuals and their moods, temperaments, motivations, and intentions. People with such an ability may become politicians, good leaders, and psychiatrists, though other abilities are needed for such occupations.

As mentioned earlier, women on average are better at this ability. Indeed, the classic sex stereotypes have males as cooler and more aloof, often not noticing their wives' many signals of distress and unhappiness.

Intrapersonal. In contrast, intrapersonal intelligence is inner-directed. It is the ability to understand one's own motivations, quirks, moods, separate selves, strengths, and weaknesses. Some novelists excel at such self-understanding and description, as do many individuals from more introspective cultures. They know well many of the rooms of their own minds.

Bodily-kinesthetic. This pertains to body movements; how well one can coordinate one's actions and learn new ones. Those high on it may become ballet dancers, skilled athletes, surgeons, and mime artists.

Gardner emphasises that various occupations may need a mix of strengths of these intelligences. For instance, a political leader may need high interpersonal and logical intelligence, and high linguistic intelligence to make persuasive speeches.

Some applications. This wider concept of what intelligence is has several applications, particularly in education. First, Gardner argues that every child should be assessed early in life to determine strengths and weaknesses in each area. Since the intelligences are largely genetic, a child should be pushed in the direction of his or her talents, to make best use of a society's intelligence resources. Another application is to avoid dismissing any child who does not excel at traditional academic intelligence, which some teachers seem to do. The child may have great talents in other areas which need to be nurtured.

PRACTICAL INTELLIGENCE

This ability is not one of Gardner's intelligences, and indeed probably would not meet his criteria. This important ability is an amalgam of several, plus other things, and is one of the three clusters within people's intuitive ideas about intelligence. We will briefly describe it here.

A standard figure of fun is the 'egghead'. Stock examples include the 'absent-minded professor' and high-school 'nerd'. He is usually portrayed as bespectacled, clad in ill-matched, ill-fitting clothes, shy and bumbling with women, and overconcerned with apparent trivia such as old fossils, the orbits of distant planets, and aspects of computing. He is woefully inadequate at anything practical, lacking commonsense and needing to hang about with others of his kind, but is very adept at academic topics. Two apparent real-life examples are the physiologist Ivan Pavlov and the physicist Niels Bohr, each of whom won the Nobel Prize. Pavlov's wife said that he was so impractical that he could not be trusted out alone to buy a suit. Bohr liked Western movies but needed someone to explain the plots. At the conclusion of one film, the story goes that he remarked how fortunate it was that cameras had happened to be there to capture the action.

In great contrast is the street-smart, savvy type who dominates street gangs, prisons, various organisations, and fills the ranks of the self-made wealthy. Such people excel at practical matters, though they may have done poorly at school. They can see a given fashion or trend developing and pick where it will go. They seem to know when to get into a market and when to exit. They know what most people are generally thinking and feeling, can sum up others well, and predict how they are likely to jump in a given situation. Extreme cases are 'operators', such as Milo Minderbender in Joseph Heller's novel *Catch-22*. IQ tests may class them as average or dull, but this doesn't stop them doing well in the real world.

They excel in *practical intelligence*, the ability to readily solve problems of daily life and work, to meet practical goals. A number of studies have examined this aspect of intelligence (e.g., Sternberg & Wagner, 1986) and have contrasted it with academic intelligence. Academic ability, which Pavlov and Bohr had in abundance, seems quite different; it helps in schoolwork, while practical intelligence helps in a wide range of other tasks (Neisser, 1976). In fact IQ tests, which mostly tap academic intelligence, correlate about 0.5 with school performance but only about 0.2 with job performance, which taps a wider range of abilities. School administrators sometimes talk of the 'borderline mentally retarded' people who do very poorly in school, drop out early, but 'disappear into the population'. Their school grades and IQ test scores might suggest a lifetime of super-vision is needed, but they just do not need it. They may have enough practical intelligence to get by in society, but just too little academic intelligence to perform well at esoteric school tasks.

Ceci and Liker (1986) looked at handicappers at a racetrack, who sometimes scored as low as 80 in IQ tests but who were nonetheless very high on practical *nous*. Some spent just about every day betting on the horses, and their mental feats were quite impressive. They might spend six to eight hours a day going through a form guide, juggling many bits of data together to predict a winner. In a few cases they were so adept that they could live off their winnings.

Frederiksen (1986) looked at the practical intelligence involved in supermarket shopping. Some quite low scorers on IQ tests were good shoppers, exercising complex skills in comparing prices, quan-tities, and so on. Kemp and McClelland (1986) looked at the practi-cal intelligence exercised by senior managers and noted that IQ tests are poor predictors of management performance — the skills needed to do well on such tests being different from those needed by business executives. IQ tests tap convergent thinking; their prob-lems are all clearly defined and the task is to converge on the correct answer. On the other hand, management problems are often not at all clearly defined, and the main task may be to decide what the problem is, what data may solve it, and what is the least poor (rather than the 'best') solution.

Work on practical intelligence is still in its infancy, but a major factor underlying it seems to be the knowledge base. People in a given job build up a store of domain-specific knowledge, just as in chess or computer programming. They learn to recognise certain situations and what to do. People who repeat certain tasks figure out how to make things easier: A study by Scriber (1986) found this in jobs that ranged from bartending and waitressing to various positions in a milk-processing plant. This knowledge also allowed practical reasoning to make the job easier.

Another likely factor behind more intelligent behaviour in practical situations is motivation. People are much more motivated to use their intelligence to solve problems in daily life than to complete schoolwork or IQ test items.

STERNBERG'S THEORY OF INTELLIGENCE (OPTIONAL SECTION)

This theory is a cognitive one, and its most complete statement is in Sternberg (1985), which is both an update on his earlier work and an expansion of it. The theory of what intelligence is is quite complex and vague in places, and is probably best regarded as work in progress. But it does have implications for testing and improving intelligence and for understanding what underlies such abilities as spatial relations. Sternberg also gives such notions as g and fluid and crystallised intelligence a more modern flavour. He sees his task as filling in the gaps left by psychometrics, figuring out what these things boil down to. The following account is just a brief summary, which is still complicated enough in itself.

We will start with Sternberg's criticisms of traditional psychometrics, which prompt his theory. First, he argued that the field has been largely test-driven, with IQ tests typically being the starting point of investigations. He says the reverse is preferable; one should first develop a theory of what intelligence is and then derive measures of it from that theory. He also criticises psychometrics for neglecting the uses to which intelligence is put. We use our abilities to better deal with the world. The third criticism, mentioned earlier, is that psychometrics has not much looked at what underlies abilities.

The theory itself is in three parts, dubbed 'subtheories', which do not hang together very well. Sternberg calls them aspects of intelligence but it is hard to put them together in a sensible way.

The Componential Subtheory

This was Sternberg's original theory (Sternberg, 1977), and only became a subtheory when the other two parts were added later. It deals with what underlies abilities such as spatial relations by using the notion of a *component*. A component is a process, something in the mind that takes information and does something to that information (often unconsciously). An example is a process that takes a sensory input and changes it to a form that can be stored in memory. Say a person sees a picture of a space shuttle for the first time. A component takes the image, changes it to something, and stores that in memory. Another example is a component that changes a mental image to a verbal description. If a person is asked to describe his home, a component generates an image and then words from it.

Components range in size from tiny to very large, and also come in different types. The first type are called *metacomponents*, which are very broad strategies we use to learn, think, and solve problems. An example is simple-minded rehearsal, such as repeating a poem again and again to hammer it into memory. Another is adjusting reading speed to type of written material (e.g., slowing down for a deep philosophical treatise, and rereading parts not understood, while speeding up for a comic book). Others are not acting impulsively when faced with a problem, or trying to figure out if a given problem is like any one faced before.

A second type of component is *performance*. While metacomponents help us decide what to do, performance components actually carry out those decisions. There are many such components for combining pieces of information or tackling a problem — for instance, those involved in solving an analogy problem such as:

Point is to space as _____ is to time.

One performance component figures out what the words mean, another figures out the relation between point and space, a third generates relations between time and ideas that might fit the blank, and so on.

The third sort of performance component is knowledge acquisition, which we use to learn things. These include selective encoding, which is a large-scale component that allows one to sift relevant information from irrelevant, to determine from a mass of information what is needed and is worth learning; selective combination, which is being able to combine information into a new whole; and selective comparison, or the ability to relate new information to what one already knows.

The above are some major components. The more components people know and the more adept they are at using them, the more intelligently they are likely to behave. An ability such as spatial relations may be made up of many of these components, relevant just to that domain, and some general ones that cover a variety of domains. But components are not the whole story.

Experiential Subtheory

Here Sternberg gets vague. This subtheory seems to pertain to how intelligence ought to be measured, or at least what important aspects of it should be tackled. He says that the following aspects are particularly important:

Being able to deal with novelty. A novel situation is one for which we do not have a ready-made response; one in which our typical routine ways of dealing with things do not seem to work. Much of our behaviour becomes so routinised that we don't have to exercise intelligence very much in daily life. We adopt standard solutions to standard types of problems. However, difficulties may then arise when we have to face something new. A good example is going to a different culture, where people behave in apparently inexplicable ways. Peace Corps volunteers and other aid workers in very different cultures have a high attrition rate because of culture shock. I knew someone who left Europe for Australia shortly after World War II. His job took him around outback towns selling products. Because most of the locals had never encountered foreigners before and had no idea of how to cope with such a novelty, their solution was to ignore him completely. He even had to carry around a card from his employer which apologised to each customer for sending a foreigner.

Sternberg argues that the ability to cope with novelty is an index of intelligence, which no one could much doubt. Traditional IQ tests tap this ability to some extent because the items are mostly novel to test takers.

Automating Thinking. The ability to rapidly automate thinking is the other side of the coin to coping with novelty. Much of our behaviour and thought is so well-practised that we carry it out automatically, with no conscious thought. When one automates actions, one's mental capacity is freed up for other tasks. An example is learning to drive a car. It is very difficult at first. There are lots of actions to coordinate and one must pay attention to events occurring on all sides. A novice driver is all thumbs. But with practice the actions become more integrated, until they are virtually out of awareness altogether. Learning to read is much the same. First, one struggles with letters and individual syllables, but after a time the whole operation becomes so automated that one can scan lines without much conscious thought. Indeed, some psychologists believe that much of our everyday behaviour is so automated that we rarely think much about what we are doing. These automated actions become the learned equivalents of animal instincts. People even become very upset when their automated actions are broken and they have to stop to think. Sternberg argues that this ability to quickly automate actions and thinking processes is itself a sign of intelligence. Again, some IQ tests tap this ability with certain items.

The Contextual Subtheory

This involves the uses to which intelligence is put. Intelligence helps adjustment to the environment, or at least better coping with it, but psychometrics said little about this, preferring to see intelligence as intrinsic to an individual. Intelligence can promote adaptation in three major ways, which again no one could really dispute. The first is to change oneself to better fit a situation. Some people are particularly skilled at this, being able to figure out the game in just about any situation and alter themselves to fit it. (It helps to have certain attitudes as well.) The second is to try to change the environment to suit oneself. Extreme examples include dictators such as Mao Zedong, who may remake an entire society to suit themselves. Sternberg gives the examples of workers in an area of psychology (learning theory) in the 1960s who changed the field to suit their mathematical talents. The third is just to leave an environment that does not suit one's interest and talents, if it is possible. Lots of emigrants and refugees do so.

As mentioned, the three subtheories are aspects of intelligence. Sternberg describes some ways in which they interact, but they are all hard to grasp. However, the theory still has its uses. It may lead to better ways of measuring intelligence, as Sternberg has developed an intelligence test based on his theory which is somewhat different from traditional IQ tests (see Chapter 3). However, it is still being tested. It also suggests some ways to improve intelligence. One can train people to better cope with novelty, teach them metacomponents and knowledge-acquisition components, and so on.

So, according to this theory, intelligence is a many-sided thing with a number of aspects. Underlying the abilities, however, is a set of 'components'.

Intelligence is not the only thing that helps us adapt to our environment or cope with it, and Sternberg (1986) considered 'Why intelligent people often fail'. He lists a number of factors, based on personal observations, including trouble in delaying rewards, being too impulsive, and having poor motivation.

CREATIVITY AND COGNITIVE STYLES

Finally, here is something that intelligence is not (though with which it is often confused) and something intelligence is like (but is not the same as).

Intelligence and Creativity

An American government inquiry once asked a scientist whether funding a certain line of research would help the nation's defence effort. His famous reply was, 'No, but it's one of the things that make this country worth defending'. Indeed, one thing that makes Western culture worth preserving and passing on is its great achievements in arts, literature, music, architecture, science, and so on. Some commentators argue that most of the really fine work is done by a relative few. Only a handful of people in any generation break through the usual modes and forms and come up with radically new ideas. They borrow heavily from others, but push things forward as well, stimulate our thinking, re-organise existing ideas, and mark out new directions. We usually call this kind of person 'creative' and the highest expression of this creativity is 'genius', described in Chapter 4.

However, creativity is not the same as intelligence and should not be confused with it. Scores on IQ tests and creativity tests (which admittedly are often very poor measures of creativity) show a modest correlation of O.3. A person can be very bright but not creative, or very creative and not particularly bright. Everyone knows people who do very well at school, perhaps score high on IQ tests, but contribute little original work. Indeed, Wallach (1976) uses this consideration to criticise the use of IQ tests to determine entry to graduate schools. He says that they tell little about talent, and that creativity is more important beyond certain intelligence levels. Many students who consistently get top grades lack the creative spark that makes a good researcher or practitioner and flounder when they set out on their own. They may be adept at solving problems with standard sorts of solution, but poor at finding problems that need to be solved, which is the hallmark of talent. Einstein once said that half the battle in research is finding what problems need solving.

What is creativity, then? Like intelligence, it is an ill-defined concept and just as hard to pin down. Definitions abound, however. Mackinnon (1962) defines it as behaviour with three characteristics. First, it must be novel or at least rare. For example, say one is asked the distance from London to Sydney. A standard response would be about 20,000 kilometres. A creative, very rare one would be about 12,000 if you go through the centre of the Earth, or even less through hyperspace. Lots of humorous quips come into this category. Second, the response must be appropriate; it must solve a problem, fit a situation, or accomplish some goal. For example, a quip must be relevant to a situation if it is to be creative and funny. Einstein's theory of relativity is creative because it solved some major problems in physics. An ad campaign is creative if it actually does change attitudes and persuade people to buy a product. Third, it must sustain an insight, for certain sorts of creative works, anyway. It must develop, extend, and evaluate some initial idea. Lots of new ideas need a lot of refinement. Bits are added, discarded, and modified continually. Indeed, many great creative works such as Wagner's opera series The Ring and Beethoven's Ninth Symphony developed over years. The creator continually tinkers, refines, and reworks until not too unhappy with the final result. Many creative people tend to be compulsive perfectionists. A creative person is one who makes responses with these three characteristics.

Because of its importance, creativity is something schools and society should foster. But the reverse is too often true. School systems, for example, tend to stress convergent thinking, getting the right answer, doing things according to set rules, and doing work set and prescribed by others. Indeed, some teachers seem to regard very creative children as a nuisance, upsetting lesson plans or going off on unusual tangents, and finding unusual associations or subtle humour in all sorts of places. One example is the distance question above. Another is a teacher who asked her children to draw a person. One child asked whether from the inside or outside? Some teachers do not understand such responses or they feel threatened by such playfulness. A not uncommon response is to stomp on the child, discouraging creativity.

The very creative may suffer a similar fate in the sciences, and to a lesser extent in the arts. Often the world is less than grateful to people who introduce new ideas. Wagner satirises this situation in his opera The Mastersingers of Nuremberg, where the mastersingers would not initially accept a newcomer with different ideas. People with very unusual ideas or novel works outside the usual patterns may be ignored or ridiculed. Wagner himself had such problems with his 'music dramas', which are now seen to have greatly developed opera. He and other artists may only be recognised after a long struggle, or even long after death. In science, work that does not fit prevailing prejudices may be rejected and kept out of professional journals. University jobs and promotions tend to go to people producing work much the same as everyone else's. Radically new ideas may get serious attention only when a champion promotes them or a field is in crisis and the new approach solves the problems (Kuhn, 1970).

Intelligence and Cognitive Styles

During World War II, a researcher was intrigued by an observation. He noticed that some pilots would fly straight into a cloud bank and come out again upside down or at some strange angle without realising their position until they emerged. Other pilots always came out just as they went in; bolt upright. They seemed to differ in the extent of what is now called a *cognitive style*, this one being field dependence/independence (FD and FI).

A cognitive style is a preferred way of taking in information and as such is midway between an ability and a personality trait. A few examples should make the notion clear. Those with an FI style tend to make judgments by reference to themselves, rather than to the external world. They are not much affected by the contexts in which things appear. Thus, the bolt-upright pilots judged position internally, and did not need external cues such as the sky and ground. FD persons are the opposite. Being greatly affected by their surroundings, they may be lost without external guides to judgments. They tend to be much more social than FI persons, more group-influenced, and able to blend in with others easily. But FDs are less able to analyse things like complex figures, tending to see them as a whole rather than as composed of parts. They also have trouble driving, being less skilled at picking out the hazards ahead. The style affects many things. For example, FDs tend to prefer people-oriented occupations like social work and teaching, while FIs prefer science, mathematics, and lighthouse keeping.

There are many other cognitive styles. 'Scanning' refers to the way in which people focus their attention. Those high in scanning have a very sharp focus of attention, can readily resist distractions, and can concentrate on what they want to. They can also take in more of a scene at once. Those low on scanning have a short attention span and are easily distracted. Then there is impulsiveness/reflectiveness. Impulsive people do things quickly and with little thought. If asked a question, they are apt to give the first answer that comes to mind. The reflective tend to ponder everything, weigh up alternatives, and think deeply before acting. They make poor quiz show contestants and are sometimes dull conversationalists because of the time they take to answer questions.

Cognitive styles are continua. A person is usually not just one or the other, but closer to or further from an extreme. There is probably some optimum point for any particular sort of task.

The relation between cognitive styles and intelligence is close, but it is not fully worked out. Intelligence is a capacity, an ability to do things at maximum effort, whereas styles are more preferred ways of doing things that only have elements of ability in them. Another way to look at a style is as a metacomponent, as a large-scale information-processing component, learned in the same way as one can learn to analyse a text or rehearse a poem. This suggests a person could be more or less field-dependent or independent according to task requirements. Indeed, some work has suggested cognitive styles can be trained. For example, children can be trained to be less impulsive, a useful thing for schooling (Baron et al. 1986).

3

MEASURING INTELLIGENCE

The nineteenth-century phrenologists measured intelligence in a simple, no-nonsense way. They stuck a tape measure on to selected bumps on the head and read off the numbers. They seemed little concerned with the validity of such measures as indexes of intelligence and of other things, leading Bierce (1906) to define phrenology as 'the science of picking the pocket through the scalp'. Nowadays, most people recognise that more sophisticated measures are needed.

Measurement involves assigning numbers according to some rule. We assign 'two metres' to a plank's length, 'three kilos' to a cat's weight, and 'seventeen light years' to a star's distance. A lot of purely physical measurement is straightforward. As long as the measuring stick is applied accurately, its validity is hard to dispute, and physical measurement rarely rests on shaky ground.

However, psychological measurement is quite different from physical measurement. We cannot usually use simple devices like rulers and scales to gauge extroversion, neuroticism, intelligence, and aptitudes. Such psychological attributes are quite different kettles of fish, although it may one day be possible to measure them this way if the traits can be tied down better. Perhaps we may count up a person's total of certain genes, or gauge some physiological function such as the evoked potential to measure their innate potential. But even then, it would only tap Eysenck's (1987) intelligence A (or fluid intelligence) and not B, or crystallised, which may be much more important for the test user's purposes.

So, indirect gauges are needed. The basic test principle that is mostly used today goes back to Alfred Binet at the turn of the century. A set number of questions (or problems) are arranged in order of difficulty. The problems are called 'items'. The subject answers as many as possible, often but not always in a set time period, or with the time spent on each problem being recorded. The number correct (and/or time taken) is then compared to norms based on other people who have done the test. A score on most intelligence tests only means anything in relation to other scores. Without any norms, it is meaningless. The test designers further assume that testees are highly motivated and are working at capacity. Naturally, this assumption is not always true. Test takers may not be very interested, may dislike the examiner, or just not want to do the test. Indeed, one reason for lower mean black IQ scores in the U.S.A. appears to be that blacks are less motivated to do the tests. In an experiment to see if more motivation would improve scores, Ayllon and Kelly (1972) simply paid children for each correct answer, and scores indeed rose.

Tests based on Binet's principle are used widely in schools, industry, the armed forces, for entry to the civil service, and in clinical practice. Why would such organisations want to measure someone's intelligence? To what uses could the scores be put? There are several major practical purposes, each of which is important enough to ensure that millions of IQ tests are given every year.

The first use is diagnosis, which is a concern in education in particular. For example, if a student is doing poorly in school, the first question to ask is whether the schoolwork is beyond his or her ability, which an IQ test may indicate. One also would look at motivation, home life, and a counsellor's own judgment of the person. Most traditional intelligence tests are fairly blunt instruments for diagnosis though: They give a global measure of ability but do not pinpoint exact deficits. However, a newer test called the British Ability Scales (discussed later in this chapter) gives such data. IQ tests also may pick out the gifted. Some very bright children underperform in school and may misbehave and continually disrupt the class because they are bored, not challenged by the work, or resentful at having to proceed slowly. Teachers may not identify them as gifted, but IQ tests may pick this up.

Intelligence tests also are used in clinical work. Certain brain disorders or mental problems may be indicated by patterns of scores on subtests of a test, although this belief is supported more by clinical lore than by hard evidence. For example, schizophrenics are thought to score low on the similarities and comprehension subscales of the WAIS test, while a large discrepancy between verbal and performance IQs on the WAIS may indicate minimal brain damage. An IQ score may also help a clinician plan psychotherapy, with the patients' level of intelligence suggesting appropriate therapies.

A second use is selection, which again is particularly important in education. Places in universities, selective high schools, grammar schools, and in various training courses (e.g., for pilots, mechanics, and aid workers) are often scarce. Those running the course need to pick out candidates most likely to finish and to perform well on the job itself. An example mentioned in Chapter 1 is the eleven-plus test used in England. IQ tests also help pick out candidates for classes for the retarded or very gifted. In higher education in the U.S.A., medical, law, dental, management, and graduate schools typically use special tests of applicants' aptitudes for the profession. Most American universities require applicants for undergraduate admission to take the SAT — a test of scholastic ability which overlaps with general intelligence — and set a minimum SAT score for entrance. Tests to some extent predict how well applicants will do, although sometimes the correlations with performance are modest.

Selection is also important in industry and the civil service. An organisation needs to pick out the best people for its jobs. An executive position may attract many candidates and a personnel officer needs to determine who is most likely to do the job well. IQ tests typically correlate only about 0.2 with such job performance, but the score gives some indication of general ability. Some civil services give all applicants to join an IQ test, and pick out those with the highest scores. For all their faults, as long as they are used together with other data, such scores have their uses. Previously, the main criterion for entrance was an interviewer's judgment, notoriously unreliable.

Another use is counselling and placement. The latter is typically important when a student is in his or her last few years of school or when a large organisation has a lot of recruits to place in specialised jobs. How to allocate them? One can first look at their interest, personalities, and attitudes. What kinds of tasks do they like doing? Do they prefer working alone or with people? Many tests are available to gauge such things (e.g., Anastasi, 1988). A further question is what their abilities suggest they should do. If general intelligence is high, one can counsel a student to try for university or a highly selected occupation such as medicine. If it is not, and grades and other evidence support this assessment, one can recommend some other occupation. Certain occupations need high scores on more specific abilities. For example, spatial relations ability is important in architecture and air traffic controlling, each of which involves the ability to visualise things readily, and to rotate the images. One can give persons to be counselled or placed a series of ability tests, see if they match up to their desired occupations, and if not, suggest some that they do fit. Tests also are used for basic research in psychology.

Here are some major principles of psychometric testing, commencing with an outline of some of the simple statistical concepts underlying them that are also used in other chapters of this book. Then we look at how to construct an intelligence test, which is an essential part of understanding how they work and what they can be used for. Then follows a description of some of the most widely used intelligence tests. Finally, we look at some criticisms of IQ tests and how they are used.

SOME BASIC STATISTICAL CONCEPTS

Statistics is a branch of mathematics applied to domains of great variability and uncertainty, such as human behaviour and quantum physics. It enables us to come to grips with this variability. Some of the following statistical concepts (such as the normal curve) have been touched on before, but will be expanded upon here.

The Frequency Distribution

This notion, which was mentioned in Chapter 1, is simply a way of graphing a set of scores to make their spread easier to take in. First, one obtains a set of scores, which may be IQs, heights of male Venezuelans, reaction times, or blood–alcohol levels. These single measurements are *raw* scores. Nothing has been done to them; they have not been processed. Such a large set is hard to work with, take in at a glance, or compare with other distributions, so one processes them by summarising them in an easily understood way. With a frequency distribution, one simply determines how many in the sample got a certain score and graphs that. This distribution can then be processed further with more sophisticated statistics.

Percentiles

This statistic — which simply tells where a given score lies in the distribution — is a useful way to summarise how a person scored in comparison to others. Thus, if John Smith's percentile rank for height is 80, his height is higher than 80 per cent of those in a sample. If it is 40, it is higher than 40 per cent.

Raw scores are easily converted into percentiles by ranking them and then seeing how many fall above and below particular ones. They summarise right away how a person compares with others. Intelligence test scores are sometimes reported as percentiles which can be converted to IQs. Thus, an IQ of 100 is equal to a percentile rank of 50.

Mean and Standard Deviation

The mean is a measure of the average of a set of scores. It thus gives some idea of a typical score and is a very useful statistic for comparing different groups (e.g., average IQs in different countries) and also in doing certain operations with a normal curve. The mean is calculated by summing up all of a set of scores and dividing the result by how many there are. Thus, the mean of the scores 3, 4, 4, 6 and 8 is

$$\frac{3 + 4 + 4 + 6 + 8}{5} = 5$$

The score gives some idea of the distribution's average.

Another important characteristic of a set of scores is its variation, its spread. In some distributions scores are very scattered; in others they may be much less so. Thus, in the distribution 4, 4, 4, 4, 4 every score is the same and it has no variation at all. However, the distribution 10, 156, 2,300, and 10,000 is very scattered, having a lot of variation. Similarly, IQs in a given family may be much less scattered than in another. We need some measure of variation, some statistic that allows us to directly compare variability in different distributions.

A very useful one used in conjunction with the mean is the *standard deviation* (sd). It is calculated by the formula:

$$sd = \sqrt{\frac{(x-X)^2}{N}}$$

Where   X is the mean,
        x is each score, and
        N is the number of scores.

Briefly, one takes each score, subtracts from it the distribution's mean, squares it, and adds all these together. Then one divides by the number of scores and takes the square root of the result. It is a very useful measure when dealing with the normal curve.

Here is an intuitive idea of what a standard deviation is. Each score that is not exactly the same as the mean differs from it by a certain amount. Some scores are close to the mean and differ little, while others are far from it and differ much. Thus, say we have a distribution with a mean of 6. A score of 7 differs by 1, a score of 10 by 4, and a score of 3 by –3. We could try to get an idea of the average amount each differs from the mean by adding them together and dividing by that number. However, we will always end up with zero because the negative numbers and positive numbers will cancel each other out. The standard deviation formula gets around this by squaring each deviation (to get rid of the negatives) and then taking the square root of the result.

The statistic has many uses. One is that, with a normal distribution, a certain proportion of scores will fall between the mean and a set number of standard deviations. That allows us to see what a given score (e.g., an IQ of 120) means. Standard deviations can also be used to convert raw scores on any distribution to scaled scores called standard scores. These are like percentiles. They tell us where a given score on a distribution is in terms of standard deviation units. Thus, a score one standard deviation above the mean is 1, a score one below is –1, and so on. The mean is 0.

Correlation Coefficients

Correlation, which has been mentioned in several places already, is another important concept in the study of intelligence. A correlation is a relationship between two variables such that as values on one vary, so do values on the other. As one variable changes, so does the other. Consider the variables height and weight. As the height of a person increases, typically so does weight. Tall people tend to weigh more than short people. Another correlation is between success in American society and years of formal education. The more years of education, in general, the greater the success.

Correlations are positive or negative. A correlation is positive if values increase together. For example, height and weight are positively correlated. As height increases, so does weight. A correlation is negative if values of one go up as values of the other go down. Age after thirty-five and running speed are negatively correlated: As age increases, speed decreases. Temperature and weight of clothes worn are negatively correlated: As temperature increases, weight of clothes that people typically wear goes down.

We can be more precise about correlations by using various statistical tests to measure the extent to which two variables are correlated. These yield a coefficient of correlation, which have values between 1 and –1. A value of 1 represents a perfect positive correlation and –1 a perfect negative correlation. Zero (or a value close to 0) represents no relation at all.

Correlation coefficients are a useful research device in the study of intelligence because we can correlate various variables with IQ scores. Some examples of such variables are social class, level of education, and also kinship status (e.g., identical twins, sisters, foster parent and child, and so on). If, for instance, we asked if intelligence is largely genetic, we could correlate IQ scores with degree of kinship and see if the two are strongly related.

Correlation coefficients can be a dangerous weapon in some hands, because they say nothing about what causes what. They merely note that two variables are linked. A classic example is the very high correlation between the number of people in Norway and the number of storks. How to explain it? Perhaps the more storks there are, the more babies they can bring, and hence the more people. We recognise this right away as nonsense. The reason for the high correlation is that migrating storks nest on rooftop chimneys, and the more people there are, the more chimneys and so the more storks. The variables themselves have to be looked at closely to figure out what is actually going on.

HOW TO CONSTRUCT AN INTELLIGENCE TEST

It's a rainy Sunday afternoon. There's nothing much to do. All your friends are out of town, so you decide to construct an intelligence test . . .

Teachers and personnel officers sometimes misuse tests and sometimes misinterpret test scores because they do not fully understand how the tests are constructed. To really understand how a test works, what a score on it shows, and a test's limitations, one must see how it was developed. Test development is a long, tedious process and is so expensive that only a few rich test publishers can undertake it. Some newer tests are constructed in a different way from the one described here.

First, one should start with a specific test group in mind. It could be eighteen-year-old high-school students, infants, the general adult population of a nation, or anyone scoring in the top 5 per cent of the IQ distribution. Ideally, one also should have a theory of intelligence and a basis for believing that a specific task or tasks will tap it. This aspect has been neglected to some extent. Many test developers only have a vague idea that their test is measuring g. Often, tasks such as words to define or analogies to solve are chosen simply because they appear to measure intelligence. Some tests simply use a number of tasks, with no clear rationale for choosing them rather than others.

The next step is to write some test questions. The items can be words for a vocabulary test, nonverbal or verbal analogies (A is to B as C is to _____), puzzles to put together, or shapes to identify. The items ideally should cover a range of different tasks. Test publishers hire highly skilled freelance or in-house item writers who are very adept at creating such questions. They write about twice as many as the final version of the test will have. Editors then check over their questions for error, ambiguities and so on, and discard or rewrite bad items.

Then the publisher's coffers must open, as the next two phases are both very expensive. The surviving items are given to a large group of subjects (a group numbering in the hundreds or thousands) and their responses are analysed. The difficulty of each item (defined as the percentage of testees passing) is determined. An easy item is one that most people get right, a hard one is one that most fail. Unreliable items, that is, those that do not correlate well with the final score, are discarded. One also sees if the test produces a roughly normal distribution of scores. If it does not, selected items are discarded until it does.

The surviving items form a first version of the test, which is customarily arranged in order of difficulty, with the easy items first.

The test is then given to a large *standardisation sample*, another group often numbering in the thousands. From their scores, one determines norms (means, standard deviations, percentiles, etc.) which give the scores of later test-takers their meaning. For example, the original sample for the Scholastic Aptitude Test (SAT) consisted of 11,000 candidates for university who took the test in 1941. The original group's mean on the test's verbal and quantitative sections was scaled to be 500. Scores given to testees today are scaled in comparison to that 1941 group, allowing different years to be compared. Only about 20 per cent of present-day takers score as high as 500 on the verbal section, however. For IQ tests, norms are often given for different age groups, as raw scores may change with age.

Finally, one determines the test's reliability and validity. A test is seen to be reliable if it gives much the same score when taken at different times, just as rulers are reliable measures of length because they give pretty much the same result (within limits) whenever used. An unreliable test is not much use. Unreliability can be due to ambiguous questions or faulty administration of conditions. Reliability can be measured in several ways. The first is just to give it to a group twice, some months apart. One then correlates the scores to see if they are much the same. A second is to construct two or more versions of a test. One administers both versions to the same group and correlates the scores. A third method is called split-half. One correlates scores on half the test items with scores on the other half, say the odd numbers with the evens. If a test is too unreliable, it may go back to the drawing board for redevelopment. Many tests are very reliable, with a correlation between scores of over 0.9.

Validity is much trickier to determine. A test is valid if it measures what it is supposed to. A ruler is a valid measure of length and a balance scale of weight. Size of head bumps is an invalid measure of intelligence, extroversion, and dress sense. An intelligence test is valid if it does measure intelligence. But a problem crops up right away. As we saw in Chapter 2, there is no good definition of intelligence, so how can a test be validated?

Some critics say that test developers do not adequately solve this problem, while designers usually consider a test validated if it meets several criteria. One is that scores on it correlate well with scores on an old, established test: The Wechsler Adult Intelligence Scale (WAIS) is a benchmark here. They may also correlate test scores with some external criterion such as school grades, achievements in life, and so on. One can also see if the test yields an age progression, at least with children. Do scores get progressively higher with different groups of older and older ages? The validity of tests of specific abilities, such as mechanical aptitude, are a bit easier to determine. One can simply see if people who score high on a test do better in practical tasks or in specific mechanics courses.

When these steps are completed, and the test is deemed to have sufficient reliability and validity, you have a test. You can now write a manual giving the test's rationale, instructions on how to administer and score it, all the norms, and research done on it . . . and then set about selling it.

SOME INTELLIGENCE TESTS

There are literally hundreds of intelligence tests in existence, all of them listed in catalogues as books are. Tests are available for many groups — amongst them the gifted, mentally retarded, infants, Mensa candidates, children from two to seventeen, or the general adult population.

These tests tend to have a number of characteristics. Most are timed: A testee usually has a set time to do the items. Many high-level tests are designed to be so difficult that no one finishes in the set time. This means that mental speed is considered an important aspect of intelligence. (In other cases, as mentioned, time to do a certain item is recorded.) The faster the time, the higher the score. Whether speed should be part of tested intelligence is sometimes questioned (Sternberg, 1985) since a test might class as dull a wise person who always makes the right decisions but ponders everything deeply before acting. Second, tests typically yield IQ scores or percentiles, or standard scores of some type. Some tests give only a single score, others give scores on a number of subtests.

The nature of most tests and the way they are given means that tested IQ, assumed as the measure of intelligence, consists of three main factors (Eysenck, 1979). Doing well on all three yields a high score. Eysenck maintains that we can split IQ into these three parts. The first is speed, as mentioned above. All other things being equal, the faster one is the higher one's score. The second is answer-checking, a useful strategy that test-wise persons know. One simply looks at items completed later on to check their accuracy. Not everyone does. The third is simple persistence, the capacity to struggle on with the test and with the tougher problems. Some of these factors — especially persistence — have more to do with personality and test experience than intelligence. That is another reason why IQ tests are imperfect measures of intelligence.

The three-part split also means that people can get the same IQ score in different ways, again highlighting the point that a single test score does not tell a lot about mental capacity. One person can be fast but not persistent, not bother to check answers, and score 110. Another person could be slow, persistent, check carefully, and also score 110. The first person might attempt many more items but make many more errors. However, some newer tests are constructed in a different way, and as we will see, they get around such problems to some extent.

As mentioned, publishers list their tests in catalogues. Each entry briefly describes the test, its target group, and similar details. One simply orders test materials such as answer sheets, scoring keys (when scoring is not done by computer) and manuals, and other bits such as puzzles, blocks, and so on, which are used in some tests. Most tests can only be bought by trained users, such as professional psychologists. There are several reasons for this, the first of which is simply security. Tests are used to make important decisions and their validity would be destroyed if anyone could find out the answers. Tests used to control entry to university or graduate schools (such as the SAT and Miller Analogies Test) are kept under very tight security indeed. A second reason is to prevent misuse. As mentioned, test scores must be interpreted carefully by trained people. Given the weight that many people ascribe to IQ scores, an inexperienced tester let loose on the world can do a lot of damage by giving out scores indiscriminately.

Test manuals tend to be fairly self-congratulatory. It's hard to get any serious evaluation of a test from them. One can do so, however, by checking reviews of a given test in a weighty tome by A. Buros called *The Mental Measurements Yearbook*. Reviews in it look at the validity and reliability of various important tests, and at research done on them.

Good tests are often revised, just as textbooks are. The meaning of words used in them may change (such as 'gay'), educational practices may mean that certain classes of item lose their validity, and the norms themselves may have to be updated.

The tests available fall into a number of categories. First, there are individual and group tests. *Individual* tests, such as the WAIS, WISC, and Stanford-Binet, are administered by a skilled tester to just one person at a time. Typically, the tester sits across a table and gives items one by one. Instructions are given verbally, and any problems in doing certain items are noted. This procedure is expensive but is best. One can see if the testee understands what to do, is motivated or not, and can spot problems (e.g., due to cultural differences) that affect the test's validity. *Group* tests, such as the Ravens Progressive Matrices and Otis-Lennon, are given to several people at a time. Typically, a printed form with instructions is given out (or the examiner may give these verbally). All the items are on the form. This procedure is inexpensive and easy but problems of motivation and lack of understanding may occur. Indeed, in the Army Alpha tests of 1917, many inductees were unclear what to do and scored zero.

Second, there are general ability and specific aptitude tests. General ability tests give a single final score (such as an IQ) which purport to measure 'general intelligence'. Though a test may consist of several subtests, in the end one sums them up to a single number. Aptitude tests, however, tap more specific abilities and in that sense are not measures of general intelligence at all. Thus, one might tap specific aptitudes such as numerical or mechanical ability, clerical speed, aptitude for flight training, or officer candidacy. As mentioned, such tests are useful for choosing people for specific jobs or training courses, or in finding a niche for a particular person. General intelligence may not be such a useful predictor of performance in more specific cases.

There is also a major distinction between verbal and nonverbal tests. Verbal ones rely largely on words. They usually consist of vocabulary items (define palindrome), verbal analogies (duck is to hatch as refrigerator is to _____[build]), general knowledge (the capital of Paraguay is?), and so on.

Here are some specific tests. Those arising mainly from the psychometric tradition are covered first, and then some based on newer models of intelligence.

The Stanford-Binet
This test is the grandfather of many later ones. First developed in 1916, versions of it are still widely used. Materials needed to administer it include some toys, books of printed cards, beads, and pictures of animals.

The age range is from about thirty months upwards, but the test is not all that useful for adults. It is administered individually by a highly trained examiner. At the early ages, children need to identify objects, repeat digits, and identify the uses of certain objects. At later ages they define words, describe the similarities and differences between things (e.g., cars and trucks), attempt vocabulary and analogy problems, and show comprehension of aspects of life. Questions for older testees mainly tend to tap verbal skills.

The test's rationale is that it is measuring g, broken down into fluid and crystallised intelligence, and working memory. Each of these is tapped by a variety of subtests. For example, crystallised ability is tapped by vocabulary and by comprehension tests (e.g., Why do people obey laws?). The test's early versions determined mental age and converted it to IQ. The latest version shuns the term IQ for 'standard age score', which is pretty much the same thing.

The test's validity seems sound. There is a reliable age progression; children of progressively older ages get more and more items correct. Scores correlate well with school achievement and with other IQ test scores, and the items look as if they measure intelligence (Murphy and Davidshofer, 1988).

Wechsler Scales: WAIS and WISC

The WAIS and Wechsler Intelligence Scale for Children (WISC) are both benchmarks of intelligence testing. They are veteran work-horses used extensively for purposes ranging from education to clinical work. As such they are so highly esteemed that anyone publishing a new test will proudly display its validity by showing high correlations with WAIS or WISC scores. Both tests are

Table 3.1   The Scales on the WAIS Test. Each Sums to a Verbal and a Performance IQ That are Added Together to Get the Final IQ

Verbal Scales

Information. This scale taps general knowledge (e.g., What is the capital of Paraguay? What are the Gnostic gospels?)

Similarities. Several pairs of words are presented and the testee has to say how they are similar (e.g., pencil and pen; colt and duckling)

Vocabulary. The testee is given some words to define

Arithmetic reasoning. One must solve several arithmetic problems (e.g., if apples cost 60 cents a dozen, how much do three cost?)

Comprehension. A series of questions that tap understanding of why some things are the way they are (e.g., why do governments require drivers to be licensed?)

Digit span. This tests short-term memory. One is given a series of digits in rapid succession and must repeat them

Performance Scales

Object assembly. This is like a set of jigsaw puzzles. The testee puts together a number of pieces to form a picture of something. Time to do so is recorded

Block design. There are a number of small blocks, with half of a side on each coloured in. The testee must arrange the blocks in a series of patterns

Picture arrangement. A series of pictures go together in a sequence to make a story (e.g., the steps in making a meal). They are jumbled up and must be put together in the correct sequence

Digit symbol. This scale taps clerical-type speed. There is a code in which a number from 1 to 5 is paired with a geometric symbol. The testee must put the code number by each symbol. Score is number correct in a set time

Picture completion. A series of pictures of objects with a feature missing which must be supplied (e.g., a bicycle without one wheel)

descended in part from the Army Alpha test, David Wechsler adapting some of the tasks and item types of that famous test. Another predecessor is the Wechsler-Bellevue Intelligence Scale, published in 1939 as an adult equivalent of the Stanford-Binet. The first WAIS version came out in 1955, and was revised in 1981. The new version is called the WAIS-R, the R standing for 'revised'. The WISC is an easier version of the WAIS, with most of the same scales.

The WAIS-R has eleven subscales: Six scale scores sum to a verbal IQ and five to a performance IQ, these adding up to a single IQ score. The scales are described in Table 3.1 The test's major rationale is that it taps g, the verbal scales mostly tapping crystallised intelligence and the performance one's fluid intelligence. The pattern of subscale scores may indicate various disorders, or at least a pattern of a person's strengths and weaknesses, although all subscale scores correlate with each other. The WAIS also shows a clear ageing pattern, as we see in more detail in Chapter 6. Raw scores in the performance scales decline at an earlier age, and more precipitously than those in the verbal ones.

Ravens Progressive Matrices

There are three versions of this test — one for children, a 'standard' version, and an advanced test for very bright testees — which was published in 1938 as a 'culture-fair' measure of g; abstract reasoning ability, and eduction of correlates. Figure 1.2 shows some examples of items. The general trick is to figure out how the patterns change, and what rules govern the changes from part to part. Rules in the earlier problems are quite simple, such as 'add one figure', or 'superimpose one over another', but they get very difficult. Since the test has no verbal items, it was assumed to be less biased against persons from other cultures. This assumption is questionable, however. The Ravens is an untimed, group test.

The Differential Aptitude Test (DAT)

This test, which has eight scales, is a cross between an aptitude test and a general intelligence test. The scales include several thought to tap g — verbal reasoning, numerical ability, and abstract reasoning (which has nonverbal problems) — which can be summed to an IQ score. The others tap specific aptitudes; spatial relations, mechanical reasoning (the ability to recognise everyday physical forces and principles), clerical speed and accuracy, and language usage.

The main target group is final-year high-school students. They take the whole test and a profile is used for career counselling. For example, journalism or writing requires good language usage and verbal reasoning, architecture requires high spatial relations, and engineering needs mechanical ability and perhaps spatial relations as well.

Miller Analogies Test

This is a very high level test used mainly for graduate-school admission in the United States. Consisting of several complex analogy problems based on concepts from many fields, it is held under strict security because scores control admission to greatly prized graduate schools.

Scholastic Aptitude Test (SAT)

The SAT, which is given to high-school students in their last years at school, is not strictly an IQ test. Rather, it is a test of academic ability, which is what many see most IQ tests as being. Scores are used to select people for colleges and by counsellors to give career guidance, and for these reasons the SAT is held under high security. The test takes about half a day to do. There are two sections. The verbal part uses analogies, sentence completions, and antonyms to tap ability to extract meaning from and answer questions about obscurely written passages (a useful academic skill!). The quantitative part involves various arithmetic and mathematics problems that tap computational ability and understanding of some mathematical concepts.

Instead of giving an IQ, the SAT supplies a separate score for each section on a scale from 200 to 800. These have a mean of 500 and a standard deviation of 100. As mentioned, means are given for the original 1941 standardisation sample. Though new versions of the test are constructed every year, scores on each only have meaning when compared to the original standardisation sample, with a tricky statistical procedure too complex to delve into here.

There has been a steady decline in mean scores since the 1960s which, though it was halted slightly in 1980, has prompted much soul searching and research to find its causes. One reason is simply that more people are taking the test and the sample is less selected. But at least part of the decline seems to be due to the general decline in scholastic standards in the U.S.A., lamented by many (e.g., Hirsch, 1987), who feel that schools are teaching less and less.

Alice Heim Tests

A problem with many tests is that they have a low ceiling and do not discriminate well (or at all in some cases) between people beyond IQ 120 or 130. But Aliee Heim has constructed two important tests for people at the upper end of the intelligence distribution. The AH5 and AH6 tests cover verbal reasoning by analogies and classification, and some quantitative problems, and are quite tricky and hard to do. However, one problem with these tests is that there are no norms. The standardisation sample which really gives the scores meaning has been omitted. But they are useful for certain purposes.

Kaufman Assessment Battery for Children (K-ABC)
This is a relatively new individual test, published in 1983, which has proved very popular. It partly taps fluid and crystallised intelligence, and is also based on recent findings in cognitive psychology. The test's age range is two and a half to twelve and a half years and the items are mostly nonverbal. The test itself is divided into a Mental Processing section (measuring fluid) and an Achievement section (measuring crystallised). The latter has traditional tests of general knowledge, arithmetic, and reading comprehension. The Mental Processing section also uses a fundamental distinction between *sequential* and *simultaneous* processing, which are considered to be different ways of thinking. Sequential is solving problems one step after another like a computer. Simultaneous processing requires taking lots of information and integrating it to solve a problem. It's almost like having to write an essay; taking diverse information from many sources to answer the question.

Sternberg's Intelligence Scale
This test is another of the new breed, based on cognitive psychology and more explicit theories of what intelligence is. Sternberg believes that traditional intelligence tests focus too narrowly on academic intelligence, at the expense of practical intelligence and other aspects of intelligence, such as the ability to deal with novelty, and the ability to automate one's processing. Traditional tests tap novelty and automatisation to some extent, but perhaps these can be more directly measured. Sternberg's test measures a broader range, including the ability to automate, to cope with novelty, to show insight, and the components that a person knows and can use adeptly. Here are some examples of items.

The ability to deal with novelty is assessed by sample items such as these, from Sternberg (1986):

1. Villains are loveable. Hero is to admiration as villain is to:

    (a) Contempt
    (b) Affection
    (c) Cruel
    (d) Kind
2. Lemons are animals. Lime is to green as lemon is to:
    (a) Yellow
    (b) Orange
    (c) Row
    (d) Pick

The problems are tricky. They are novel in that most people have never done anything much like them before, and one must figure out how accepting the premise will create a novel situation. The items also tap an aspect of 'insight'. One must figure out if the premise really is relevant. In the first, it does change the analogy (the answer being b) but in the second it does not (the answer being a). The items also tap various components; for example, metacomponents of figuring out what to do, and so on. The following two questions also tap 'insight', figuring out what information is relevant to solving the problems:

3. In a town 20% of adults have unlisted phone numbers. You take out 100 names at random from the phone book. How many would you expect to be unlisted?

4. In the Jones family, there are five brothers and each brother has one sister. If you count Mrs Jones, how many females are there in the family?

The first answer of course is zero, as the unlisted names will not be in the phone book. In the second, the answer is two, as all the brothers have the same sister. One must read the questions carefully to decide what is relevant.

    The next question type taps a variety of components, performance, knowledge acquisition or meta:

5. Classify the relation between these words.
    (a) clue: hint
    (b) dial: laid

The first pair are synonyms, and the second two are anagrams; dial is laid spelled backwards. The items also tap understanding of relationships, an aspect of fluid intelligence.

    The next item taps practical ability:

6. Rate the following factors in importance as qualities of a good

manager.
(a) critical thinking ability
(b) willingness to take risks, etc.

There is also a digit symbol pairing test like that on the WAIS, which taps ability to quickly automate. Sternberg argues that testees will score higher if they can quickly automate the components involved in doing the task.

It will be interesting to see what unfolds with experience with this test; how well it correlates with school performance, work performance, and so on.

The British Ability Scales (BAS)

This test is quite a departure from traditional intelligence tests. Originally titled the British Intelligence Scale, it is an individual test developed over fifteen years for use with children aged between two and a half and seventeen years. The first version came out in 1979 and a revised version emerged in 1982. It comes in a large suitcase stuffed with toys, cards, printed forms, and a variety of objects all of which are very hard to fit back into the case.

The test has a number of interesting features. First, it is soundly based on psychology theories. The BAS makes use of information-processing theories of the mind, Jean Piaget's developmental theory, and Lawrence Kohlberg's theory of moral development. Second, it samples a wide range of cognitive abilities, of powers we associate with intelligence. There are no fewer than twenty-three scales that cover such mental functions as working memory, spatial relations, speed of thinking, and social and moral reasoning. These allow a profile of a person's intellectual strengths and weaknesses. Thus one can do what most IQ tests do not allow; pinpoint the nature of a child's learning disabilities or gifts.

The twenty-three scales fall into five categories: reasoning, spatial imagery, perceptual matching, short-term memory, and retrieval and application of knowledge. One can also sum up scores on several scales to get an IQ.

The test is unusual in another respect. It uses a statistical procedure called Rasch scaling (see Anastasi, 1988). This method gets away from the traditional idea of an IQ meaning something only in relation to a group. Rasch scaling gives a more absolute measure of ability. However, discussing the intricacies of this procedure is beyond the scope of this book.

A major use of the test is diagnosis, and as mentioned, one can get a clear idea of what deficits a child in school may have which lead to poor performance. One first entertains some hypotheses about what problems may exist, and gives a set of scales to determine this, rather than all twenty-three. The test's manual gives some examples. Here is one. James (aged four) showed poor attention in class and difficulty in motor coordination. Six BAS scales were given. They revealed deficits in three scales which involved visual material: copying, visual recognition, and naming vocabulary. His verbal comprehension was at least average and his verbal–tactile matching was above average. The problem seemed to be difficulty in dealing with visual materials and he was recommended for a lot of practice in tasks with them, including language tasks with pictures.

Computerised Intelligence Testing

Tests are still largely based on the technology of 1904; pencil, paper, and a human examiner. To be sure, the mathematics behind many of the tests has become very sophisticated, but the general technology has not. Updating by using computers has a number of advantages (Murphy & Davidshofer, 1988). First, there is no examiner to like or dislike, which can affect motivation. (Against this, a disadvantage is that the computer cannot readily judge things like testees' motivation, anxiety, and so on.) It is easier to record times to take items, and it is also much easier to tap an individual's ability level. Most tests start with a number of items that may be too easy or too hard, leading to frustration or a feeling of being insulted. One can just start with a moderately difficult item and then adjust other items given according to how the testee responds. It is also much easier to make the test interactive, presenting branching versions of a test. Research suggests that testees like taking computerised tests and their scores correlate pretty highly with pencil and paper ones (Murphy & Davidshofer, 1988).

MISUSES OF INTELLIGENCE TESTS

In the 1970s and early 1980s, psychometrics and intelligence tests came under fierce attack. Gould (1981) and Evans and Waites (1981) launched broadsides on several fronts. They charged that the whole testing enterprise discriminated against minorities and the working class and that the theoretical basis of tests was built on sand. The derogatory terms 'pseudo-science' and 'unnatural science' were hurled freely.

Though much controversy was generated, their charges are mostly about how tests have been used. Tests have many limitations and just a few restricted proper uses. Their scores should not be taken as gospel or used alone, and in some circumstances they are just better than nothing at all. Here are some common misuses.

Giving a Score Undue Weight

In Douglas Adams' *Hitchhiker's Guide to the Galaxy* series, a computer is run billions of years to find out the secret of the universe. The famous answer turns out to be '42'. Forty-two is rather unsatisfactory, partly because we do not know the exact question.

An IQ score sometimes seems a bit like '42' as an answer, given the limitations of tests and the varying motivation, care, and fatigue of testees. A single IQ score gives little guide to a person's strengths and weaknesses, and only covers a limited part of human intelligence. Most tests, for example, tell little about such things as musical and practical ability, and are limited as predictors of performance. A good illustration is a story told by Seymour Sarason, who had arrived to take up a job as a psychologist at a training centre. Several inmates had just engineered a difficult escape from the institution. Yet, after recapture, they performed abysmally when tested on a simple maze learning test. Clearly the test was not tapping their practical ability.

Another problem that makes interpretation of scores difficult is test-wiseness. People who do a lot of tests may just get adept at taking IQ tests. Their intelligence has not changed, just their test-taking power. The item types are no longer novel, they develop strategies for dealing with them, and even recognise that the same items come up in test after test (point is to space as — [moment] is to time). I once knew someone who wanted to join Mensa. Since Mensa's IQ test was given infrequently he decided not to leave his entry to chance and did an intelligent thing: He went to a university psychology department's test library and just practised doing IQ tests for a few weeks. Though not able to attempt the specific tests that Mensa used, he became so test-wise that he passed easily, even finishing time-limited tests that no one is meant to finish. The final score must have been astronomical.

Most experts know of such problems with IQ scores, but many test users and takers do not. They interpret a single score as an infallible measure of intelligence, set in stone. The score acquires a hallowed status and what it is supposed to predict goes out the window.

Examples of this problem abound and it is a major reason why many schools and psychologists will not tell anyone their IQ scores. A 1975 CBS documentary called *The IQ Myth* gave a horrendous example. A Mexican-American schoolboy with poor English was diagnosed as mentally retarded from a single test and consigned to a special class for the 'educable mentally retarded'. Years later he was allowed into university, but only on sufferance because of his score. Yet he graduated with honours, still on probation, and the university still regarded him with suspicion because it took that test score as gospel and disregarded the performance it was supposed to predict. He now teaches in a university!

Another example is recounted by Sternberg (1985). A student wanted to enter a small teachers college in the United States at which condition of admission was a score of 25 on the Miller Analogies·Test, just about chance performance. She scored below 25 but was let in on sufferance. When she completed the course with distinction the college required her to retake the test before awarding a diploma! The sole value of the test was to predict how well she would do. At graduation, her test score was totally irrelevant.

Poor Administration of Test Conditions

For a score to mean anything, a test must be administered under the conditions set out in the manual. The tester must give the instructions clearly, be sure that everyone understands them, give any prescribed practice problems, and follow prescribed time limits. The tester should create the right atmosphere and scan the crowd to prevent cheating. As well, many individual tests like the WAIS need highly trained testers.

In some cases, the set conditions are not followed and a score becomes meaningless. Jensen (1981) recounts some bizarre examples from testing in schools. Though most teachers follow the manual, some do not and in one school a test with a forty-five-minute time limit was given in anything from fifteen minutes to several hours. Some teachers altered test questions to make them easier. One read aloud items from a reading comprehension test because some pupils could not read them! Another teacher filled in items that testees had left blank if she thought they should have known them. Many errors were also found in scoring and in converting raw scores to scaled ones. From such tales, Jensen argued that group intelligence tests should not be given in schools. An error could have a profound effect on some unfortunate pupil's life course.

Forgetting That Tests Only Predict Performance on the Average

Many people make many judgments by thinking only of very familiar cases; themselves or a few others they know. For example, some discount the smoking/cancer link by citing their own good health despite two packs a day for twenty years or their Uncle Ned who has smoked heavily since age sixteen and is fit, active, and healthy at seventy. Similarly, some people discount the value of IQ tests because they sometimes fail to predict something. It is not hard to come up with cases where a person scores low on a test but goes on to great deeds. For example, James Watson, Nobel Prize winner for codiscovering the structure of DNA, says he has a tested IQ of 115, which is just bright/normal.

But this overall strategy is fallacious. Tests (or statistical correlations like that between smoking and cancer) only hold on the average. There are always exceptions and failures of prediction, for a host of possible reasons. Human behaviour is incredibly complex. But in general, people with high IQs tend to do better in certain courses or at various tasks than people with lower IQs. Lots of factors such as motivation, emotional stability, and so on intervene to affect prediction in individual cases.

As a Justification for Certain Practices
According to Gould (1981) and Evans and Waites (1981), IQ tests have been used to oppress minorities and the working class because they are heavily biased toward middle-class persons. Many test questions involve things only the latter are likely to know.

Virtually anything can be misused by someone with an agenda to fulfil. For example, politicians quickly become aware of how reporters can select out a few of their words to make a point. The evil is not inherent in IQ tests, just in how they are used. Similarly, while Darwin's theory of evolution did much to make sense of the biological world, it was misused by people with other agendas. It became part of the Nazi doctrine of Aryan racial superiority, helped justify great extremes of wealth in the United States (social Darwinism), and even the inevitability of Communist revolutions. An idea with much value could be put to very nefarious purposes. So it is with intelligence tests.

CAN WE ACTUALLY MEASURE INTELLIGENCE?

The answer must be yes and no. No one really knows what intelligence is, and so in that sense we cannot directly tap it. However, we can certainly measure something that has something to do with intelligence. IQ tests have been severely criticised, but if used very judiciously they have some value. The newer tests such as K-ABC and BAS also are tapping important functions, and we await further experience with these and new developments in testing.

4

EXTREMES OF ABILITY: TALENT, GENIUS, AND RETARDATION

In Poul Anderson's 1954 novel *Brainwave*, the Earth passes out of a field in space that had bathed the planet for millions of years and where the radiation had slowed down neural transmission. Overnight, the brains of every human and animal work faster, and all get much, much more intelligent. Farm animals get nasty and resentful. They are no longer content to be locked up and are bright enough to learn how to escape; just keep kicking a fence in the same place until it crashes. Human society collapses quickly. Most people become too bright to want to do dull, routine jobs day in and day out, to do the tasks needed to keep society going. Also, they no longer swallow official propaganda. The formerly mentally retarded now have what would have been average intelligence, but they are still bewildered by the very bright and the changes.

Daniel Keyes' 1966 novel *Flowers for Algernon*, which was made into the film *Charly*, explores the same theme in much more depth. It has two heroes; a mentally retarded man named Charlie Gordon and a mouse named Algernon. Both receive experimental brain cell transplants and go through a remarkable series of changes in general intelligence. These are described in Charlie's diary entries, which are very cleverly written to reflect his changing intelligence. Initially, the text is ungrammatical, full of spelling errors, and shows that he understands little of the world around him. His co-workers laugh at him and play savage pranks. But he learns and learns, and as the entries become more grammatical they also show more understanding. He sees how his co-workers make fun of him, detects criminal dishonesty in one, and learns and learns. His powers of observation and reasoning grow until he reaches genius level. He becomes a speed reader; librarians gather round in awe to watch him. He speaks twenty languages, writes a piano concerto, tackles major scientific problems, and even figures out what ultimately will happen to him. But as Charlie gets brighter, he becomes more divorced from people, who are increasingly uncomfortable when he is around. A world expert on economics bolts after discussing it for a short time with Charlie, who knows more. His co-workers understand him no longer and dislike and fear him.

But alas, as Charlie works out himself, the operation's effect is brief. Algernon regresses first, going from being a very bright mouse indeed to an increasingly erratic and finally a dead one. Charlie's diary entries get less literate as his powers decline. The slow bleeding away of intelligence is frightening, like the loss of functions of HAL the computer as it is slowly disconnected in the film *2001: A Space Odyssey*. Ultimately Charlie is back to retarded level, and tragically ends up in an institution.

The novel gives some insight into what it might be like to be at either end of the intelligence spectrum. The retarded Charlie learns very slowly, has great trouble remembering things, and understands very little. He is afraid of being tested for intelligence because he always fails. At the other extreme, genius Charlie thinks quickly and understands a great deal. As he puts it: 'Ordinary people can see only a little bit — each step will reveal worlds never dreamed existing'. The price is social rejection, which indeed drives many of the highly gifted into isolation.

Extremes of ability are of great intrinsic interest. People at the top end fascinate, intrigue, and delight us. Depending on their talent, the extraordinarily able are lionised, envied, rewarded, or reviled. Society largely depends on extraordinary ability to advance. At the other end, mental retardation is an enormous problem for Western societies and huge sums are spent trying to find ways to teach retardates what they need to know and even to 'cure' them. This chapter looks at these two extremes, and the light that two fascinating phenomena cast on them; the idiot savante and learning disability syndromes. It also looks at some limits to human intelligence. The first sections cover the upper extreme; savantes, gifted children and genius, and the limits. The final two look at the lower end; learning disability and retardation.

THE PHENOMENON OF EXTRAORDINARY ABILITY

Wolfgang Amadeus Mozart was born in Salzburg, Austria, in 1756 and died in Vienna thirty-five years later. His tremendous musical talent emerged very early and he was the musical genius and child prodigy *par excellence*. At the age of six he toured Europe and astonished audiences with his prowess on the organ, violin, and clavier. His talent for composition had become apparent a year earlier, and he composed for the rest of his life, eventually producing 600 works, many of which form the backbone of the orchestral repertoire. Albert Einstein said that Mozart's music was in contact with the structure of the universe, unlike that of a merely great composer such as Beethoven (in Einstein's opinion).

Samuel Reshevsky was born in Poland in 1911 and showed remarkable talent for chess very early. The story goes that he learned the moves at the age of four and that a few days later, after watching his father play and lose, Reshevsky showed him how he could have saved the game. Paraded about Europe and America as a child prodigy, he gave exhibitions and competed in tournaments. Later he became a contender for the world championship, although he never actually secured the title. In his seventies he became a prodigy at the other end of the age scale, still giving exhibitions and playing in strong international tournaments.

Like most things, such extraordinary abilities as these come in several types. First, there is extreme general intelligence, then extremes of more specific aptitudes such as spatial relations, mathematical ability, and so on. Some more types are given by Tannenbaum (1986). *Scarcity* abilities make life 'easier, safer, healthier or more intelligible'. They promote the common good. Their exercise creates a new vaccine, an invention such as the light bulb or computer, or a new scientific theory that helps us better understand the universe. Examples of individuals with this rare form of talent are Einstein, Edison, Pasteur, Bell, and Darwin. *Surplus* talents bring us to new heights of emotion or aesthetics by promoting culture, art, music, or literature. They raise our consciousness, and may get us to look at things in new ways. Examples include Mozart and Beethoven, the novelists Tolstoy and Dickens, and performers including Nureyev, Callas, and Olivier. *Quota* skills are run-of-the-mill extraordinary abilities, based largely on education. The people who have them are experts turned out by universities and other institutions. Examples are the routine high-level abilities of executives who adeptly run corporations, dentists who fill teeth, engineers who put up bridges that stay up, and doctors who can accurately diagnose and treat various disorders. The final type are *anomalous* skills — strange exceptional powers that are no longer or never were greatly valued by society. These may include anachronisms like prowess at blacksmithy or making sealing wax, and *Guinness Book of Records* type feats such as being able to drink many glasses of beer in a few minutes or stay on a flagpole for months.

Though abilities come in various shapes and sizes, the main concern here is with high general intelligence. The scarcity ones come under the heading of genius, and an insight into what underlies genius comes from the strange case of exceptional specific ability in a person of low general intelligence.

THE IDIOT SAVANTE SYNDROME

Scientists have known about the extraordinary phenomenon of the idiot savante syndrome for more than a century, but it has attracted public attention only recently (e.g., Treffert, 1989). The syndrome is surprising because it involves a person of very low general intelligence having a great talent: A neighbourhood of extreme poverty has a tiny oasis of extreme wealth. It is counter-intuitive, like a burrowing bird or flying fish, because we think of intelligence as general. We expect a person of generally low intelligence to be low on everything, and someone of generally high intelligence to be good at everything. This is often the case, but not always. Here are a few illustrative cases of the savante syndrome, some of which are discussed by Treffert.

A blind, retarded boy had cerebral palsy and rarely spoke at all. However, when seated at a piano he would begin to play and sing in the most marvellous manner. The music was so fine and the contrast between this power and his retardation was so great that the case made television and newspaper wire service reports. In 1866, the following case was described: 'A real simpleton, utterly without judgment, he has a memory which is prodigious, and a singular tendency to make puns'. The person could be given historical books and would repeat entire pages accurately from memory. A related case described by Down was of a boy with 'extraordinary memory . . . associated with a very great defect of reasoning power'. The boy

was given a book to read and on covering the third page acciden-
tally skipped a line, and retraced his steps. And then something very
interesting would happen. Whenever he repeated the passage from
memory, he made exactly the same error, skipping the line and
correcting himself. Another such case is 'Leslie', who never spoke
voluntarily, but if asked, could repeat verbatim the conversations of
an entire day, right down to the intonations of each speaker. A
retarded pair of twins scored between 60 and 70 on an IQ test, but
each could do incredible things with dates. If given a date (e.g., 4
January 1265), they would quickly say what day of the week it fell
on. If asked to name the years in the next two centuries in which
Christmas would fall on a Wednesday, they would reply quickly and
accurately.

Treffert notes that savantes favour several abilities. Calendar
calculation is very popular. They like dates. Others are music, spatial, and mechanical ability, all of which are predominantly controlled by the brain's right side. Their abilities are seldom creative,
however. They tend to 'echo rather than create'. They repeat what
they have heard before, rather than coming up with new and beautiful interpretations. Also, most savantes are male; about six for
every female.

How do they do it? How can a retardate also be a genius
without having the Charlie treatment? No one is sure, but there are
some clues. Treffert says it may partly be biological. While the brain
is developing before birth, the left side may lag behind and some of
its neurons may wander over to the right. Various areas there then
grow larger than normal. Why are there no savantes with extreme
verbal ability but abysmal everything else? Do neurons only migrate
to the right? There probably are such savantes, but we don't call
them that because Western society greatly values verbal ability, and
someone good at that and terrible at everything else would not be
called retarded.

Still, biology cannot explain it all, especially the calendar calculating. Some believe that many cases of the syndrome occur
through an enormous amount of practice. As we saw in Chapter 2,
expertise in a given area largely depends on acquiring much knowledge, which takes years of practice. Recall the person of normal
intelligence who was a genius at remembering combinations of as
many as eighty digits. The skill was entirely due to practice, and
savantes are often also immensely preoccupied with their skill area.
Calendar calculators spend most of their time juggling dates, and
when they do converse they talk about little else.

But what exactly do they learn from all this practice? Often, savantes cannot say. Studies suggest that some learn some rules and one savante can actually state the rules used. Norris (1990) speculates that they may learn such rules as we learn the obscure grammatical rules of language — just by being exposed to them. But others use different methods. The calendar repeats itself every 400 years, and one study found that a boy had exceptional visual memory for calendars. He may have memorised images for years ahead and back.

Another type of savante called 'lightning calculators' appear to learn a lot of rules and properties of arithmetic, which allow them to calculate very rapidly. There is a multitude of short cuts in arithmetic. For example, when the famous mathematician Gauss was in school, he was told to multiply all the numbers between x and y. While the other pupils laboriously computed, Gauss saw a simple short cut which gave the answer right away. There was a famous professor who used extensive knowledge of arithmetic and the properties of numbers to develop the same calculating ability, but computers and pocket calculators have made this ability 'anomalous'.

And what does the syndrome tell about genius? It suggests that genius may partly depend on some inborn talent, lots of practice, a lot of specific knowledge, and an obsession with one domain. Indeed, the world has seen few general geniuses. Most contribute in one or two areas at most, and spend a long time learning their speciality before fine contributions come. More on this later.

GIFTEDNESS

While savantes are dull in general but have one or two talents, gifted persons are highly intelligent in general. This section will mainly look at gifted children, while the next section examines what a few of them become — geniuses.

The gifted have had much attention lavished on them in the last few decades. Earlier, many got little. People thought that they needed no special treatment from teachers or parents, or anyone else. Most generally competent children could take care of themselves and would land on their feet. But research has shown that this is often not so and gifted children can have many problems. Some get maltreated by teachers because they ask difficult, penetrating questions, disrupt classroom routine, or look at things in interesting, novel ways. Some get bored with the slow pace of schooling and drop out early, which usually represents a tremendous waste of talent. Enough people became concerned with this squandering of intellectual capital to form gifted child organisations, and to fund research into how they could be better educated.

Society needs to improve things for its talented individuals, out of self-interest if nothing else. The gifted are needed to understand and advance the technology of an ever-more complex culture. Indeed, Norman (1988) discusses how modern technology is over-taxing the abilities of ordinary persons. He says that technology is producing goods that do all kinds of amazing things; videos, ovens, washing machines, and CD players. However, people have increasing trouble just figuring out how to operate the controls, and use all their brilliant new features.

Definition

How do you tell if a child is gifted? It is not always easy. The usual notion is high general intelligence as measured by IQ together with a few other traits. The picture is of a child who develops fast, is adept at most school subjects, and wants to work hard. Educators like formal definitions, however, and as mentioned in Chapter 1, usual IQ cut-offs are 120, 130, or 140 — with 130 being most popular. But more is involved. In 1972 the U.S. Education Office came up with a polysyllabic definition that is still widely used. A gifted child has 'Abilities which give evidence of high performance capabilities in intellectual, creative, leadership or performing arts'. Shorn of jargon, this appears to refer to a child likely to excel at one of the four areas. The leadership and performing arts ideas are fairly recent additions, and doing well at them might not require high general intelligence. Some educators plug in high motivation to work as well: Lots of bright, talented individuals are not considered gifted because they could not be much bothered to achieve and it means little to them.

Some people distinguish between giftedness and talent, seeing the former as superior general ability and the latter as superiority in a specific area. One can be gifted and talented, just one, or neither.

What are Gifted Children Like?

They are a pretty varied bunch, with a few things in common. As mentioned, they typically develop intellectually at a fast rate. They typically read much earlier than others, and may be amazed to discover on the first day of school that most of the other children cannot. A number of studies have looked in detail at their traits.

The most famous of all is a massive study begun by Lewis Terman in 1921. He inaccurately called it a study of 'genius', which was then defined as anyone scoring in the top half-percent of the IQ distribution. Terman partly wanted to see if some common folk myths about the gifted held any water. One goes back to Shakespeare: 'Early ripe, early rot'. Grandmothers used to advise holding children back so they did not burn out early and a few well-known cases at the time received much press coverage because they supported this popular prejudice. One was a very precocious child who entered Harvard University very young but ended up on society's scrapheap early, his promise largely unfulfilled. Another folk myth is that the highly gifted fit a certain type; slightly built, frail, in poor health, with a nervous temperament. The child wears thick glasses and has a nose always buried deep in books (or computers nowadays). 'Were the highly gifted really like this?' asked Terman, and anyway, how much did IQ contribute to life success.

To find out, Terman's assistants scoured California for the brightest of its schoolchildren. Teachers nominated their best and the candidates took an IQ test. About a thousand were selected, with IQ scores over 140 and an average age of about twelve. They were interviewed then and about once every five years afterward. Many are still alive, in fact. The study results have been periodically reported in countless articles and several books.

The findings were clear. The highly gifted were not frail and nervous. Rather, they tended to be fine physical specimens, taller than average and more physically and socially developed. They did not burn out as time went on, but continued to shine brightly, staying ahead of their fellows. As well, they did very much better in life than their fellows and were usually extraordinarily productive. Many took higher degrees, became professionals, and produced countless articles and books. To be sure, not all did well. Some committed crimes and spent time in prison. However, the study had a problem, as Terman himself later recognised. Teachers nominated the first batch of subjects, and teachers are likely to have some biases, notably toward very verbal, well-adjusted children with talent for leadership. They may miss the very quiet, alienated, bored child who sits at the back. Teachers in fact do not identify some very gifted children in their classrooms, who often are only picked up by IQ tests. So the sample of gifted was biased.

Indeed, work on children at the IQ distribution's very extreme suggests another picture with very bright children. As mentioned in Chapter 1, Hollingworth (1942) looked at fourteen children with IQ scores above about 180. Their performance was exceptional, they had a wide range of interests, but they had a number of problems.

Disliking routine and drudgery, they quickly got bored with repetitive tasks. Some found their classmates tedious and dull. It was as though a person of average intelligence had to spend much time with a group of retardates, perhaps nice people but not very stimulating company. Hollingworth also said that their emotions tended to lag behind their intellect. They had to learn to suffer fools gladly, as she put it, especially dull adults in authority over them. Those unable to do so became rebellious, or even misanthropic. Ill-treatment from peers sometimes led to increasing introversion and isolation. Because they had trouble finding congenial playmates they often chose to read rather than socialise. Physicist James Clerk Maxwell was treated quite savagely by other schoolboys and later wrote wryly, 'They did not understand me, but I understood them'. Hollingworth describes a child who read very early and was sent to school at age seven. One day he came home weeping bitterly, saying that the pupils there just would not read! He had taken book after book to school to show them what treasures they were, but was made fun of. Hollingworth argued that such problems may diminish with time, as the more boorish pupils drop out of school and it gets easier for children to choose their company.

What Underlies Giftedness?
Some studies have asked exactly what makes gifted children learn and perform much better than average. In part, it has to do with certain personality traits which are discussed in the section on genius. Sternberg (1985) argues that there are several mental characteristics. First, gifted children have a better knowledge base and think faster. Second, they have a superior ability to cope with novelty and they excel at 'insight'.

Sternberg defines insight as one of three things. The first is being able to bring lots of pieces of information together to form a whole (e.g., a lot of facts into a good theory; or many studies, opinions, and contradictory findings into a coherent textbook). When marking essays at university, I am sometimes struck by some students' inability to integrate data. They cannot readily assemble ideas into a coherent whole. Sternberg says that some scientists have the same problem: In journal articles reporting their research, they have trouble relating it to other work and are unable to integrate it with the rest of the field. The second aspect of insight entails knowing what is important and what is not. This ability heavily depends on the knowledge base, I would argue. Good chess players look at a position, instantly figure out the best two or three moves and ignore all the others, focusing on what is important.

Eminent scientists have a good notion of what important scientific problems need solving. Sternberg's third ingredient of insight is the ability to readily relate new information to what one already knows, by using analogies or other means. The gifted excel at all three, says Sternberg, while the retarded have little insight, a poor knowledge base, and are slow to automate their learning.

Some research has looked at what underlies a specific form of giftedness — talent. Three particularly important features are some inborn talent itself, a great deal of practice (as with the idiot savantes), and high motivation to succeed. Bloom (1982) looked at twenty-five individuals who had made world-class status in fields including mathematics, Olympic swimming, and concert piano playing before reaching the age of thirty-five. He interviewed them, their parents, their coaches, and others to find out the secrets of their success, which he listed as follows. First was strong natural talent in their area. Swimmers, for example, were said to have a 'natural affinity for water' which showed up very early. Second, they had lots of encouragement which kept motivation high. The cheerleaders were not just their family, but teachers, peer groups, and often a mentor. Many had special teachers, themselves gifted, who took great interest in motivating and training them. Each therefore had lots of help, which argues against the view that great talent will always win out.

Feldman (1979) had found much the same thing when he examined two chess players and a musician who performed at adult expert level before reaching the age of ten. All three had obvious natural talent but had also been taught by dedicated master teachers. All three were highly motivated, and spent countless hours improving their knowledge base and honing their skills. Feldman argues that great talent arises as follows. A pre-organised person is born at a time and place which appreciates his or her talent and which has the facilities to develop it. The person receives the vast amount of knowledge needed to perform well and works hard — very hard — to succeed. He cites Mozart as an archetypal example. He had enormous talent. He grew up in an environment where music was appreciated, his father also being a composer. He spent many years acquiring the knowledge to compose well and only his later works are much played in concerts. Indeed, some estimate that it takes at least ten years in a field to acquire the necessary expertise to make great contributions.

EMINENCE AND GENIUS

A few gifted children go on to eminence and a few of those few eventually get the coveted tag 'genius'. The term itself is vague, but in everyday parlance it refers to an exceptionally able person working on a lofty, exalted mental plane that ordinary or merely gifted persons cannot reach. By this view, genius is 'the ultimate in intelligence and creativity' or 'the essence of high performance'. It is a kind of gift of the gods and an enduring trait of a person, like green eyes or tallness. Some see a genius as almost a member of a different species, and even the very talented may look on in wonder. One of the great physicists of the twentieth century, Enrico Fermi, impressed physicists who themselves later secured Nobel Prizes: 'Knowing what Fermi could do did not make me humble', wrote one. 'You just realise that some people are smarter than you, that's all. You can't run as fast as some people or do mathematics as fast as Fermi.'

The idea of genius has been around for at least a couple of thousand years. The ancient Romans thought of it as a kind of spirit, a daemon presiding over his or her destiny and inspiring him on to great things. Lots of people throughout history have tried to define genius and have speculated about what it is. Baldwin gave 'superiority of ability in an unusual degree', Bernard Shaw 'seeing further and probing deeper than other people'. Francis Galton said the hallmark of genius is that the whole intelligent part of a nation mourns his (or her) death. Albert (1975) defined it as someone producing new ideas that lead to a clear break with the past, that alter the means of attack on a problem in science, or that change the way we look at things. Simonton (1988), looking at scientific genius, defined it as a person having an extraordinary impact on the course of civilisation or history. Some stress extradordinary impact and productivity in a given area, such as art, music, or science. Some believe genius to be something qualitatively different from the merely gifted and average, which moves towards the different species idea, while others suggest it is a superabundance of qualities everyone else possesses. Wechsler (1952) concurs with the latter view, noting that an extreme quantitative difference can look like a qualitative one, just as a purely quantitative rise in water temperature can produce apparent qualitative changes from ice to liquid and to steam.

Some Geniuses

But before we continue, let us make all the abstractions more concrete. Almost all history's great geniuses are male, rare female geniuses include Marie Curie and a few writers such as Emily Brontë. As mentioned in Chapter 1, the reason may involve genes, the discouragement of females to achieve, or both. It may also be that the personality traits needed are typically male ones. The best genius to start with is the genius *par excellence*.

Leonardo da Vinci. He was born in 1452 in Vinci, near Florence, the illegitimate son of a peasant girl and a local dignitary. His first great love was art. He was apprenticed to a local artist and later created some of the world's finest art treasures, amongst them the *Mona Lisa* and *The Last Supper*. He also was a sculptor, although none of his works survive, and in 1517 he became royal painter, engineer, and architect to the King of France. He died in 1519.

Leonardo's most striking feature was his extraordinary prowess at everything to which he turned his hand. He made great, original contributions in many different fields, and in many was far ahead of his time. He contributed much to the theory of art and was highly regarded as an architect, though no design was ever actually constructed. His notebooks show many original plans for palaces, bridges, a cathedral dome and even a modern city. The metropolis was to have two levels, all traffic being on the lower. He designed a fortress that could withstand gunpowder attacks. He anticipated later technological developments by designing an armoured vehicle and the world's first flying machine using principles similar to those used by the helicopter.

None of this was enough for Leonardo. He worked in biology, preparing a magnificent set of anatomical drawings of the human body, and was one of the first Renaissance artists to actually dissect and draw internal parts of the body. He worked in optics and mathematics, and he even partly anticipated James Lovelock's controversial Gaia hypothesis that the Earth is a single living organism (though in a slightly different sense). A 1550 biography hailed his ability as follows, with just a touch of hyperbole:

> The heavens . . . sometimes with lavish abundance . . . bestow upon a single individual, beauty, grace and ability, so that, whatever he does, every action is so divine that he surpasses all other men, and clearly displays how his genius is the gift of God, and not an acquirement of human art. Men saw this in Leonardo da Vinci . . . whose abilities were so extraordinary that he could readily solve every difficulty. He possessed great personal strength, combined with dexterity, and a spirit and courage invariably royal and magnanimous.

Aristotle. He was a Greek philosopher and scholar who lived from 385 to 322 BC. Born in Macedonia and later a pupil of Plato, he was tutor to the conqueror Alexander the Great. Unfortunately, little is known of his life and personality and only fifty of his 400 treatises survive. Aristotle's works have had a profound impact on the way we think and look at things. Many of Western civilisation's ideas date from him. Indeed, the rediscovery of his and other works in the Middle Ages helped spark the Renaissance. His surviving works cover a wide range of topics, ranging from ethics and categories (still used today) to physics. His ideas about motion, space, and existence were seen as revealed truth until the rise of science: No one bothered to actually do any physics experiments because Aristotle had laid out all the principles centuries before. He did much work on biology and psychology, classifying and ranking animals and listing their characteristics. He wrote a great deal on logic and on politics, looking at various types of government and noting how easily monarchy can turn into tyranny or democracy into oligarchy. He speculated about the nature of the soul. Many of our basic categories of thought and ideas about logic date from Aristotle. If only the 350 other works had lasted!

General geniuses such as Leonardo and Aristotle are terribly thin on the ground, and nowadays it would probably be impossible even to be one. There is simply too much knowledge to learn in most fields and one needs to spend years acquiring it before making original contributions. Let us look at the garden-variety type; the genius with extraordinary talent in one or two fields.

Ludwig van Beethoven. He was born in Bonn, Germany, in 1770, although his ancestry was Dutch — hence the 'van'. Unlike Mozart, he was not a child prodigy; his talent took time to develop. He studied with the famous composer Joseph Haydn, and spent most of his life in Vienna, a centre of music at the time. Beethoven's character was notoriously irascible. He had numerous titanic struggles with others, and enough disputes with landladies to induce him to frequently change his address. One possible reason is that he was the victim of an ironic twist of fate for a musician. He began going deaf around age thirty, probably due to syphilis. Indeed, some of his greatest pieces, and the most popular of all classical works, were composed when he was stone deaf. Such composition is a tribute to the power of mental imagery. Beethoven contributed quite a respectable number of works — although they did not approach Mozart's 600 — amongst them the very famous nine symphonies, many concertos, string quartets, incidental music pieces, and one opera. He worked painstakingly to compose, labouring over every note, and revising and revising. Mozart, on the other hand, apparently conceived a work as a whole and only had to set it down on paper.

Beethoven was widely recognised as a musical genius, even in his own lifetime. He was feted by many of the crowned heads of Europe, more than 20,000 people mourned at his funeral in 1827, and his works still are a mainstay of the concert repertoire. The monumental third and ninth symphonies, which are among the most popular of all works, both broke new ground in many ways and extended the symphony form: The third extended its length and breadth while the ninth, which many consider his most masterful work, introduces the chorus to a form previously only instrumental. The work is difficult to stage; it requires a large orchestra and chorus, four solo singers, whose voices are stretched to their limits, and takes about sixty-seven minutes to perform. As famous conductor Josef Krips once described it, the first two movements of the work involve struggle, with Beethoven locked in mortal combat with death. In the third movement, death has triumphed, and its final call to the composer is signalled by insistent trumpets. The fourth movement introduces the famed joy theme, which is taken up by the chorus. At the concert hall, one gets the feeling of standing at the very gates of heaven with the heavenly choir in full voice. As Krips put it: 'In my mind's eye I can see quite clearly the instant in which Beethoven enters heaven. The finale tells me of his arrival and how all heaven stands still at his presence.' The work indeed lifts the audience to new heights. At its first performance, Beethoven conducted, and the orchestra was continually interrupted by sustained applause. At the end, approval was thunderous, and the deaf Beethoven had to be swivelled around to see the audience's overwhelming response.

Richard Wagner. He led a most amazing life (1813–83), which has been detailed by several fascinated biographers. Part of this fascination lies in the contrast between impeccable work and unimpeccable personal life, which is not uncharacteristic of genius. A notorious anti-Semite, writing scathing anti-Semitic tracts and other political works, Wagner dabbled in local politics, and was often on the run from the authorities. He chased the wives of his many benefactors. He borrowed heavily from friends but rarely paid them back. He frequently had to flee a city to escape angry creditors, and spent some weeks in a French debtors prison. He felt entitled to a lavish lifestyle, even with no money to support it.

Though his personal life can be criticised, his contribution to music cannot, and the world has many thousands of dedicated Wagnerians. Many of his pieces are concert favourites, and his operas are performed throughout the world. Wagner composed only one symphony (at age nineteen) and a few assorted instrumental pieces. The most famous is the lyrical 'Siegfried Idyll', written as a birthday present for his wife Cosima. Its premiere was very early one morning on the steps outside her bedroom window. Wagner had assembled a full orchestra outside his house to serenade her.

Wagner composed almost entirely for the stage, and extended the opera form. Indeed, he preferred to call his works 'music dramas'. They are very long, some running five hours. His *Ring* cycle, consisting of four connected works meant to be seen on consecutive nights, takes fifteen and a half hours to perform. The dramas are unique in the clever way in which the music, characters, and unfolding events are all tied up. Taking an idea used previously in the pantomime, in which a character's entrance is signalled by a piece of music, Wagner gave his characters such motifs, as well as events, the hand of fate, and other things. The motifs all develop with time, and subtle changes convey weighty meanings. For example, the opera *Das Rheingold* has an assorted cast of giants, dwarves, and gods, each with a motif. The work begins with a magnificent nature theme, from which is derived the theme for the nature children the Rhinemaidens. Initially the theme is brightness, but when they are wronged it is subtly changed to reflect sadness and loss. The Rheingold itself initially has a theme derived from the nature motif but it later becomes corrupted and is slightly altered to sound evil. All these themes change and are combined and recombined to reflect the story. Today, the operas are popular, and a production of the *Ring* becomes a world event. However, Wagner's work had its critics. George Bernard Shaw once acidly commented that his music is not as bad as it sounds. Another said of the *Ring*, 'It has some beautiful moments — and some awful quarter-hours'.

Wagner was unusual among composers in that he had other talents. He had a fine sense of drama and, unlike almost every other opera composer, wrote his own story and libretto. He also designed and supervised the construction of his own theatre. The acoustics are still unmatched for Wagnerian opera anywhere else in the world.

Pablo Picasso. He was born in Spain in 1881, and lived a long and productive life until 1973. Many consider him to be the greatest artist of the twentieth century. He worked in paint, prints, and sculptures, and produced many works which have had immense influence on art, and some scholars say, on thought in this century. There were over 13,000 paintings, 100,000 prints, and 300 sculptures.

Isaac Newton. He exerted an influence on modern science and mathematics that is second to none. He was born prematurely to a peasant woman in 1642, his father already dead. His mother remarried when he was three, and farmed him out to his grandmother. He studied at Cambridge, a citadel of scholarship, and at twenty-six became Lucasian Professor of Mathematics, a prestigious post which still exists. He stayed on at Cambridge until 1696, then moving to London and a sinecure as master of the mint. He died in 1727.

Newton's contributions to mathematics and physics were enormous. He invented the calculus, an important branch of mathematics. He proposed a theory of light and of colour, and formulated the three famous laws of motion. His work on gravity, by folklore inspired when an apple fell on his head, brought together much data. Before Newton, no one had thought that the force that brought the apple or arrows to Earth was the same one that held the planets and stars in their orbits. He founded classical mechanics, still an important branch of physics. His monumental work *Principia*, written in Latin, is a classic of science. Two profoundly original contributions included using mathematics to describe the physical universe and conceiving the universe as being like an immense machine, all the parts ticking away like clockwork instead of moving through self-will or being pushed by angels. Before Newton, science was largely chaos. Afterward, it was order. Social scientists sometimes say that they are waiting for a Newton to bring order to their own diverse and chaotic disciplines. Newton gave us a picture of how the universe worked which lasted until the advent of quantum mechanics in the 1920s.

Albert Einstein. Einstein is everyone's idea of a genius. We call a very bright person 'an Einstein' or say 'If I could do that, I would be Einstein'. Born in Germany in 1879, he was not precocious, and did not speak until age four. He hated formal schooling and examinations, and after taking one physics course said that the exams had put him off so much that he gave up the subject for a year or so. He graduated from the polytechnic in Zurich in 1900 and was unemployed for nearly two years before he secured a job as an inventions examiner in the Swiss patent office. He stayed eight years, and did most of his best work there. After a round of professorships in Germany and Switzerland, he fled the Nazis in 1933 for a post at Princeton, where he remained the rest of his life. He died in 1955.

Like Copernicus and Newton, Einstein overturned our view of the physical universe. He pointed out the cosmic speed limit of the speed of light, formulated the idea of gravity as being due to the curvature of space, and proposed that energy and matter are the same, encapsulated in the famous $e=mc^2$. This equation led to the development of the atomic bomb and of atomic energy. (After the

Hiroshima explosion, Einstein reportedly said that if he had known he would have become a cobbler.) He originated the idea of light being like both a particle and a wave, and thus was a founder of quantum mechanics, though he had a deep antipathy to the theory itself.

Einstein was also an accomplished violinist, but he was not a general genius. His own mental powers were limited. He thought primarily in visual images and worked things out in images, but then had problems transcribing them into words and mathematics. Nor was he a particularly good mathematician, as physicists go, and he spent several years being taught the mathematics used for his general theory of relativity. He also did not conceive the theory of relativity in a single brilliant flash of insight. It developed over a long period. He hit blind alleys and took much thinking to arrive at its principal tenets. He also made mistakes. One famous one is his introduction of a fudge factor to stop his relativity equations predicting that the universe is expanding. It really is expanding but the idea of it being static was so fixed that even Einstein could not accept it at that time. Nor could he accept the 'new physics' to which his work helped lead the way. Last, Einstein's best work was done in his twenties and he spent the rest of his life trying to solve a problem that even today remains unsolved; unifying the forces of nature.

Einstein got where he did by ability, but also partly by self-confidence. This made him willing to tackle difficult problems and gave him sheer perseverance when the going got tough. These are essential traits for geniuses. As the inventor Thomas Edison put it, 'genius is 1 per cent inspiration and 99 per cent perspiration'.

Some Traits of Geniuses

Chapter 1 mentioned the financier who is trying to create geniuses by crossing highly intelligent women with Nobel Prize winners. The project is unlikely to work for several major reasons. The first reason is a statistical one; a phenomenon called 'regression to the mean'. If two extreme parents reproduce, the children on average are less extreme. Children of very tall parents are usually shorter than both, and those of very short parents are usually taller. A child of two very bright parents thus is likely to be less bright. The second is that Nobel Prize winning is probably not a good measure of intelligence. Winners will be much above average, of course, but the Prize sometimes has as much to do with luck, persistence, and self-promotion as with ability. The third reason is that genius does not have all that much to do with intelligence beyond a certain threshold level. Genius arises when a person has a modicum of ability, several personality traits, and the opportunity to actually work.

The world is no doubt full of geniuses who never had the chance to acquire the education needed to use their ability. Mark Twain used to tell a story of a man who died, went to heaven, and asked to see the greatest general of all time. An angel pointed him out. 'But I knew him on Earth and he was a cobbler,' the man said. 'Yes', said the angel, 'but if he had had the opportunity, he would have been the greatest general of all time.' Another kind of opportunity needed is to be born at the right time (Simonton, 1988). One cannot be a military genius if born at a time of peace, when no one wants to fight. Einstein might not have been recognised as a genius if born fifty years later. His talents and ideas were right for his time. Physics needed him then. Genius occurs when ability, background, and personality coalesce, which is why it is to rare.

Abilities. Cox (1926) was inspired by Lewis Terman to undertake a retrospective study of the IQ scores of 300 historical geniuses. Naturally, most were not around to take IQ tests, on top of which it is hard to imagine an IQ test that one could sensibly give to Aristotle, Newton, Beethoven, and da Vinci. Cox tried to get around the problem by working from biographical data, looking at when they began to walk and talk and achieve various other developmental milestones. Such data were often scanty and the study is little more than entertaining guesswork. Indeed, Gould (1981) criticises it severely. Table 4.1 gives some results, with the English philosopher John Stuart Mill at the top of the totem pole.

The estimated scores were mostly high. Does that mean a high score is needed to be a genius? Probably not. Many scientists now believe that a threshold level of about 120 is all that is needed. One must have some general intelligence to acquire expertise in a given field and a score well below 120 suggests it will be too difficult to soak up and manipulate the required knowledge. Beyond the threshold, what counts are creativity and certain personality traits. Cox's study is flawed for this reason and her estimates may all be far too high, if indeed they mean anything at all.

Some scientists doubt that even 120 is necessary. Howe (1988b) whimsically asks if anyone can be a genius, and adds that he is no longer sure that the answer is an unequivocal 'no'. He cites the savante syndrome and cases of people of average general ability developing an exceptional skill — amongst them a person who could remember eighty digits after a single hearing and another with a skill of identifying objects in a video screen accurately in about one-third the time it took others. The common factor is a lot of training in that or similar tasks, to become an 'expert'. Indeed, as already mentioned, James Watson, Nobel Prize winner and co-discoverer of the structure of DNA, said he only scored 115 on an IQ test.

Table 4.1   Estimated IQ Scores of Some of History's Geniuses

Genius	Estimated childhood IQ score
John Stuart Mill	190
Gottfried Liebnitz	185
Johann von Goethe	185
Samuel Coleridge	175
Michael Faraday	150
Wolfgang Mozart	150
Rene Descartes	150
George Handel	145
Charles Dickens	145
Francis Bacon	145
Average for philosophers	180
Average for scientists	175
Average for soldiers	140

Source: Cox (1926)

The idea that genius rests on a hypertrophied single ability based on enormous practice has been around a long time. Ellis (1904) pored through volumes of a biographical dictionary of eminent persons and argued that they were often skilled at just one area and average or below average on others. Many had poor muscular coordination and poor social perception. Chapter 2 mentioned how Bohr and Pavlov lacked practical intelligence, and Hollingworth (1942) cites the view as an old one.

However, probably more than this is needed. Studies of gifted and talented children show they have inborn talent, and they probably also need specialised abilities. Sociology and literature require strong verbal ability, which one cannot acquire just by extensive training. Physics requires strong visual imagery and mathematical ability. Painting and sculpture would seem to require good imagery and spatial relations.

Family backgrounds. In the film *The Boys from Brazil*, ex-Nazi doctor Joseph Mengele wants to unleash a horde of latter-day Hitlers on the modern world. He clones the dictator, implants embryos in women in several nations, and then tries to replicate Hitler's family background. The dictator had a doting mother and a weak father who died when Hitler was thirteen. The mothers are duly selected for tendency to dote, and the 'fathers' are killed at the appropriate time. The idea is that the right genes and family background will create a person with Hitler's abilities and personality.

Researchers into genius have believed something similar, and have examined the family background of many geniuses. Several commonalities typically turn up in many (Albert, 1983; Ellis, 1904; Simonton, 1988). One is early isolation from age mates. The child genius-to-be often had no playmates of his or her own age, and either spent much time in the company of adults or older siblings, or was alone a great deal. Sometimes it was intention. John Stuart Mill's father thought that other children would downgrade his son's capacities and kept him apart. Another shared characteristic is a lot of early stimulation, sometimes deriving from the first factor. Geniuses often were raised in a diverse, rich environment, with lots of books, interesting visitors, and so on. Indeed, rat studies have shown that a lot of early stimulation may improve the rat equivalent of intelligence (see Chapter 5). Sometimes the parents stimulate by pushing their children very hard. Mill wrote a history of Rome at six and a half years old, and his father required him to read Plato's *Dialogues* — a difficult work with which adults have trouble — at the age of seven. Mill himself said he understood little of it. Third is an unsettled family situation, stirred up for one or more of a variety of reasons. Many lost a parent early; 22 per cent in one study. Others had discordant parents. A fourth commonality is that geniuses tend to come from relatively liberal homes, either nonreligious or of liberal denominations.

These factors may lead to high ability, in the case of stimulation, and certain personality traits necessary for genius in the others.

Personality traits. The following are typical, and indeed seem necessary. First, geniuses tend to be independent, free thinkers, willing to strike out on their own and to overturn traditional ways of thinking. A study of very creative architects found that the best of them took nothing on authority and continually questioned what they were taught, even in architecture school. Being very original often involves social disapproval and a struggle to get work accepted by authorities. Being an independent nonconformist helps give the will to struggle. Such traits may derive from being alone a lot or coming from an unsettled, liberal home. The person is less socialised, less bothered by disapproval. Indeed, some sociologists have commented that really creative persons sometimes are 'marginal', not fully part of any culture.

Second, geniuses often believe strongly in their ability, sometimes to the point of having a sense of personal destiny. Such high self-esteem gives confidence when the going gets tough and the critics get rough. Believing one *can* do something also keeps a person trying much harder, a characteristic shown by Einstein.

There is a famous story along these lines that shows what belief can do. A prominent mathematician when still a student walked into a classroom late. On the board was a problem, apparently a homework assignment. He took it home, worked on it for three days, and handed in the answer. But it was not homework. The professor had put it up as a major unsolved problem in mathematics. Such self-confidence also can promote a profound dissatisfaction with the way things are in a field, and the assurance to try to change it.

Third is a tendency to introversion and isolation. This may derive from childhood isolation, and it may also select for talent. Extroverts may have the ability but not the will to create great works, which often require enormous periods working alone. Why toil when the world has many social temptations?

Fourth, geniuses show an intense devotion to their field, often to the exclusion of all else. They may think, eat, and sleep their area. Many verge on the compulsive when it comes to work. Such single-mindedness means lots of knowledge gets acquired and that lots of work gets done and improved. Again, we see the parallel with savantes. Great artistic and scientific works often require an enormous amount of time and effort. Few emerge complete in a single burst of creation. Wagner took twenty years, on and off, to write the *Ring* and Beethoven tinkered with every note in a work for months. Darwin developed his ideas about evolution over many years. Someone must have a compulsive devotion to work to put in the hours.

Simonton (1988) further points out that geniuses tend to be prolific. Bach's musical works take up many volumes, and apparently would take a lifetime just to copy out by hand. Einstein contributed 250 publications and Picasso many thousands of artworks. Simonton says that devotion leads to productivity, which in turn leads to a better chance that a few works of the many will be great ones.

Simonton mentions two more traits of scientific genius. While many scientists live in dread of being in error or upstaged and so may contribute little, the genius tends to be a risk-taker and not afraid to be wrong. As well, many a genius has a sense of playfulness, manifested sometimes in an odd sense of humour.

Other factors. Both Simonton (1988) and Albert (1975) point out that a person only becomes a genius when others judge him or her to be one. Self-opinion is not enough. Important persons in the field must accept it. Even so, great talent often goes unnoticed. For example, in the early 1960s the author John Toole committed suicide after repeated failure to find a publisher for his novel, *A Confederacy of Dunces*. Later it was published, due to his mother's efforts. It won the Pulitzer Prize and the film rights were sold. In the 1970s someone wanted to show how hard it was to publish a great novel in America. He took Jerzy Kosinski's novel *Steps*, which had won the American National Book Award, typed it out and sent it to many houses, but could not find a publisher. Richard Wagner had enormous difficulty getting his own work accepted. Einstein's special theory of relativity was published in an article in the German Journal *Annalen der Physik* in 1905, but it did not immediately set the world on fire, probably because few actually read it and fewer still could understand it. Only many months later did a letter arrive from prominent physicist Max Planck, who was so impressed that he persuaded colleagues to look at it. Often, a genius needs such a strong champion to get new ideas accepted.

If a genius lacks such a patron, he or she must be a tireless self-promoter, ready to constantly battle tradition and the critics. Those who curl up in despair after initial setbacks rarely get anywhere. Once more we see the importance again of traits such as determination, belief in oneself, and ability to work hard.

These findings lead to an interesting paradox. On the one hand, society depends largely on geniuses to advance, to solve its difficult problems, or to push forward the frontiers of science and the arts. However, society often treats them badly, rejecting both them and their work before their work is recognised. One reason is innate human conservatism. Few like it when ideas that they have lived with and with which they are comfortable are demolished. Many have a vested interest in traditional ideas as well. In addition, because of our social nature, humans tend to prefer extroverted, conforming, group-oriented persons, just the opposite of many geniuses.

The ill treatment that many receive has been noted time and time again. John Stuart Mill commented on the pressure to conform and the difficulty that geniuses, individual by nature, may face:

They are less capable of fitting themselves into any of the small number of moulds which society provides . . . if they break their fetters they become a mark for the society which has not succeeded in reducing them to common-place, to point out with solemn warning as 'wild' or, 'erratic' or the like.

Ellis (1904) commented:

It is practically impossible to estimate the amount of persecution to which this group of pre-eminent British persons has been subjected, for it has shown itself in innumerable forms, and varies between a mere passive denial to have any-thing whatever to do with them or their work and the active infliction of physical torture and death . . . The person of genius is an abnormal being, thus arousing the instinctive hostility of society, which by every means seeks to put him out of the way.

MENSA — THE HIGH IQ SOCIETY

An IQ test arrives in the mail. You open it and read the instructions, which admonish you to adhere strictly to the test time limits to avoid later embarrassment, complete it, and then return it. You do so. Some time passes, and you receive an invitation to take some supervised IQ tests. You spend a morning doing two tests; a verbal one so difficult that no one is ever meant to finish in the time allowed, and a nonverbal Ravens-type test. More time passes. Even-tually word arrives that you may join Mensa, which is an exclusive club for the gifted, the genius, and those just good at doing IQ tests. All you need do is pay a small membership fee that allows you to attend meetings and receive a monthly magazine. You are in, certi-fied as having scored in the top 2 per cent of the population, as only one person in fifty would do. Sometimes the test routine is different. British Mensa used to operate drop-in testing centres in which anyone could take a test immediately.

Mensa began after a radio broadcast in England in 1945 in which Cyril Burt discussed the new public opinion polling and suggested that it would be interesting to know the opinions of the very brightest of the population. The following year, the lawyers Roland Berrill and L. L. Ware set up a panel of the very bright, as measured by an IQ test, feeling their views might be of interest to governments and other organisations. The panel was named *Mensa*, Latin for 'table', because the group would be a 'round table where no one has precedence'. It grew mightily from there. A U.S. branch began in 1961 and Mensa now has branches in many nations and about 90,000 members worldwide. It does not, however, much bother to advise governments, which often do not heed the advice of committees they set up themselves. Mensa's primary purpose now is to provide a social club and a stimulating environment for some of society's talent. Many people say that they join simply to be able to talk to other bright people. Too much everyday conversation is dull for them and they have to 'talk down'. As one member put it: 'I like to have conversations where I don't have to wait half an hour for an answer'. Some quite famous people are members, for example the writer Isaac Asimov, but members come from just about all occupations and walks of life.

Serebriakoff (1965) gives the following description of some of the traits of Mensa's earliest members. He says in a crowd they are hardly distinguishable from any other group, but after being with them you notice they are more at ease, humorous and informed, and that discussions among them are very wide-ranging. They are less conventional than normal, and one must be aware of hidden wit.

The Limits of Human Intelligence

Limits are of intrinsic interest. People want to know the maximum speeds of cars, planes, and rockets; the maximum height that helicopters can reach, depths submarines can dive to; and the maximum lifetimes of anything from vacuum cleaners and dams to subatomic particles and the universe itself. Much scientific and engineering research probes such limits, both for practicality's and curiosity's sake. Scientists have determined many limits; the cosmic speed limit of about 305,000 km/hr, the minimum possible temperature of about -273°C (no one knows what the maximum is), and the possible size of the observable universe at perhaps 14 billion light years across. Practical limits are ones such as the maximum load a bridge, floor, or rope can take.

Plant and animal limits also are tested. Biologists investigate them not just out of curiosity, but because physical limits explain why many things are as they are. For example, animals have strict size limits. Once they get too large they collapse under their own weight, as a beached whale does. Insects cannot grow beyond a certain size because their breathing system of tubes into the body gets too inefficient if the tubes are too long. Birds cannot get too large or heavy and still fly. Most species have maximum lifespans, from the day of a mayfly to the thousands of years of the sequoia tree.

Lots of questions about human limits have been asked, and *The Guinness Book of Records* continually updates some. They include rather unpleasant ones like how long we can survive without food or water and the extreme temperatures that we can take. Athletes keep pushing back some apparent physical limits, improving their performances through better training methods, psychological preparation, and even drugs like steroids.

What are the limits of human intelligence? We can look at this question in several ways. First, what are the brain's limits? It has an enormous number of neurons and connections, but neural transmission is fundamentally limited because it is agonisingly slow by computer standards. The brain partially overcomes this problem by performing many tasks at once. But it does limit speed of reaction and of other things. For example, reading has an estimated physical limit of about 800 words per minute. The eyes cannot move faster to increase this. Speed readers overcome it by skipping words, of course.

First, consider IQ. What is the maximum IQ? Is there one? Probably. Wechsler (1952) argues that variation in a species is limited. He says that set ratios of the highest to the lowest are common, and that for IQ the ratio is about 2.86 to 1. Unfortunately it is not really clear what the lowest IQ should be for the comparison. Table 4.1 gives J. S. Mill as having the highest estimated score of 190, while *The Guinness Book of Records* lists two people as having scored 197 on the Stanford-Binet. We can tentatively argue that maximum human IQ score is about 200, which is also what Lewis Terman estimated that Francis Galton would have scored. However, it is not all that clear exactly what such a score means. Persons with very high IQ scores often are not particularly creative, but they think very quickly and are extremely adept at solving well-defined problems with clear-cut answers. They are good at 'converging' on the right answer. Perhaps a well-endowed individual might exceed 200 if given enormous amounts of education, and a very stimulating early environment. Genetic engineering may possibly also produce people who score above 200.

The limits of some of the elements of intelligence are much more clear-cut. Our senses have very impressive resolving power, but they have limits. For example, vision is restricted to a short band of wavelengths (from about 400 to 700 mm) and hearing to a certain band of frequencies. The limit of vision is about seven photons — a photon being the smallest unit of light — while an ordinary light bulb emits tens of billions of photons every second. Our noses can detect some chemicals diluted by one part in trillions of air. Table 4.2 presents some sensory limits. They are only approximate, however, as factors such as fatigue can alter them. People do differ greatly in sensory acuity, and some animals have keener senses than humans (see Chapter 8). We partially overcome our limits with telescopes, microscopes, stethoscopes, X-ray scanners, and so on.

Table 4.2   Some Sensory Thresholds

Vision	Candle from about 50 km away on a dark night
Hearing	Tick of watch from about five metres away
Taste	Teaspoon of sugar in 9 litres of water
Smell	Drop of perfume in volume of three-room apartment
Touch	Wing of bee falling on cheek from one centimetre away

Source. Galanter (1962)

Memory also has limits. Working memory span is only about seven items, although we can improve it by chunking, while long-term memory capacity, as far as anyone knows, is infinite — at least for all practical purposes. Some studies supporting this idea were mentioned in Chapter 2. But there is other evidence, such as the verbatim memories of some savantes, while *The Guinness Book of Records* describes Mehmed Ali Halici's memory as so good that he recited 6,666 Koranic verses from memory, taking six hours to do so. Chapter 2 also mentioned the Russian journalist described by Luria whose memory was so good that he virtually could not forget anything. His talent was only discovered when an editor handing out the day's assignments noticed that he was not writing instructions down. He did not need to, and thought that everyone else had his particular talent.

What is limited is how much we can take in at a time. Chapter 2 mentioned the limits on our attention, that we can fully focus on just one stream of information at a time. We are partially overcoming this with computers, which not only store vast amounts of information but can manipulate it. Computer simulations of atmospheres, economies, and even the universe's formation make it possible to study things that the limits of our intelligence previously made impossible.

One more limit is on the number of domains in which a given person can become an expert. But this is difficult to quantify. Most of us become experts in several domains for which we have innate wiring — language, dealing with other people, and so on. It is much easier to acquire expertise in some fields because they contain much less knowledge; Trobriand Island folk-dancing and Wagnerian opera versus quantum mechanics. Let us just consider complex fields containing a lot of knowledge. By one estimate it takes ten years to become an expert in a domain such as chess or music. The practical

limit, based on motivation and on a maximum age of about seventy
is probably around five or six fields. Very few excel in more than
two or three, however. Persons such as Leonardo da Vinci are truly
exceptional.

LEARNING DISABILITIES

And now from heights to depths; to ability well below average, to
disability. The first case is a very interesting syndrome which is the
mirror image of the idiot savante syndrome; a person with at least
average general intelligence but abysmal ability in one or two areas.
An oasis of poverty lies in a middle-class or affluent suburb. Here
are two illustrative cases, from Kirk and Gallagher (1986).

George is a university student with good grades in science and
mathematics, an excellent grade in art, but dismal performance at
subjects based on words, such as English and history. He failed
first-year English twice and only barely scraped through on the
third attempt. Why was there such a disparity in a person of above-
average intelligence? An intrigued university counsellor gave him
some tests to find out. They revealed good spatial relations and
quantitative ability but verbal ability well below average.

At age twelve, Sampson came to a clinic because his arithmetic
was dreadful, although he could read well. He had had a car acci-
dent four years before, which left him able to do little arithmetic
beyond adding and subtracting. He could not grasp the idea of place
value, which is an essential concept needed to multiply and divide.
Special tutoring helped little.

Such cases are called *learning disabilities*, a term coined in
1963. A learning disabled person has average or better general
intelligence (as measured by IQ tests) but a perplexing deficit in one
or a few specific (disability) areas. The most common disabilities are
in language, and particularly in reading. Other disabilities may be
perceptual, involving problems in recognising objects or faces, or
motor; a person has poor coordination and poor muscle control, may
walk with an odd gait, and have problems handling tools and toss-
ing and catching balls. Further deficits may be in memory (e.g., a
child easily forgetting words, facts, and teachers' directions); in
attention (e.g., a child having difficulty concentrating for long); or in
social skills (e.g., a person having difficulty learning to read
nonverbal cues, assess intentions, or behave appropriately in social
situations).

The deficits can range from mild, which often can be compensated for, to quite severe. They are often picked up early, when a child has trouble with a school subject or two, and although they may persist into adulthood they become less of a problem because people can select work to minimise their weak spots. However, a lot of learning-disabled children get very frustrated in school and drop out early. It is also a widespread problem, and by one estimate, about 4 per cent of all schoolchildren are learning disabled to some extent (Kirk & Gallagher, 1986).

Causes

Kirk and Gallagher (1986) note that it is usually impossible to spot the specific cause of learning disability in a given case, but say that about half of all cases may have a specific brain disorder. Since many functions are localised, damage in a given brain area can zap one function and not others. The cause may be an injury, or it may be genetic. DeFries and Decker (1981) found some evidence for genetic predisposition, establishing that reading disabilities tend to run in the family. Other possible causes include severe malnutrition, biochemical factors, early environmental restriction, and a poor learning environment.

Lots of research has tried to tease out exactly why the learning disabled cannot perform tasks in particular areas. Sternberg (1985) argues that they have trouble automating processing in a domain; they automate slowly or not at all. Other work suggests they have problems learning strategies to deal with their problem domain. A strategy is a general plan of attack on a problem; for example, rehearsing a list of items again and again to recall it, or consciously chunking items (see Chapter 7). A lot of remedial work has involved teaching strategies. Sometimes they improve the situation, but sometimes they do not. A problem seems to be that the learning disabled don't think that strategies will help, and need a lot of persuasion to even try them out.

This and the savante syndrome show that intelligence is not always general, though on average it seems to be. Again, this work fits Gardner's ideas that there are independent intelligences, at least to some degree.

MENTAL RETARDATION

Finally we reach general poverty, unmarked by any oasis of wealth. Mental retardation is low general intelligence, and affects about 5 per cent of the population. The diagnosis is sometimes made soon after birth (or even before it). Some syndromes are obvious then; the child looks retarded. But sometimes it is made much later. The child is slow, not meeting the usual developmental milestones, and by school age the reason why becomes all too obvious. Parents often greet the label with shock. In extreme cases it can necessitate a lifetime of care, sometimes in a custodial institution or a sheltered workshop. For some retardates, what they can do and achieve is fundamentally limited and life holds very dim prospects. Others lead fulfilling lives. Intelligence is not all-important. But, mental retardation limits independence and what can be understood and is a great problem for technological societies. Some nations spend massive sums on prevention and education programs and some, like the United States, will not allow retarded immigrants.

Definition

As mentioned, a disability is an incapacity to do something; jump three metres, toss a javelin 100 metres, learn calculus, or do long division. In mental retardation the disability is general, and with the very rare exceptions of savantes, it covers all areas. A widely used definition of the condition is that used by the American Association of Mental Deficiency: 'A general disability manifested by an IQ less than 70 and deficits in adaptive behaviour'. The latter part means that the individual has problems getting by in society independently. He or she finds it hard to find and hold a job, manage finances, find places to live, and meet social demands. Such things are 'adaptive behaviours', which are assessed by observation or specific tests. But IQ alone is not everything and a person may score below 70 but behave adaptively enough to not merit the diagnosis. Maladaptive behaviours are responses such as banging one's head to gain attention, repeatedly stealing, or rocking back and forth. These disturb others, of course. Many retarded persons have physical problems as well, such as palsy, seizures or inability to walk (Snell & Renzaglia, 1986). Nature treats them very unfairly.

There are three degrees of retardation, usually indicated by approximate IQ ranges. These give some idea of what an individual can and cannot do, but only an approximate notion (Snell & Renzaglia, 1986).

Mild retardation is indicated by an IQ score of 69 down to about 55 or 50. It usually is not so bad, involving difficulty in school but a good chance of holding an unskilled or semi-skilled job and having an independent life. *Moderate* retardation ranges from there down to about 40 or 35. It usually necessitates custodial care and the prospect of possible supervised work in a sheltered workshop. *Severe* retardation is anything below that, and is very bad news indeed. Such retardates usually require constant attention, which Snell and Renzaglia illustrate with the case of a six-year-old child who sits in a wheelchair and has little facial expression. Her movements are floppy because of poor muscle tone. She will learn little that year, perhaps just to brush her teeth, take off her coat, or help someone feed her. She may learn to 'talk' with an electronic communication board. Children in this category may behave in unpleasant ways as well. They can be very aggressive, throw temper tantrums, self-mutilate, and typically do not pick up social cues well. Some nontechnological societies living in harsh environments have neither the time nor the labour to spare for them. Western society is rich enough to care for some of nature's mistakes.

Causes

The number of factors that can cause retardation are so many that it seems a minor miracle that more persons are not affected. A lot of the causes are quite preventable, either through genetic counselling or altering habits during pregnancy. Health authorities lavish large sums on such education programs, a little prevention being worth many tonnes of treatment.

First, there are many genetic causes (Snell & Renzaglia, 1986). Several specific syndromes are carried on the genes, with two of the most common being Down's syndrome (Mongolism) and phenylketonuria. Down's results from the child gaining an extra chromosome (47 instead of the usual 46) and was first described by Langdon Down in 1866. He gave it the racist tag because sufferers looked a bit Oriental. Most cases are born to mothers over thirty-five years old, one reason why reproducing late becomes progressively more dicey. Phenylketonuria is quite intriguing in that it is a rare example of a treatable genetic disorder. The child's body cannot break down a chemical called phenylalanine, an unpleasant substance that builds up in the blood and eventually damages the developing brain. If the child is kept on a very low phenylalanine diet until adolescence, when the brain is no longer developing, the problem is solved. But this can be difficult to achieve as children do not like special diets. The syndrome is a psychologist's classroom favourite because it shows how hard genes and environment are to disentangle. Environment is having an effect through the genes. Another genetic disorder, recently discovered, is 'fragile X syndrome', where an X chromosome lacks something. The child usually is male, and has a long face, pointed jaw, and protruding ears. There are other genetic syndromes. Other cases of retardation are genetic in the sense that the child just gets too few genes that involve intelligence.

There is a host of environmental causes, some of which strike during pregnancy itself. The developing fetus has a lot of protection from the outside world, but does not live in a fortress. Several diseases contracted during pregnancy may lead to retardation; German measles in the first three months, syphilis, and a number of viruses. Sometimes the child's major threat is its mother. Taking substances such as lead and alcohol during pregnancy may cause retardation. One well-known problem is the 'fetal alcohol syndrome', which by one estimate can be induced by the mother drinking only three ounces a day. A few children have even sued their mothers for alleged abuses during pregnancy. Malnutrition, before or after birth, is another cause. One legacy of widespread famine in a nation may be a lower intelligence level in the next generation. Finally, a number of diseases contracted after birth are causes; for instance meningitis and encephalitis.

Yet another cause is an impoverished environment. Occasionally, children come to light who have spent their entire lives concealed in an attic or cellar. Usually they were illegitimate, and were kept from the world's sight out of a deep sense of misplaced shame. A solid regime of attic walls will produce a very dull child indeed, as may a generally unstimulating environment. One of Head Start's aims was to stimulate at-risk children to counter the effects of dull environments, to ensure that any IQ score decline was not as severe as might be.

A particular child might be retarded for more than one of the above causes. In nearly half of all cases, the exact cause is not known. There may also be many other causes still awaiting discovery.

The Deficits

Psychometrics hardly tackled the question of deficits, doing little more than noting that the retarded score low on IQ tests. But why? What deficits make them score low and behave unintelligently. Why can't they learn easily? Cognitive psychologists became very interested in finding out why (e.g., Ashman, 1990; Campione et al., 1982). Understanding what is wrong may suggest ways to improve their intelligence or give better methods to teach them things.

It would be nice if there were only one deficit, but research has turned up a number. First, the retarded generally think and respond slowly; they are generally mentally slow. They have a poor knowledge base, which partly derives from their inability to learn readily. A poor knowledge base also means that new things are harder to learn. The more one knows about a domain, the easier it is to learn new things. Retardates also have poor judgment and face problems deciding what is relevant and important in a given situation. They have great trouble keeping their attention focused, which is necessary to think and learn well. They have poor working memories and do not readily chunk. Most are poorly motivated to learn, probably because it is so hard for them and they have a long history of repeated failure. When they do learn, they need very explicit instruction (Berry, 1989). They hardly ever find out or figure things out for themselves.

Research has turned up another major deficit: The retarded know little about strategies. They don't understand how their own thinking and memory works, and they do not try to use strategies to remember and learn. Even when they do know a strategy, they do not spontaneously use it (someone has to tell them to) and they don't switch to another if it is not working. A simple example is rehearsal, continually repeating items that one wants to remember. Very young children have to learn to do this, too. Another example is simply noticing redundancies in material to be learned. Say one had to recall the digits 172172172165165165. Most retardates would not spontaneously rehearse them, and would not notice the repetition of digits, which would simplify the task of recalling them.

The strategy-lack suggested a plan of attack. If they don't know and use strategies, let us teach them some. Let us teach them to rehearse and to chunk and to look for redundancy, and how to improve their learning. Lots of researchers have tried, and it works to some extent. Some retardates learned strategies and their performance often improved dramatically, but then things got less promising. Often they would abandon the strategy, or not use it spontaneously. They also would very rarely use the strategy beyond the situation in which it was learned. Say one taught a retarded child to rehearse to remember a series of digits. The child uses the strategy and his memory improves. Then one gives him letters or shopping list items to recall. The child does not rehearse and performance plummets; he does not *generalise*. Lack of generalisation is a problem in education with all children, but to a lesser degree. Many teachers get frustrated with their children's failure to extend something beyond the situation in which it was learned. Indeed, Skemp (1979) tells an amusing story along these lines. A child told his father that he had learned his seven-times table. The father then asked what seven times five was, and the child answered correctly. The father then said, 'You are seven little boys at a party and you have four balloons each. How many balloons altogether?' The reply showed no generalisation: 'I don't know ... we haven't done balloons'. The retarded never seem to realise that in a sense they have done balloons.

Much research on strategy training is still going on. Some researchers are looking for ways to improve generalisation. Others are trying to find out if the retarded do not use them for other reasons; poor motivation or because they don't think that strategies will help. Various programs have also tried to improve the general prowess of retardates or 'cure' them. Some make extravagant claims, and these are examined in Chapter 7.

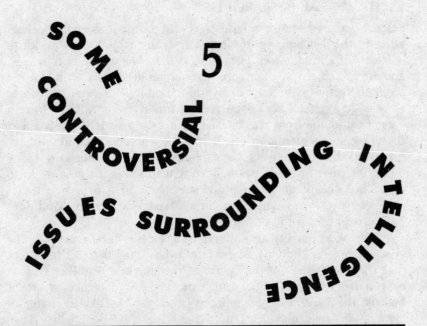

SOME CONTROVERSIAL ISSUES SURROUNDING INTELLIGENCE

5

Intelligence is an emotion-laden topic, often cloaked in controversy. New findings and ideas about it can easily provoke heated arguments, partly because decisions made from them or from test results may be far-reaching.

The controversial issues fall into two broad categories. The first consists of research issues like 'Are differences in intelligence between people partly genetic?' and 'Are there race differences in average intelligence?' Lots of people lose their rationality when such questions come up. They accept only one answer, or say that no one should even try to tackle the question. For example, in the early 1970s the American Anthropological Association wanted to halt all research on racial differences in IQ. However, the questions have answers and the answers are important, even if no one much likes them.

The second category includes ethical and philosophical issues, such as 'How should society deal with the mentally retarded?' and 'Should intelligence be treated as a national resource?' The answers largely rest on values and practicalities. Here they are just outlined along with some opinions about them.

CONTROVERSIAL RESEARCH ISSUES

Science works because scientists try to be dispassionate seekers after 'truth', just hunting 'the facts'. In reality, this is only an ideal. Scientists are human too. They have beliefs, wishes, and prejudices, and are influenced by their culture. Such influences sometimes blind them to facts, or at least delay their finding out how the world more-or-less actually is. Even such a luminary as Albert Einstein was not immune from bias caused by his deep-seated beliefs about the universe. As mentioned in Chapter 4, when his relativity theory predicted that the universe was expanding he introduced a 'fudge factor' because he could not believe that this was the case. He also could not accept quantum physics because of a firm belief that things have causes, summed up in his famous statement 'God does not play dice with the universe'.

The wider society also affects what facts will be accepted. The best example is church leaders' refusal for many decades to accept that the Earth was not the centre of the universe. Another famous case comes from the Soviet Union in the 1930s. Science had to fit Marxist theory, and the Soviets put geneticist Lysenko in charge of genetics because his ideas fitted the ideology. Though his views about genetics verged on the crackpot, Soviet geneticists had to heed them and all dissenters were suppressed. Even much agriculture had to be based on his ideas. The result was disaster for Soviet genetics and agriculture.

Much the same problem has surfaced with some issues to do with intelligence. Many researchers and the wider society will often accept only one favoured answer. They are partly justified in this, because unpalatable data can be used for nefarious purposes. For example, racial differences data may be used by racists for propaganda, or by governments to abolish specific programs. But we still need answers, and for several major reasons. The first is that they are needed to understand intelligence. Answers will help build a theory that cannot be complete without them. Second is simple curiosity. Third, the answers have dramatic social policy implications. Intelligence enters into welfare, education, and a host of related areas. Policy-makers need a solid knowledge base to make intelligent decisions. They need facts, no matter how unpleasant they may be. Of course, values and wishes and ideology always intrude into government decision-making, but planners still need data.

When decisions are made on a tenuous knowledge base, problems can arise (Zigler & Seitz, 1982), and examples abound. Consider the issue of whether intelligence differences are partly genetic. If planners believe they are not, they may spend vast sums trying to 'cure' retardation or to try to raise intelligence levels in others through heroic environmental means. School systems also are less likely to stream children in classes by ability or to select out the best talent early for special training. As Spitz (1986, 1988) points out, this rabid environmentalism has prevailed in the United States and underlies a great deal of social policy. Planners don't much believe that genes affect IQ scores. The same assumption and the idea of fair play mean they don't much believe in racial differences either, at least not in genetic ones. Black/white differences are seen as due to poor environments or past discrimination. If a planner believes such things, then money may be spent trying to raise black average intelligence rather than on other things. Similarly, many resources have been poured into trying to do something about the poor average performance of schoolgirls at mathematics. Planners assume there are no innate sex differences in ability, and work from that belief. But if there really are differences, the money will be best spent in some other way.

Planners need sound information. Let us look at what research has to say about some of these questions.

Group Differences

Many studies have looked for possible group differences in general intelligence or in more specific abilities (e.g., Cattell, 1987; Eysenck, 1979). The usual method of investigation is to give IQ tests to many members of various groups and see if average differences occur. The results may satisfy curiosity and guide decision-making.

Two problems immediately arise. IQ is a poor measure of general intelligence, and if IQ tests are biased against a particular group, this may produce the apparent group differences. One such case arguably is the 15-point mean IQ difference between American black and whites. Investigators have tried to overcome this problem by eliminating biased items or by developing culture-fair tests. Whether or not such tests can be fair is still a matter of controversy. Here we will merely survey some studies. In view of the problems listed above, it is a bit unclear exactly how they should be interpreted.

Before launching into the data, a caution needs mention. A finding of a group difference between, say, the sexes, does not mean that every member of one group scores higher than every member of the other. It merely means that the averages differ. In practice, the distributions usually overlap greatly. It is much like height. On average, males are taller than females, but lots of females are tall and lots of males are short. Some females are taller than the male average of about 180 cm and some males are shorter than the female average.

Sex Differences

Chapter 1 mentioned that there are no mean sex differences in IQ (Cattell, 1987), but that more males are at the extremes. However, a few scientists have argued that perhaps there are mean differences and that IQ tests are cooked to eliminate them by dropping items that favour one sex. When one looks at more specific abilities, things get more interesting. Females consistently score higher, on average, in verbal fluency (the ability to produce lots of words quickly). Indeed, girls generally begin talking earlier than boys. Females are also better at social skills, being better able to deal with others, and to pick up and send nonverbal messages. Males score higher on spatial relations, the ability to visualise spatial arrangements, and to manipulate the images. Males also score better at mathematical ability (Benbow, 1988). The latter difference is quite marked and seems to emerge early. Indeed, female mathematicians are very thin on the ground. Educators have expended much effort to try to encourage more females to study mathematics, believing the difference to be entirely environmental, and perhaps it is. But perhaps it is not.

Why do these differences occur? One favoured explanation is that it is all environmental. Females are trained differently. They are taught to nurture, to cooperate and not to out-do, and so excel at social skills. One researcher has even argued that young girls do not venture as far from home as males, and so do not learn the same spatial skills. Females may avoid mathematics because it is traditionally a male subject, and so their ability at it remains dormant.

Others say that the differences are partly genetic. Nature selected for them. There is a lot of evidence for this idea. Male and female brains may be organised differently because selection pressures on males and females are different. Consider sexual behaviour, of which differences are usually pronounced. Females typically are very choosy about partners while males are more indiscriminate. It is to the male's advantage to impregnate as many females as possible; he does so very cheaply. For females, however, pregnancy and giving birth constitute a long and risky process. Best if they select a very fit mate so that the offspring will be fit too. So the behaviour differences arise. In a few species, the roles are reversed. The female cheaply lays eggs and then takes off, leaving the male to care for and feed the young. Males then are typically choosier about partners and females more indiscriminate.

Why would natural selection produce such human ability differences? For most of its existence the human race has been employed as a hunter-gatherer. The men trooped off together to hunt game while the females stayed close to the camp to gather fruit, seeds and roots, and to mind the children. Since males ranged over wide areas, those best able to find their way around (and back to camp) had a selective advantage. For women, traditionally keeping groups together and bringing up children, great skill at human relations was an advantage. Much the same sort of pattern occurs in other species. For example, in some bird species the males outperform the females at spatial tasks and in others there is no sex difference. Studies suggest that species where males perform better range over wider territories, or at least the males do, and so ability is selected for. It may well be that the human sex differences are entirely due to upbringing, but it seems likely that they are not.

Again, the variation in sexes and overlap between them is great. The differences are only on average. As Dr Johnson aptly asked, when quizzed about sex differences, 'Which man? Which woman?'

Race Differences

Humanity is sometimes classified into three major groups: Mongoloid, Caucasoid, and Negroid. Each group also has subgroups, though of disputed validity (e.g., Alpines, Nordics, and Celtics within Caucasoids). The races shade into each other. There has been a lot of mixing of genes, and some scientists dispute that such things as 'races' even exist. Certainly, no one is certain when humanity split into the groups: One estimate is about 250,000 years ago, but others say much less. In fact, it is not unusual for a species to break into such groups. A major cause, and probably the one in humanity's case, is geographical isolation. When one group is cut off from another (e.g., birds flying to an island), genetic drift and natural selection over many generations may produce a new species. Some say that if the human races had been isolated much longer, different species may have arisen, unable to interbreed.

Races differ in average height, skin shade, and a few other physical things. Not surprisingly, people have asked whether they differ in intelligence as well. Beliefs that they do go back a long way and are of course still current. In 1869 Francis Galton argued the Caucasians are the most intelligent race and he ranked all the others down to the Australoids (Australian Aborigines) at the bottom. In 1986 then-prime minister of Japan Nakasone created a storm by telling a Japanese audience that Japan held an economic edge over the United States because of the low intelligence of American black and Hispanic minorities. The Nazi racial philosophy of the 1920s postulated an Aryan 'master race' superior to others in all ways, including intelligence. There is no master race, however. J. B. S. Haldane debunked the idea in the 1930s, while Noble in 1978 surveyed many studies of all kinds of perceptual and motor skills and debunked the idea of one race being superior to others in every way. (There is not even an Aryan race!)

Nazi propaganda gave the whole study of race differences a very bad name, which persists. Even studying it nowadays can lead to trouble. Consider Phillippe Rushton, a professor at the University of Western Ontario in Canada. He has written extensively on racial differences but is very unpopular because of it. Academic critics and the media have dealt with him harshly. He has been charged with faulty scholarship and was banned from speaking at a scientific conference.

What do studies show? The data are mixed, and are often hard to interpret. It is, as mentioned, difficult to find usable IQ tests because of the cultural problems. However, Rushton (1988) wrote a very controversial review of many studies. Some of his arguments are listed below, along with those of some other studies, and they seem to show that there might in fact be some racial differences. But such a conclusion is very tentative.

Rushton first argues that there is a lot of evidence for behaviour differences between people in the three major race groups, at least on the average. He argues that Mongoloids on average have more placid temperaments, and are less prone to swings of mood and excitability. Caucasoid children are noisier, more aggressive, and more disruptive. Negroids, in turn, are more aggressive, impulsive, and dominant than whites. He says that some such differences are apparent soon after birth, and further argues that Negroids mature faster. Then he gets very controversial indeed. He argues that there are race differences in 'sexual restraint', with Negroids having least, Mongoloids most, and Caucasoids being in the middle. Indeed, that was the typical pattern in many measures; Mongoloids, Caucasoids, then Negroids. Some critics dismissed this all as pseudo-scientific rubbish, particularly criticising the studies used.

And what of intelligence and other abilities? Rushton argues that the same pattern prevails; Mongoloids have most, followed by Caucasoids and then Negroids. He cites studies which show average brain sizes fitting the pattern; 1,351 gm, 1,336 gm, and 1,286 gm, respectively. He mentions the 15-point black/white difference in the United States. He cites studies of Africans in Jamaica with average IQ scores in the 80s and with even less in Africa. On the other hand, some studies suggest that the average Japanese IQ score is higher than the 100 of Caucasoids. Lynn and Hampson (1986) cite studies finding Japanese means of 106 and even 113. Rushton argues that Chinese and Japanese average IQ score together is higher. Some studies also suggest that the Japanese have a different mix of abilities, being stronger in spatial relations but weaker in verbal comprehension on average (Lynn & Hampson, 1986). Other studies have looked at narrow racial groupings. For example, Humphrey (1988) suggests that Amerindians and Puerto Ricans score lower on average than Caucasians. Rushton finally gives 107, 100, and 85 as averages for the three major groupings.

And now the real controversy starts. Assuming these differences exist, why do they occur? It may be genetic. The races may have different numbers of the genes for intelligence. Proponents of this view say that it explains the chronic poverty and underdevelopment in Africa; the bad, self-indulgent leaders of some African nations; and the consistent failure of most government programs to much improve the lot of American blacks. Some say that it partly explains the current commercial ascendancy of Japan. But others deny all this, claiming that there is no real evidence of innate racial differences (e.g., Kamin, 1974). The differences are due to environmental factors; years of discrimination, poverty, neglect, poor nutrition, poor education, and biased tests. The higher Japanese average may be due to intensive education and test wiseness. Japanese children take countless tests, become good at doing them, and know a lot more than Caucasians. However, some have investigated such possibilities and say they account for only some of the difference (e.g., Lynn, 1982).

The question is as yet unresolved and possibly will remain that way, perhaps because many feel it should not be studied. A major reason why it arouses hostility is that such data can be misused. Governments can use it to cut back social programs. Far right-wingers can use it to justify various practices. Racists can use it for propaganda.

Other Ethnic Factors
Race is one 'ethnic' factor. Many studies have looked at others,

notably nationality and social class. Again, such comparisons are fraught with peril. But findings are suggestive. The nationality question ties in with the race one to some extent. One study suggested average IQ differences between various Caucasian nations (Lynn, 1979). The average IQ in Ireland was supposed to be 96, versus a bit over 100 in England. One explanation is selective migration. Ireland has traditionally exported its people in hard times, and the brightest may have been more likely to shift to England or elsewhere.

Another factor is social class. Western societies traditionally are divided into upper, middle, and working classes, with various gradations in between (e.g., lower-middle, etc.). A new term is 'underclass', used to classify a vast body of people who depend on welfare or very low-paying jobs and are permanently locked into poverty. Class structures differ across nations. In Japan, England, and various European nations, there are great differences in accents, interests, behaviours, attitudes, and so on between classes. It is also difficult to shift from one class to another. Indeed, H. G. Wells' *The Time Machine* extrapolates the English class difference to the far future, where the upper and working classes have become different species. The upper live in an upper-air Athens, while the working classes have become troglodytes living underground. In the United States and Australia the behavioural differences between classes are much less pronounced, and are largely based on wealth rather than family background.

Studies suggest that there are class differences in average IQ (Herrnstein, 1973; Jensen, 1981) at least in meritocracies. IQ correlates with socioeconomic status. The bright tend to rise in society and the dull fall. Of course many other factors operate, such as motivation, personal connections, and so on. A major way in which class operates is through education. The better-off can afford more schooling for their children, and are more likely to value education, encourage it, and to be able to pay for university. In addition, the better-off are more likely to provide stimulating environments for their children. This plausible argument got Herrnstein into much trouble. He said that if classes are partly based on intelligence, and intelligence differences are partly genetic, then social class position is partly genetic. Many critics could not accept this idea.

There are also regional differences. Average IQ is typically higher in urban than in rural areas. In English children the difference may only be three or four points. In American blacks it may be seven to twelve points. As with Ireland, selective migration may be one reason why. The brighter may be more likely to move to the city for its stimulation. Teasdale, Owen, and Sorenson (1988) say that education differences may be the main cause. Urbanites on average are better educated.

Heredity or Environment?

Genes or upbringing? Nature or nurture? Are differences in intelligence partly genetic? This question generates heat second only to the racial differences issue, but the answer is important and lots of matters ride on it.

There are two extreme views. At one extreme, environmentalists such as Kamin (1974) hold that there is no evidence at all for genetic determination. They concede that some could exist, but at present there is just no evidence. They say that differences are caused by environmental factors such as diet and stimulation. Brighter children have had much more stimulating environments. This assumption underlies much American social policy and it fits in well with the official ideology that all are created equal. Similarly, the Soviets used to assume much the same. Marxism says that environment is everything. Despite this official line, in practice the Soviets selected out young talent very early for special schools and training. At the other extreme are such geneticists as Jensen (1969) and Eysenck (1979). They hold that genes cause at least some differences between people and that if the effects of environment were somehow nullified, if everyone's environment was exactly the same, differences in intelligence would still remain. A prime example is Cyril Burt, for whom it was an *idée fixe* (Gould, 1981). No one seriously proposes that environment has no effect at all and geneticists dispute how much of the scatter in intelligence is due to genes. Some argue for 80 per cent, others say 50 per cent or even 30–40 per cent (Plomin, 1989; Vandenburg & Vogler, 1985). This means that X per cent of the variation in IQ scores is due to genes. For example, say the figure is 80 per cent. If the effects of genes were somehow cancelled out, the scatter would only be about one-fifth of what it is. Eighty per cent is a lot!

What is the answer? Both genes and environment seem to create differences. First let us consider logical grounds. Whatever it actually may be, intelligence is a very important trait. It gives a great selective advantage. There is natural selection for it across species which one would expect to be partly coded in the genes. Chimpanzees are almost genetically identical to humans, but are fundamentally limited in what they can do. A few scientists have tried raising young chimps as human children, which leads to an above-average chimp but not a brilliant one. Within humans, differences in many traits such as height, extroversion, and neuroticism are partly genetic, and one would expect intelligence to be as well. A second source of evidence is the existence of prodigies, children who flower very early and brilliantly, sometimes in the least fertile soil imaginable. If environment alone mattered, how could such prodigies come about? Third, some cases of retardation are due to genes, again suggesting other intelligence differences are partly genetic.

Many studies have been carried out. Some early ones used animals, trying to breed for the supposed rat equivalent of intelligence; maze-learning ability. The trick is to run rats in mazes, and pick out the fastest and slowest. Then one breeds the fastest with each other, and the slowest with each other, over several generations. Over time, clear differences emerge, which show an effect of genes.

Another tack is to correlate IQ scores of relatives with different degrees of kinship. The logic is as follows. The more closely two people are related, the more genes they share. If intelligence is partly genetic, close relatives should show higher correlations than far ones. The best test is with identical twins separated at birth. They are genetically identical and presumably have had somewhat different environments. Cyril Burt apparently studied several such pairs. They are hard to find and often their environments are not so different, however, since they typically get farmed off to relatives. Some pairs in such studies even lived on the same street and played together. Also, as mentioned in Chapter 1, Burt's data may have been falsified. One also could compare identical twins' IQ correlations with that of fraternal twins, who are not identical but who have had similar environments.

Willerman (1979) presents a summary of results from many studies. He found that as kinship gets closer, so does correlation between IQ scores. The results are suggestive, but they do not separate out environment from genes since the closer the kinship, the more likely it is that the environments will be similar.

Is it all genetic? No. Many studies have shown environmental effects on intelligence differences. A very stimulating environment with lots of interesting things to do certainly may raise it, as has been mentioned. Several rat studies have demonstrated the effect. Very young rats are divided into two groups. One group gets the rat equivalent of an upper-class private-school education. They have lots of interesting things to do; puzzles, activity wheels, objects to investigate and so on . . . all that a young rat could want. The second group gets an underclass, impoverished upbringing in a very restricted environment. When the groups reach adulthood, the upper-class rats tend to test as much brighter. In addition, their brains are physically different. They have more neurons and more connections. The human parallel is clear and was a spur to the Head Start social planners. Children who have grown up in very restricted environments tend to score lower on IQ tests. Studies of orphanage children who have led restricted lives with few outings and little adult attention suggest they also score much lower. Stimulation differences may partly cause social-class IQ score differences.

One way to think about the effects of genes and environment is with the idea of a *reaction-range* (Weinberg, 1989). One's genes set limits for adult IQ score (see Figure 5.1). Given a very rich environment, individuals may get near the top of their range; given a poor one, they will be near the bottom. People have very different genetic endowments, but can have the same IQ score due to a rich or poor environment. A good analogy is to height, where the major environmental factor determining it is nutrition. Height is partly genetic in that tall parents tend to have tall offspring, but the genes do set a range. Given a very good environment, a person may reach the limits set by his or her genes. Indeed, average height in Japan has risen many centimetres since World War II, during which time the typical diet has included much more protein. Though the mix of genes is little different, children of parents born before the war typically tower over them.

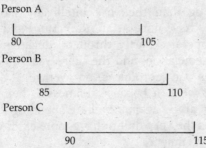

Fig 5.1 An illustration of the concept of IQ reaction-range. A person may inherit a certain potential range for adult IQ score of 20–25 IQ points. Given an excellent environment, he or she may reach its limits. Given a poor one, he or she may stay near its lowest end. Individuals have different reaction-ranges because they inherit different genes.

Many genes are involved for intelligence, and there certainly is no single one. No one knows exactly where they are or how many are involved. Eventually scientists probably will. A major project is underway to map out the entire human geronome, to figure out where all the genes for various traits are. That knowledge, when it comes, will raise the possibility of breeding extremely intelligent persons by genetic engineering. The very prospect frightens many people, but technology ultimately may make it possible.

Mapping the genes for intelligence will answer another question; exactly what is the neural basis of human intelligence differences. Biologists are usually very happy when they locate a gene for something because they may eventually figure out what that gene is doing or is not doing. For example, a genetic disease might be caused by lack of some chemical or oversupply of another, and one can find this out by comparing the same gene's action in normal and abnormal persons. No one knows exactly what might underlie intelligence differences. Eysenck (1979) speculates that the genes may code for number of neurons or increased availability of transmitter chemicals, or a host of other things. Some day we should know for certain. It may even be possible to develop drugs to increase intelligence.

Is Average Population IQ Score Changing?

If intelligence differences are in part genetic, then perhaps the eugenics worriers were rightly concerned. Perhaps the human species' future is dim. The eugenicists' concern was that average population intelligence would drop because the dull outbreed the bright. Family size and IQ score correlate negatively. The dull do indeed produce more young than the very intelligent. Nowadays many professional couples have none at all. Retherford and Sewell (1989) say that the link operates partly through education. The brighter tend to have more education, and the more years of education one has the fewer times one reproduces, on average. If so, our genetic stock may steadily weaken because dullness is being selected for. Some conservatives argue against welfare spending for this reason, saying it encourages the very dull to have more children to get more money from the government.

There is a degree of ammunition for these critics in the clear decline in academic standards. Many American universities have to run remedial reading and writing courses for their first-year students. Average SAT scores have plummeted since the 1960s (see Chapter 3).

What in fact has been happening? Have average IQ scores been dropping at a rate such as the alarming three IQ points a generation that Cattell (1937) tipped? Are we *en route* to the world of Kornbluth's Marching Morons? No! The scores have been increasing.

First consider some anecdotal evidence. Many teachers who have been in the classroom for ten or twenty years say that today's children are much brighter than those of an earlier generation. They seem more 'with it', they learn more easily, and can learn a lot more. To be sure, teachers say the children have their faults. They have short attention spans and are not much interested in academic work, but they seem much brighter than their parents and learn better when they feel like it.

IQ test score studies show much the same thing. On average, raw scores on standard IQ tests have gone up massively in the last fifty years. Flynn (1984, 1987) conducted some heroic studies on population trends, putting together data from fourteen nations, including Norway, Japan, West Germany, England, and Australia. The data were scores on standard tests such as the WAIS, WISC, and Ravens. On average, the IQ point gain was 13.8 points between 1932 and 1978. Indeed, the tests had to keep being renormed because previous norms kept becoming obsolete. More than half of test-takers did better than the mean. Teasdale and Owen (1989) looked at average IQ scores of Danish draftees and found increases up until the latest year studied, 1987. This suggested that IQ scores are still going up. (Where will it end?) Their data also suggest that the increase is mostly occurring at the scale's lower end; the dull are getting brighter.

What is going on? Now the controversy starts. Flynn argues that people are not really getting any brighter. They are just getting better at solving abstract problems such as those on IQ tests, which he believes only weakly measure intelligence. But this argument is not convincing. People probably are getting brighter, as the teachers think and the IQ tests indicate. Intelligence is not the only trait to increase lately. Average height has risen 7 or 8 centimetres and head circumference 1.5 to 2 centimetres since World War II, almost certainly because of better nutrition (Lynn, 1989). Nutrition affects intelligence too, and Lynn says it has pushed up average intelligence.

Another environmental factor that has improved is sheer stimulation, which also may have increased average intelligence. The world today is a much more stimulating one for Western children than was that of the 1930s. They have television, computers, many more books and magazines, overseas trips, teaching aids, and stimulating video games. The children of today have more years of education as well.

But the gains raise an interesting question: Just how long can they continue? We may soon reach the limits of what environment can do, just as increases in height may soon level off. Environment can only do so much. The effect of the worsening genetic potential may set in and average IQ score may start to decline. We may yet reach the world of the Marching Morons, just a lot later than was thought.

ETHICAL/PHILOSOPHICAL ISSUES

Governments have to face a number of issues concerning intelligence. Many have to do with education, such as how to educate the gifted and whether to stream students by ability. These are covered in Chapter 7. Some issues touch on social engineering, all the rage in the 1960s but with a bad name now. Whether a government should in fact do anything about some of these issues is controversial. As mentioned earlier, to effectively deal with them, planners need a solid knowledge base about intelligence. Zigler and Seitz (1982) point out several cases where bad decisions based on poor understanding waste much time and money; for instance, efforts to 'cure' retardation in the 1960s. This section will look at three issues that social policy-makers need to deal with, and about which a society as a whole needs to make decisions.

Should Intelligence be Treated as a National Resource?

Every human society has to make a living in a tough, competitive world. The competition each battles might be the climate, landscape and other species, or it might be other nations. Some nations compete strongly and live well, examples being Germany, Switzerland, and Japan. Others do not, such as several nations in Africa and Asia for example Chad and Bangladesh. A major reason for success or failure in global economic battles is a nation's resources. First there are physical ones such as mineral wealth, climate, and amount of agricultural land. Second is population; its size, educational level, and motivation to work hard. It is not enough just to be blessed with such resources. The government also has to manage them wisely, but some nations do not do this. Argentina and Burma have excellent resources but poor management has meant inept use of them.

Some say that a nation's intelligence should be regarded as a resource. The idea goes back at least two centuries to Adam Smith. Cattell (1987) is a firm believer, and expounds on the theme in depth. He argues that the stock of fluid intelligence is largely fixed (finite like coal and arable land) and should be hoarded, developed, and used wisely. He gives several reasons why. First, the exercise of intelligence may help a nation survive in time of crisis: One bright inventor can mean the difference between survival and destruction. Examples include the weapons invented by the ancient Greek Archimedes to defend against attack, and radar and the atomic bomb in World War II. Second, intelligent research has led to improved food production, cures for diseases that once ravaged populations, and so on. Third, the application of intelligence allows a nation to compete in the international marketplace and partially transcend its physical limitations, as the Israelis have done by making their deserts bloom. Fourth, Cattell argues that a high level of intelligence improves an individual's and a society's quality of life and produces more responsible citizens and better democracy. (The last point could be disputed.)

And what should governments do to hoard and use such resources? The first goal is to try to raise average population intelligence. Governments attempt this in many noncontroversial ways. The first is by providing education, since knowledge is crucial to intelligent behaviour. Governments provide schools and universities, incentives to attend and to stay past minimum leaving age, and may fund scholarships for their best students to study overseas. A second way is to greatly reduce the incidence of retardation by prevention programs. There are education programs about preventable causes such as drugs taken during pregnancy. Governments also encourage genetic counselling for prospective marriage partners, and may fund screening programs for fetal abnormalities. Zigler and Seitz (1982) argue that governments should help support families by providing both minimum incomes and adequate health care, which may reduce the incidence of retardation. A somewhat more controversial method is by controlling immigration. If a nation has many candidates for entrance, it can raise the average level of intelligence by taking the best, brightest, and most highly educated and refusing the poorly educated and retarded. Many nations do this.

Finally, there is a very controversial method; directly controlling the reproduction of the nation's population. An early but fictional case was described in Aldous Huxley's novel, *Brave New World*. The government created castes of workers with differing intelligence levels and fixed numbers in each category. This kind of intervention is common, but has a very bad name. In Romania, Nikolai Ceaucescu increased population size by virtually requiring women to produce many children and by banning contraception and abortion. Nazi Germany bred blond-haired, blue-eyed 'Aryan' types, and tried to exterminate non-favoured groups such as Jews and

Gypsies. Some American states advocated eugenics (Gould, 1981). The low in measured intelligence were sterilised or forbidden to marry.

Though many greet such policies with horror, others want to go further. In 1975, Nobel Prize winner William Shockley argued that welfare payments should be stopped for low IQ test scorers unless they 'volunteered' for sterilisation. Various persons advocate cutting welfare payments completely because it 'encourages the people on the bottom of society to breed'. Kamin (1974) gives the following quotes from Lewis Terman, who thought along these lines:

> in the near future intelligence tests will bring tens of thousands of these high-grade defectives under the surveillance and protection of society. This will ultimately result in curtailing the reproduction of feeble-mindedness and in the elimination of an enormous amount of crime, pauperism, and industrial inefficiency.

Terman also argued that an IQ score in the 70 to 80 range

> is very common among Spanish Indian and Mexican families of the Southeast and also among Negroes . . . Children of this group should be segregated in special classes . . . There is no possibility at present of convincing society that they should not be allowed to reproduce, though from a eugenic point of view they constitute a grave problem because of their unusually prolific breeding.

One nation in particular takes eugenics very seriously indeed. In Singapore, Lew Kuan Yew is a firm believer in intelligence as a national resource. The method of controlling it is reward rather than punishment. Poorly educated mothers qualify for large cash payouts if they get sterilised. University graduates get payouts for having children. As briefly mentioned in Chapter 1, the government went even further when it recognised that its highly educated high achievers actually need help to get married. According to statistics, 40 per cent of female graduates were not expected to marry at all. Many graduates are apparently very self-centred, see making money as their major activity, and have little knowledge of how to meet and approach the opposite sex. The government therefore set up the Social Development Unit, for university graduates only, which organises moonlight cruises, blind dates, a computer dating service, and even lessons on courtship and finding a mate. Those who run it make no bones about why it exists. As one put it: 'The problem is that the better educated are not replacing themselves. We will end up with a net loss in human capital . . . since human resources are Singapore's strongest asset, we can't afford that.'

The second major thing a government can do is make the best use of its talent. This means identifying it early, developing it, and giving individuals every opportunity to use it. Again, the education system provides one way to identify the talented; examples include the eleven-plus system in England and the Soviet Union's early selection of its best talent for special schools. A nation also tries to distribute its talent to where it is most needed. Jobs that contribute most attract the best rewards, at least to a point.

Societies differ enormously in the opportunities they give to their talented citizens. Some are largely meritocracies (e.g., the United States) where the university postings and the best jobs largely go to the most talented. Obviously, even the United States is not a perfect meritocracy, as discrimination exists on racial and other grounds. But the very talented can rise. Other societies are much less meritocratic. Family connections and caste or wealth are what is important. In many Third-World nations, government posts are bought and sold, just as military commissions once were in Europe and seats in the House of Commons were in England. A good example is India, where caste bias and nepotism are rife. Incompetence can rise to high places and talent sometimes cannot even get a foot in the door.

Misuse of talent may mean poor competitiveness and one historian has attributed the decline of Great Britain since last century partly to important positions going to members of the aristocracy, establishment, and 'old-boy networks'. Often such people had little ability and the wrong sort of education, such as classics instead of business management. Eysenck (1979) recounts an old joke which shows this sort of policy in action. A man has three candidates for a secretarial position and gives each various tests. Then they are ranked on performance and the results given to the boss. The boss admires the series of tests and then employs 'the one with the big boobs'. Personal and other factors often outweigh ability. Many large organisations have strict policies on employment and promotion by merit alone, but they often are circumvented.

How Should a Society Deal With the Mentally Retarded?

The retarded pose many questions for social policy-makers. The issues are not always so stark for the moderately and severely retarded, who often need to be institutionalised. The major issues in such cases are when to do so (what criteria to use) and what conditions inside should be like. Drew et al. (1984) point out that such institutions often are dreary and restrictive places, run for the ease of staff rather than the welfare of the inmates. There are cases of petty practices like opening inmates' mail, imposing severe punishments for mild offences, forcing inmates to share clothes and wardrobes, restricting visits, prescribing unwanted sedatives, and so on.

Another major issue is how much society should do to reduce the burden that the severely retarded may impose. At one extreme this amounts to reducing their numbers. A not-uncommon practice is to let newborn severely retarded and/or physically handicapped die at birth. Doctors undertake no operations or may simply not feed them. This practice leads to outrage from those who believe any life is sacred, and sometimes leads to court cases to force medical treatment or even prosecution for manslaughter. Another controversial practice is to stop the retarded from reproducing, because they are more likely to produce retarded offspring. Some American states had compulsory sterilisation or forbade the retarded to marry or even have sex. In 1895, the House of Representatives of the American state of Connecticut passed this bill: 'Every man who shall carnally know any female under the age of 45 years who is epileptic, imbecile, feeble-minded or a pauper, shall be imprisoned in the state prison not less than three years'. In 1897, a law to prohibit marriage of the 'feeble-minded' and insane in the United States received much support but was never actually passed.

The mildly retarded pose more problems and subtler ones. One major issue is just how much society should do to restrict or protect them. One long-standing policy is paternalism (Khan, 1985). The general approach is much like that to young children, who lack the knowledge and skills to get by in society: They need to be protected and handled in certain ways, for their own welfare and for society's. The policy can extend far and involve telling the retarded where to live, whom they can live with, and even when they can marry and have children. The paternalistic argument is that the retarded may have enough problems without the added burden of children, and need to be protected from themselves.

But some advocate as little paternalism as possible (Khan, 1985). They argue that the retarded often want nothing more than to live free of restrictions, as people in the rest of the community do. Since their inability to do so causes much unhappiness, the proposed ethical principle is that society should let them go their own way as much as possible, and provide money and advice to help them do so. Society should only step in when things really do go wrong; for example, by paying bills that the retarded have not budgeted for, or by halting obvious exploitation by others. To some extent, many governments already do this with the general population. There are consumer laws to save people from being fleeced and advice bureaus to deal with various problems.

Workers with the mentally retarded are guided by some major ethical principles. One is *normalisation*, which advocates that the retarded get conditions which let them live as much like normals as possible. Another is the *equal rights principle*, which advocates that they be given rights equal to normals as much as possible. A third is *deinstitutionalisation*, which holds that institutions generally are not a good thing. They induce inmates to become dependent, and the institutionalised retarded often end up with fewer skills than those who live independently. There are a variety of measures between the institution and complete independence, such as sheltered work-shops and half-way houses. A fourth principle, adopted in schools, is *mainstreaming*. This advocates that the retarded should go into classrooms with normal children as much as possible. It seems meritorious, but sometimes the other children do not accept them, in which case it does more harm than good.

Should Intelligence Tests be Used?

Chapter 3 described some major uses of tests and noted that their use was often controversial. Indeed, a major issue is whether tests should be used at all, and many school districts have either restricted or even banned them. Court cases have sought to ban them for employee selection. Some American states prohibit use of test scores to assign children to classes for the 'educable mentally retarded'. California and New York force test publishers to make test items public; the so-called 'Truth in Testing' laws.

Opponents of tests have several major avenues of attack. First, they charge that tests have often been misused, which of course is true. They further say that many handlers of tests and test results, such as teachers, do not understand their limitations and so on. The solution may well be to better educate test-users rather than ban the tests.

Another criticism is that the tests don't measure intelligence; that no one knows what intelligence is, let alone how to measure it. Eysenck counters that scientists could measure temperature before knowing what it is. IQ tests do tap something to do with intelligence, although they are not the best measures. Few argue nowadays that IQ tests tap some inherent, biological capacity rather than a number of learned skills. Newer tests such as BAS and Sternberg's may prove better measures of cognitive abilities. Who knows what will be developed in the future?

A final major criticism is the one taken most to heart — that of test bias (Caplan, 1985). The argument runs as follows. Many tests rely heavily on words, language, and other skills that members of minorities are much less likely to possess. The tests tap knowledge rather than specific ability, or as one judge in a California case put it, 'The issue is whether the tests are measuring ignorance or stupidity'. So, they violate the rule that all should be treated equally. They are used by middle-class whites in Western societies to oppress minorities.

How well does the argument hold up? Some studies have tried researching the issue, and Caplan (1985) briefly reviews some. One study tested whether American blacks' command of English biases standard IQ tests against them and suggested that it did not; they understood standard English about as well as black dialect. Other studies looked at specific test items and found that not all that many were actually biased, at least when one considers a subculture in a society. Eysenck (1979) also points out that, biased or not, the tests often do what they are supposed to do. Many tests are given to predict how well students are likely to do in, say, a university or a law course. Entrance is sometimes relaxed for minorities under 'affirmative action' programs, and they are allowed in even if SAT or other test scores are too low. However, they tend to fail in large numbers and this may be because they cannot do the work. He mentioned a study of UCLA Law School graduates where a quota system operates for minorities. In one year, only about 10 per cent of blacks admitted passed the bar exams on the first try, while about 85 per cent of whites did.

Eysenck (1979) also argues that tests may help talent rise, regardless of minority status. In England, large numbers of talented working-class children who otherwise would not have made it to universities did so because of the eleven-plus. As well, he says that tests can reduce the number of square pegs in round holes. Tests give better guides to abilities, aptitudes, and prospective occupations than do personal interviews. Organisations such as the armed services have to place recruits somehow, and tests are one way. Despite all their faults and limitations, what alternatives are there to ability tests? No one has anything much better, goes the argument.

6
THE GROWTH AND AGEING OF INTELLIGENCE

L ife usually involves change. Nature seems to abhor not just vacuums but stagnation as well. So, higher animals such as humans rarely stand still; each continuously alters in many ways throughout its lifetime. The most obvious change is in our physical form. A newborn baby has a large head and small undeveloped body which will alter dramatically over the years to come. These changes are so striking and so predictable that we can pretty accurately pick an individual's approximate age at a glance. Along with the physical alterations go a host of mental ones; in personality, social skills, emotional range and control, morality and, of course, intelligence.

Physical and mental development in higher organisms often obeys an inexorable rule; growth to a peak followed by a decline that is either precipitous or gradual. The physical changes are well-known. Our bodies grow up until age eighteen or nineteen, at times gradually and at times in spurts such as in adolescence. Many physical abilities peak at the end of the growth phase; running speed, jumping and throwing prowess, and so on. Some abilities peak much later. Endurance improves throughout one's twenties, which is why marathon runners in their thirties or older can still win. Muscular strength in males peaks in the early thirties. But most abilities decline at the end of the growth phase. In some sports, athletes are washed up and pushed aside by the younger generation by their early twenties. In others they hang on until later; experience turns out to be more important. Tennis players can stay on the top into their thirties and baseball players into their forties. By age twenty-five, the bones undergo a major change as they calcify and become more brittle. Most joint and back problems date from that age; football players' injuries get more serious and make them think about retirement. Later on the skin gets thinner and starts to wrinkle. There are individual differences in ageing rate, and different body parts age at different rates. Exercise also may slow the pace of deterioration, summarised in the saying 'Use or lose'.

Just why we age physically is still not known, but there are two major theories. The first, and the one that most laypersons probably hold, can be dubbed the 'wear-out' theory. We age because we constantly use our bodies and they wear out as do inanimate objects. The body's ageing is like that of a new car. Initially, it hums and purrs and the parts work together beautifully, but as components age and wear down, disorder increases and things begin to go wrong. Eventually, disorder is so widespread that it is often best to toss away the vehicle and buy a new one. Human bodies simply have longer lifespans (70 or 80 years and a maximum of about 120 years). However, this view has serious flaws. The first is that ageing is not so inevitable. Cancer cells are essentially immortal, as are many one-celled creatures. There also are wide differences in lifespan between species, from the year or two granted to small mammals to the few hundred of the tortoise and the thousands of the sequoia tree. Bodies are also self-repairing, while unfortunately, vehicles are not. The most telling fact is that the changes that ageing bring on are so predictable as to suggest that a lethal clock is steadily ticking away, rationing out our years, rather than disorder merely increasing.

So the second theory was born, which proposes that ageing is due to planned obsolescence. The latter was not invented by American industry to keep its products moving fast in the shops. Nature may have come up with it many millions of years before. According to this view, our bodies are programmed to self-destruct after a certain time, not all at once like a *Mission Impossible* tape, but slowly. Our genes contain a clock which gradually increases our disorder, and like machines, our lifespans are strictly limited. Nature's idea seems to be to clear away a generation after it has reproduced, thereby giving its offspring better access to the environment's resources. The species benefits over the long term because the young are genetically different and may be better able to cope with the challenges of changes in the environment.

There are lots of extreme examples of this effect. One is the strange life cycle of the salmon. It hatches in mountain pools, but when it is mature it makes its way down to the sea and swims about in the oceans for years. Near the end of its life it makes its way back upstream to the pool in which it was hatched. Only the fittest survive the hazardous journey. There they mate and spawn for the first and last time and, within hours of laying the eggs, are all dead: Their genes have programmed the body to deliver a massive dose of a killer hormone. The fish are superfluous and would just take up the resources needed for the hatchlings. Some rodent species have a somewhat similar cycle. The males live one year and die soon after impregnating females, but if their mating was not carried out for some reason, they live another year.

Most cases of the clearing away of the previous generation by ageing are less spectacular. What kills many animals is the pervasive physical slowing-down that begins when the growth phase is over. This can be readily observed in a human family consisting of three or four generations together. The very young child seems almost ceaselessly active, running rather than walking, and finding it hard to sit for long. Teenagers also are hard to keep up with. But people slow down and by their fifties and sixties they sit still and ponder for long periods, and rarely hurry to do anything. In nature, this slowing can mean that a predator gets too slow to reach the prey or a prey species gets too slow to escape its predators. They do not survive. Old animals are quite rare outside homes, farms, and zoos.

Intelligence changes systematically with age. Indeed, its development in some ways parallels the physical changes we undergo. Our mental abilities typically grow until a peak around age twenty. Children know and can do more as they get older. Indeed, many IQ tests use this fact as their guiding principle, the Stanford-Binet being a prime example. But mental growth peaks, and afterwards some functions decline — some slowly, some quite rapidly — although some abilities actually increase until the sixties. Paralleling the physical slowdown is a mental slowdown. The changes are predictable enough to suggest that the same clock timing out our physical ageing is also controlling our mental ageing, at least in part. Perhaps our intelligence, our adaptive trait *par excellence*, is programmed to deteriorate in the same way our speed and agility do. However, we have partially outwitted nature here, as we will see.

This chapter will briefly survey what is known about the growth and ageing of human intelligence. The first section looks at the growth phase, beginning with general intelligence as measured by IQ, before examining some things that are known about the development of more specific abilities and capacities, such as memory, attention, and categorising. We can ask when they actually start (e.g., when can we first categorise things into groups such as plants, animals, red things and blue things?) The second section looks at ageing, examining both changes in IQ and the decline in such functions as memory and attention. These two things are of course connected, but it is useful to consider them separately.

However, before we look at intelligence, first let us examine what changes occur in its underlying base; the neurons. They grow and age, and somehow this causes the changes in intelligence.

THE GROWING AND AGEING BRAIN

Neurons grow profusely in the first few months after birth, but by age one they get out of the habit completely. Thereafter they do not reproduce at all and the stock of neurons has to last us a lifetime. It is fortunate that we have 10 billion or so, because we have only our capital to live off.

Our neuronal capital also matures. Neurons age and die like other cells. By our mid-eighties, an estimated 11 per cent of brain weight is lost, and certain brain areas lose more neurons than others; the frontal cortex more than the cerebellum, for example. Because many functions are localised in certain areas, particular abilities deteriorate more with age. Neurons are killed off even faster by factors like heavy alcohol use. Twenty years of hard drinking may lead to brain damage syndromes such as Korsakoff's syndrome, where a person has enormous trouble learning new information. Neurons also get more inefficient with age. Their metabolism declines, which among other things can mean that they have trouble making the transmitters needed to communicate. Neuronal links and circuits may also vanish with ageing.

The neurons are even attacked on another front. A variety of brain diseases linked with ageing can lead to weakening or loss of various functions. Perhaps the best known and most common is Alzheimer's disease, often dubbed 'dementia'. The disorder strikes down very few persons under sixty years old, but hits at least 20 per cent of those who survive past eighty. Often so many intellectual functions are impaired that social life and work performance are greatly affected. Some functions so affected are memory, judgment, and abstract thinking. An individual may have great trouble remembering things, and may be unable to pick out similarities and differences between various words (e.g., apple and orange), to define words, or to interpret proverbs (e.g., 'He who has only a hammer sees nails everywhere'; 'Strike while the iron is hot'). Brain damage is always present but the cause, which is not fully understood, may be slow and steady neuronal deterioration with ageing. Some recent work has suggested a link with accumulation of aluminium in the brain.

GROWTH

'Mental growth' and 'intellectual development' mean different things to different psychologists. It can mean changes in IQ, or the beginning of specific mental functions and their development. A vast amount of research has tried to map out the general pattern of growth and what affects it. A lot of people want to know because it affects many things; education, for example. There are also grand theories of human development, such as Jean Piaget's, which have had enormous influence in schooling. There are also great gaps in knowledge, but some notion of the broad outlines of intellectual growth are becoming apparent. First let us examine changes in IQ.

Changes in General Intelligence

A lot of studies have looked at changes in IQ over the growth years, using it as a measure of general intelligence. The question is important for several reasons, as Anastasi (1988) notes. School administrators usually assume that IQ scores are reasonably stable; a person tested at age six will score pretty much the same compared to others at age ten or sixteen. Decisions to stream classes or send children to different schools on the basis of ability (as in the English eleven-plus system) assume such stability. We can also ask, if IQ indeed is relatively stable, what is the earliest age at which it can be usefully tested? The question is also important in programs to raise intelligence. For example, Head Start workers assume that the children selected really will be at risk of low IQ test scores later. They assume that their low IQ scores are stable, and that improvements are likely to persist. As well, if certain individuals show dramatic IQ score changes, we can ask why and perhaps manipulate such factors to raise intelligence.

What do the studies show? The following borrows from reviews by Anastasi (1988) and Murphy and Davidshofer (1988). The studies are fairly consistent, suggesting that IQ score is relatively stable after about age three or so. Though there are a number of intelligence tests for infants, they don't predict later IQ much at all. This may be because no one has hit on the right measure, so the question is open. Still, infant test scores correlate weakly with IQ at ages three or four but very little with IQ beyond that. Beyond about age two or so, IQ scores settle down. One study found a correlation of 0.78 between IQ scores tested at 13 and 18; another of 0.72 of tested IQ at age 10 and 20; and a study of children tested at 6, 12, and 17 found correlations of at least 0.75. To sum up, someone who tests as bright at age 3 or 4 or 10 is likely to test as bright at age 15 or 20 as well, and someone who tests dull at such ages is likely to test that way later. This finding would be expected if intelligence differences are partly inherited.

But some individuals help confuse the issue by showing IQ test score changes over time by as much as an astronomical 50 points. Such changes may occur because of poor testing in one session; the child was unmotivated or did not like the examiner or became test wise. Anastasi also suggests that environmental factors may operate. A child may go from a rich, stimulating environment to a poorer one (or the reverse), as parents move or the child is farmed off to relatives.

Origins: The Intelligence of Infants

Humans everywhere ask origin questions: Where did this come from and when did that start? Children begin to ask such questions very early. They want such information about cars, clouds, stars, and themselves. Every human culture asks where it and the Earth came from. Many answers arise; creation myths derived from folklore such as the dreamtime of the Australian Aborigine and the Norse one of the giant Ymir, whose body formed the Earth. Science gives answers based on archaeological digs, biology, geology, and astronomy, which are still creation myths to some people. Questions about origins interest just about everyone, though the answers may not be palatable.

One origin question about human intelligence is when it diverged from that of other animals. Others ask, when does consciousness itself begin? Before birth? At birth? A few months later? When do we first recognise objects seen before, learn and remember, and become able to focus our attention?

Different people give different answers. Proponents with vested interests say that intelligence of some sort arises well before birth. They say the fetus is aware, that it can learn at quite an early stage, and they promote a wide range of products to exploit this idea to give the discerning mother's child a head start. Products promise to make the child a genius or a master musician. Some provide tapes to play, or readings for unborn children. The famed Suzuki method of music instruction advocates very early instruction, though after birth, and appears quite successful. Other claims are hard to evaluate. The fetus is almost impossible to study, although some work has been done on its nascent mind. Infants also are very difficult to study. Infant researchers need a sturdy temperament, a lot of patience, and much resistance to frustration. Infants sleep most of the time, being awake only about two hours a day, and there is some evidence that they can learn while in some sleep stage (Maurer & Maurer, 1988). It is very difficult to get them to cooperate in tasks, because they lose interest quickly, but people try to study them. Much of the discussion below is borrowed from a fascinating book by Maurer and Maurer (1988), who have surveyed the vast literature on infant intelligence.

Let us start with the fetus. Countless mothers-to-be talk to their infants-to-be. Freudian psychology implies we have some sort of consciousness in the womb and memory of it, because a cornerstone of the theory is that we all have some wish to return to our days of peace and tranquillity there. But the womb is no oasis of peace. As the mother moves about and smokes and drinks it turns out to be a thoroughly noisy, foul-tasting, and bumpy place. The fetus can detect these things, even though its senses are not very developed. Studies suggest that the noise level alone is a quite high 85–95 decibels, equivalent to a loud motorcycle going past an adult, and the child's senses can pick it up. At birth, infants do feel some pain, but not a great deal; their senses are not developed enough. Still, the fetus can actually learn and an early study showed a simple form of conditioning in a fetus only a few months past conception. Another showed that the fetus can learn and remember its mother's voice, at least in the last five to six weeks before birth. No one really knows when consciousness arises, but a newborn child goes through the sleep/waking cycle, showing different brainwave patterns as well, which implies consciousness. Perhaps it emerges very gradually, like an adult waking up very slowly in the morning and becoming progressively more aware of things until fully awake (at noon for some people).

What does a child know at birth and what can it do? This is

not an idle question and it is hard to imagine one that has caused more controversy or more affected child-rearing and schooling. Philosophers have speculated about it from the time of the Ancient Greeks and the views people take have profoundly affected human history. There are two extreme philosophical views. The first, called empiricism, holds that the child's intelligence at birth equals its age; a large zero. The seventeenth-century philosopher John Locke even coined the phrase 'tabula rasa', or blank slate, to sum it up. The mind was blank at birth, a tablet on which experience would write. The nineteenth-century psychologist William James thought so too, describing the brave new world of the newborn as one 'blooming, buzzing confusion'. The child's mind was blank and he or she experienced the world as an overwhelming jumble of sensations. The child had no way of imposing any meaning or order on it, so it seemed as a very abstract painting might to an adult; just a meaningless chaos. Swiss psychologist Jean Piaget, though not an empiricist, held the same view of the newborn. Until the second year of life, the world was just a meaningless clutter of fleeting impressions. Piaget believed that infants do not even have an idea that objects are permanent. If an object disappears, say a person behind a wall, to the child it has gone forever. Only slowly does this idea of continuing existence emerge, argued Piaget.

The opposing view, nativism, goes right back to the Greek philosopher Plato and holds that the mind is far from blank at birth. A lot of knowledge is programmed in by the genes. We are not like computers with no knowledge base or programs, but are closer to dedicated ones that are already up and running. Basic ideas like *time* and *space* and *causality* are innate: They are so abstract that we would never learn them otherwise. According to this argument, the newborn infant already knows and can do a lot.

This clash of views is much more than an obscure academic dispute, and the view to which one leans has enormous ramifications. Consider education. Schools and teachers with empiricist leanings tend to see students as empty vessels to be filled with knowledge. They tend to be much more directive, handing down knowledge to the children from on high rather than letting children find things out for themselves. Nativist-leaning schools tend to be more experimental, sometimes to a fault. Children are seen as active, curious explorers, with much of their knowledge already present. They need to be left to explore things and bring that knowledge out. The 'open classroom' movement of a few decades ago was based on this view. There was hardly any discipline or set lessons, students followed their own inclinations, and the teacher was there to consult with if need be. Individual teachers also tend to favour one extreme, and teach accordingly.

Consider politics. The great ideological clash of the twentieth century has been Capitalism versus Communism. A basic tenet of Communism is empiricism: the mind is blank at birth and the adult mind is a reflection of society; change society and you change people. All communist societies tried to do this, to create a new sort of selfless person who worked for the common good rather than narrow self-interest. As Mao Zedong once put it: 'The Chinese people are like a blank screen. You can paint beautiful pictures on a blank screen'. The usual capitalist view is more nativist. People are seen as more-or-less innately selfish and will work only for personal gain, though that tendency can be organised to ultimately benefit everyone. The collapse of Communism and its widespread failure to change human nature suggest that the nativists are partly right. Research suggests much the same thing. A lot of our knowledge is innate. We have a lot of genetic programming to learn certain things. That means that the newborn infant is not a blank slate. As well, it can sense the world, can remember and learn, and is quite capable. One practical result of this finding was applied in Venezuela, where the minister for intelligence suggested that mothers begin training and intellectually stimulating their infants right from birth. Let us look at some of the infant's capabilities.

To a newborn child, the world is not at all a blooming, buzzing confusion. It may bloom and buzz a bit, but not all that much. Some of the child's senses are working well already. They can distinguish between checkerboards that differ in size and pattern, and look at certain patterns longer than others (showing they can tell them apart). They can distinguish between various colours when only a few days old, and can recognise objects seen before (Fagan, 1984), tell where sounds are coming from, and are particularly attentive to speech (Seigler, 1986). At birth, a child also has some idea of size constancy, which is the knowledge that objects look smaller when they are more distant, even though really the same size. Infants do not have to learn this fact.

The infant has some capabilities but has to learn much to use its senses fully and to recognise patterns. Perhaps the most dramatic demonstration comes from studies of persons blind from birth, who as adults gain their sight through an operation. This event is sometimes portrayed in films. The operation takes place and everyone awaits with trepidation the fateful day when the bandages are removed. Off they come, and with a radiant look, the newly sighted gazes upon her friends' faces with joy and says 'So that is what you look like!' The reality is quite different. A lot of learning is needed before objects such as faces can be readily identified, and before eye and touch can be coordinated. Most such individuals never learn very well, and the operation can make them unhappy. One famous case involved a cheerful man who became very depressed soon after the visual world was opened up to him, and who died some months afterward.

The infant's memory has been much studied. Infants have to remember to recognise objects, but questions arise about their memory span. Studies suggest that memory is present before birth. After birth, infants can recall things for at least two days. By age seven months, memory span is at least one to two weeks. Some basic concepts are present at birth and children start learning others very early; a rudimentary idea of *face* at about ten months, *female face in general* at thirty weeks, *animal* at about eight months, and simple dot pattern concepts at just three to four months.

The beginnings of intelligence are not, then, a humble zero. Olson and Strauss (1984) say that the infant is still mostly a bundle of reflexes but that these soon disappear to be replaced by more complex responses. They say that by age three or four months, the basic components of intelligence have emerged and are busily developing to prepare the child to cope with the world; these include functions such as attention, imitation of others, and classification. Children soon use these abilities to begin building up that all-important knowledge base. They seem to be programmed to be curious and to want to actively explore the new world, another useful human quality that appears to be innate.

The elements of intelligence emerge early. But before the first year of life is gone an ability develops that gives the intelligence of children a quantum leap and that sets us dramatically apart from even the most intelligent of other animals. That ability is *language*. Much of our problem-solving, thinking, and learning is based on it. It allows each individual to rapidly build up a knowledge base from books and other people. Animals have primitive communication abilities, but nothing really like language. Various researchers have tried to teach simple languages to chimpanzees and dolphins (see Chapter 8), but without great success. The animals do not learn anything as impressive as human language, though they can do some things and the noted investigator David Premack believes that such language training improves chimps' thinking ability, just as language does for people.

Language does not emerge at birth, but regardless of the language or culture, the pattern and pace of its beginnings and development are pretty much the same all over the world. We can no more stop children from learning language, within limits, than we can stop them learning to walk. Its universality suggests an innate program unfolding. The pattern is as follows. The first words generally appear around age ten to twelve months, but in various individuals much earlier or later (about age four for Albert Einstein). The first word, greeted with joy by most parents, is preceded by a few months of meaningless verbalising called babbling, from which the first word is shaped. Early words usually refer to objects with which the children interact, such as 'mama' and 'papa'. By about age eighteen months, the child knows about fifty words and by age six the vocabulary has expanded to an average 14,000 words. The early word meanings often are quite different from those of adults. A child may use a word to express what he or she wants it to. Classic examples are of a child referring to all men as 'dada' or just to moving cars as 'car'. Children also may invent their own words, being disappointed that English has no terms for something like 'red objects moving quickly'. They lose this habit, but may regain it later if they become scientists, educators, or bureaucrats.

The first sentences emerge at about twelve to eighteen months, consisting of just a single word intended as a sentence. A child may say 'Eat!' or 'Door', meaning 'I want to eat' or 'Close the door'. Two-word sentences, such as 'Me eat' or 'They go' begin about age eighteen months. Around age twenty to twenty-four months children enter the famous 'telegraphic speech' stage. They use sentences stripped down to their essentials. There are no adjectives or adverbs or articles if they can help it; it is as if the child was sending telegrams which cost a hundred dollars a word. Examples are 'Me play dog' or 'He go shop'. This kind of talk has its limitations, of course, as anyone receiving an obscure telegram or reading newspaper classified ads will realise. There is a classic story about a slightly ambiguous telegram sent to actor Cary Grant, who wilfully misinterpreted it. A journalist was writing an article on the ages of various Hollywood stars and cabled 'How old Cary Grant?' The reply was, 'Old Cary Grant fine. How you?' At around twenty-four to twenty-six months, the child begins using more complex sentences and adding plurals, past tenses, and adjectives. By age five or six, the child is speaking pretty much like an adult, and is connected to the vast amount of knowledge that human cultures accumulate. Vocabulary continues to expand throughout the lifetime.

When do individual differences emerge? Are later differences in intelligence in some way apparent early? As mentioned, infant IQ tests do not correlate very well with later IQ scores. However, some believe there are indicators. Fagan (1984) argues that differences in recognition memory become apparent in infancy and that they correlate with IQ scores. Perhaps the ubiquitous g makes itself apparent very early.

The Pattern of Growth
The origins of intelligence are not humble, but a lot of growth is needed. Just how intelligence does grow over the early years is still a matter of controversy. From birth to age sixteen or eighteen, we go from being rather limited beings with a small knowledge base to a quite complex one with an enormous knowledge base, numerous skills and abilities. How does it happen? How do we acquire it all? What actually changes in the growth years and what spurs these changes on? It is another question that affects many things.

There are so many ideas about the growth of intelligence it is beyond this book's scope to try to cover them all. But two major, though opposing, views are briefly covered. They differ in several ways, especially as to whether intelligence develops in discrete stages — a stage being a period in which the child is thinking differently and can and cannot do certain things — followed by a quick leap to the next stage, in which the child can do more things. An analogy is to the growth of a caterpillar into a crystallis and then a butterfly. The stages are dramatic and can be quite strikingly different. Some insects, for example, can fly in later stages. Perhaps the mind grows in this fashion too. Let us look.

Piaget's Idea of Stages
Jean Piaget was born in Geneva, Switzerland, in 1896, where he remained and worked until his death in 1980. A precocious child, he published his first scientific article at the age of eleven. It appeared in a naturalist journal, and described an albino bird he had found. He rose to greater heights from there, gaining some reputation in his teens, and it is said that a museum director offered Piaget at eighteen a position as curator, knowing him only from his work. Piaget declined, deciding to finish high school instead.

His writings span seventy years and include dozens of books and countless articles. His writing style is very obscure, however, while his theory, which was developed over many years, is quite complex. Piaget's early training was in biology and, like many scientists who switch fields, he brought the ways of thinking of one to the next. He often used biological analogies to try to understand intellectual growth, the best-known being the growth of the embryo from a fertilised cell. That growth is not a steady continuous one; it occurs in stages like the caterpillar's. Piaget eventually postulated four stages of mental growth, with sub-stages within each (that we will not trouble with here). Another idea from biology is the import-ance of adapting to the environment. As mentioned earlier, intelli-gence allows us to better deal with our environment. The more intelligence, the better the adaptation, at least in principle.

Piaget also stressed the importance of knowledge in adapting us better, and put forward two major ways in which we increase and improve our knowledge base. One is simply adding information to existing knowledge, just taking in what fits our ideas, and is much like the way some people flick through newspapers and magazines, just taking in what fits their prejudices and ignoring anything else. The second is much harder, and one that all of us are loath to do; altering our existing ideas to fit the world. It happens when we meet with facts that our existing ideas cannot handle and that we can no longer ignore. If I believed that all swans were white, I would have to change my ideas upon encountering a black one, after I had made sure that it was not painted or dyed. If I believed the Earth to be flat, I would alter the view if seeing it from space. These two ways of changing what we know go on continuously, as we continually refine what we know to make ourselves more adaptive (in theory, anyway).

And now for the stages. They were largely derived from Piaget watching his own three children grow up.

Sensory-motor: 0–2 years. We all start in this one. Piaget believed that we can do little at all here, just experiencing the world as fleeting impressions. The child has no concept of *time, space, causality*, or *object* and only sees himself as separate from the world toward the end of the stage. However, as we have seen, Piaget greatly underestimated what infants can do.

Pre-operational: 2–7 years. Here the child's intelligence has grown impressively. The world now appears more stable, rather than just fleeting impressions. But the child's thinking is still lim-ited. He or she is bound to appearances, taking the way things look for reality. The child also is very egocentric, being unable to see anything from any perspective but his or her own. A good illustra-tion of the limited mental capacity is a quite striking effect called conservation. You need two jars, one wide and short, the other long and narrow, and a child. You pour some water into the wide jar, show it to the child and then pour it all into the tall jar. If you ask which jar has more water the child invariably says the tall one. The child cannot *conserve* quantity, cannot see that the water quantity was the same. The child cannot deal simultaneously with height and width, said Piaget; cannot work out that the thinner a jar is, the less water is holds for the same height. The child only can integrate the two in the next stage.

Concrete operations: 7–11 years. A major shift in thinking seems to occur around the ages of five to seven. According to Piaget, the child has got to a new stage. He or she is no longer egocentric, or dominated by appearance, and can shift between viewpoints. The child can integrate two dimensions such as height and weight. But there are some deficits which are not overcome until the final stage begins, about age eleven. It is interesting that age eleven is also the usual age of progression from primary to secondary schooling.

Formal operations: 11+ years. The stage of typical adult thinking is Piaget's final one (although some argue that there is a fifth stage beyond it that only a few adults reach). A person can think much more flexibly and logically, can reason abstractly, can form and test hypotheses (If X is true, then Y follows). A child can learn much more abstract concepts, which require a more complex mental apparatus than that of earlier stages. Some argue that many adults do not in fact reach this stage, and that formal operations thinking is largely a product of Western schooling, which stresses logic.

According to Piaget, these stages are universal. Every child in every culture goes through them at about the same ages, though some go through faster than others. The stages are given which have to be accepted, and in large part are due to maturation, a genetic program unfolding. Many other things, such as a child's moral reasoning, depend on the stage it has reached. Children cannot learn certain complex moral concepts until they have the mental apparatus of the appropriate stage.

There are implications for education. Indeed, much of the curriculum in nations such as England was based largely on Piagetian ideas. The scheme gives a guide, albeit a rough one, as to what may be taught at certain ages. For example, learning algebra requires certain cognitive abilities. One can ask when children have these powers and use that to guide when to introduce algebra. Piaget's views influenced many alternative schools into believing that children need a lot of free play to explore the world.

Piaget's influence has been enormous but his theory has been much criticised. It is clear that he underestimated the abilities of children, who can do a lot more much earlier than he thought. But he also got a lot right. From the Middle Ages, children had been viewed as miniature adults, but Piaget observed that children do not see the world as adults do, which is an important point, and his ideas about how knowledge grows also are widely used in education. But there is an alternative view to stages, to which we now turn.

A Cognitive View of the Growth of Intelligence

A TV commercial is being shot. It features a group of very young children walking past the camera, followed by a woman who makes a comment on them and then launches into a sales pitch while the children march off into the distance. After many takes, one is almost right. However, a curious child then straggles back to the woman who is repeating her spiel and asks her, 'How come you always say that? Why do you always say that?' Filming halts as the woman shakes uncontrollably with laughter.

An older teacher of five-year-olds wears shoes with fashionable rough leather. A child with smooth shoes and unlined face looks at the teacher's wrinkled face and shoes and asks if his own shoes will also wrinkle as he gets older.

Such cutenesses delight parents, and some TV programs even feature them. But while they suggest that children think differently from adults, if one looks closely, they simply suggest their lack of knowledge. The children really did not know much about TV commercials and takes, or about the causes of wrinkles. It takes a vast amount of knowledge to really understand such things.

This observation, problems with Piaget's views, and some recent research have led to some cognitive views on the development of intelligence. Siegler (1986) lists several theories, and this section will briefly outline a somewhat idealised sampling to give their flavour. The view covers development from newborn infancy to late adulthood (Rybash et al., 1986).

This cognitive view says that no stages of development exist. There is no unfolding maturational program, no invariant order of stages in which a child can and cannot do certain things. There is just a change in certain things. Most important of these is the child's knowledge base, as it increases with time and the information that it holds gets better and better organised. The change from child to adult thinking is like the change from novice to expert, at least in many domains. Children are general novices. Adults are general experts (within limits!). However, adults and children sometimes specialise in certain domains that might include baseball, stamp-collecting, ancient history, Wagnerian opera, Trobriand Island folk-dancing, quantum physics, sewing, or Freudian psychology. Children also early on may become experts in limited domains, such as chess. As well as acquiring knowledge in such a domain, we learn broad strategies for handling it (metacomponents). Working memory capacity also improves in general. Its capacity grows from about four or five items in young children to about seven in adults, and then may diminish in late adulthood.

Rybash et al. say that the same trend goes on until late adult-hood. We get caught up in a few domains of special interest, and develop our knowledge of them throughout a lifetime. Examples are our job-related one, and perhaps chess, baseball, and classical music. We become adept at dealing in these areas but find it harder and harder to learn things in domains in which we are not experts. We also find it hard to learn information about other domains (you can't teach an old dog new tricks) because our thinking gets ossified.

There is indeed evidence for the idea that what really matters in development is knowledge growth. Perhaps the most convincing is the existence of prodigies and idiots savantes. Samuel Reshevsky was a chess prodigy around age six. Judit Polgar is the strongest chess prodigy ever, a recognised expert before the age of ten. Chi and Koeske (1983) discuss a child with an unusual interest in the domain of dinosaurs, who was an expert at a very early age. These children dealt very well with these domains, though they may have been of only average intelligence according to IQ tests. Piaget would say they are still in early stages, and should not be able to do what they can. One cannot argue that they are going through his stages fast because they may be average in general. Idiots savantes also cannot be accounted for.

If this cognitive idea is correct, it has many implications, one of which is that education can be structured differently. If children are limited by their knowledge base rather than their stage, this is something that teachers can do something about.

AGEING

What happens after the peak at age twenty or so? What changes and what does not? Are declines in intelligence inevitable? Can they be slowed down or even halted by such measures as exercise or drugs or a healthy lifestyle? All these are important questions, and we need a good knowledge of what does happen for a number of reasons. Again, one is simple curiosity. Ageing happens to all of us, and we need to know what is likely to occur. Second, it is useful to know what is inevitable and what is due to factors such as disuse or an unhealthy lifestyle. Physical ageing seems to be slowed down to some extent by exercise, for example. Many of the declines in physical functions once thought due to ageing turn out to be the result of inactivity. Third, it is useful to know because of the great proportion of older people to come with the ageing and increased life expectancy of the baby-boom generation. The average lifespan in the West just this century has jumped by an astronomical twenty-six years (Labouvier-Vief, 1985).

There is much folklore about intelligence and ageing. Employers tend to favour younger workers in most fields. A 1990 survey in England found that many were reluctant to hire anyone over thirty-five because they believe them to think too slowly and to be too set in their ways. Folklore also has it that a person's best work is done when young, though this varies across fields. In physics and mathematics, the feeling is that the best work is done before age thirty, though not until the late thirties and early forties for psychologists and even later for historians. Isaac Newton reportedly was unable to understand his brilliant early work later in life. Bertrand Russell, perhaps facetiously, described his own decline as taking him from the difficult discipline of mathematics down to philosophy, the easiest of all. But not everyone declines like this. A prominent exception is Winston Churchill, who became British prime minister at sixty-five, and later again in his seventies, while in his eighties he wrote brilliant histories. Some think that the tendency to do one's best work early may not be so much due to a later loss of ability as to people losing interest and enthusiasm, being given many administrative tasks, or just getting lazy. With some, however, it may be that their knowledge domains do get ossified, and it takes the radical unossified young to really shake things up and come up with new ideas.

Much research has tried to map out the course of the ageing of intelligence, but such map-making is very difficult for several reasons. One is that the nature of intelligence changes as people get older (e.g., Labouvier-Vief, 1985). After school, people diverge into all sorts of lifestyles that require knowledge of quite different domains; farming, administration, business, sport, and so on. Each involves different skills and abilities and people learn new ones while they let some of those acquired in school fall into disuse. How can we compare the intelligence of two persons who have led very different adult lives? Indeed, the typical finding is that IQ increases in people who work in educational settings, and may decline with people who do not. This probably reflects a limit of the tests themselves. People have varying opportunities to exercise their intelligence.

A second problem is a major bugbear in any research on human development; the inconvenient existence of *cohorts*. A cohort is a group of people born at about the same time, though the bounds are rough. Thus, one cohort is all those born in 1937 or those born in 1972, or all born between 1940 and 1950. People in a cohort are *different* from those in another one, and comparing cohorts is almost like comparing people in different cultures. People in a cohort get different educational experiences (e.g., the three Rs and lots of rote-learned facts versus training in how to think), different amounts of education, and undergo different rearing experiences (permissiveness versus strict, moral discipline). They undergo different historical experiences, which can leave a mark on a whole cohort. The generation born in the 1920s went through the Great Depression and it left its mark on many, making them more concerned with material things and financial security than the generation which followed. The baby-boom generation differs in many ways from previous ones. The major historical events were the unpopular Vietnam War and the social upheavals of the 1960s. They also are much more concerned with their looks. Early this century, youth was something to be got through as quickly as possible. To be accepted as an adult one had to look the part, and people willingly lost their youthful looks early. Youth was hung up in the wardrobe at thirty at the latest. There are other differences. People born in the 1950s also are much better educated than those born earlier, who tended to leave school quite young. Many more people go to university than did early this century, when a degree was a rarity and a doctorate almost unheard of.

All these differences make it hard to compare intelligence across the generations. As we will see, it was once thought that IQ declined precipitously past thirty, but this apparent drop was due to the cohort effect. One solution to the question of IQ and ageing involves following the changes in one group of people over a long period, rather than just comparing intelligence in groups of different ages. It is expensive and time-consuming, but a few heroic investigators have done so.

First, we look at changes in general intelligence, as measured by IQ, and then in some more specific mental functions.

Changes in General Intelligence

How does IQ alter past twenty? What obvious changes do those ageing neurons produce? First, relative position does not change all that much, though there are individuals for whom it does, because they are in education systems or whatever. But raw scores decline, and more precipitously after age thirty. To deal with this fact, most IQ tests are 'age-corrected'. To convert a raw score into an IQ, one looks at a conversion table which gives different IQ equivalents for different ages. The underlying assumption is that raw scores will decline and one wants an IQ for that age group alone. Plotting IQs that are not age-corrected may give frightening curves like that in Figure 6.1, which suggests a rather sharp age decline in ability. But that does not accord with commonsense, which suggests that people are not all washed up and over the hill for mental work by their early thirties. The younger generation does not start to push the older one aside for some years. One curve is based on people of different ages and therefore of different cohorts. Earlier cohorts had much less education and so on, which is why the scores are lower. One follows the same group over many years, and the pattern is different.

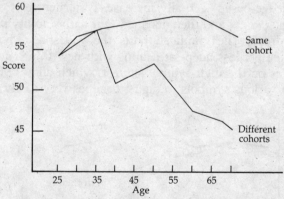

Fig 6.1 Changes in ability with ageing. The two curves show a cohort effect in scores on a test of educational aptitude. The rapidly declining curve shows average scores of people of different ages from different generations. The second curve shows changes in the same group of people, tested at different ages. Ability does not drop as precipitously as once thought. From Schaie and Strother (1968). Copyright 1968 by the American Psychological Association.

Schaie and Strother (1968) show this effect with the two curves. Schaie (1983) updated this work by looking at 500 people ranging from age twenty to their sixties. He followed the group from 1956 onwards and the picture his findings suggest is much rosier. IQ seems to be fairly stable until the sixties, with a significant decline after that. He also found individual differences in the rate of decline. Some individuals hardly declined at all until age seventy or so, while others did quite a bit earlier. There may be several reasons for this, and one of them is the exercise of intelligence. A person such as a political leader who continually has to deal with and solve a myriad of problems exercises intelligence much more than a person forced to retire or placed into a custodial care institution where he or she has little say in affairs. There may also be some physiological difference, people ageing physiologically at different rates.

Things get even more revealing and rosy when general intelligence is split up into fluid and crystallised. As mentioned in Chapter 2, fluid is one's native ability, while crystallised is heavily knowledge-based — the learned skills and knowledge that allow a person to behave more intelligently. They are roughly measured by the WAIS test: The performance IQ measures fluid and the verbal IQ crystallised intelligence. Scores on various WAIS subtests reveal distinctly different ageing patterns (Kaufman et al., 1989) that are shown in Figure 6.2. The verbal IQ changes little beyond age twenty or so, and scores on vocabulary and information subtests (both heavily knowledge-based) actually increase. Performance IQ score peaks about age twenty and then declines. Our native ability to deal with novelty drops. The graph supports the widespread popular view that people get less adept at dealing with new things as they get older. Scores on the digit-symbol subtest, which allows 90 seconds to match various symbols to digits, declines very easily.

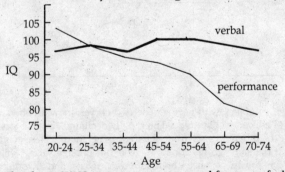

Fig 6.2 The classic WAIS ageing pattern, corrected for years of education. Verbal IQ score changes little with age, but performance IQ declines from about age twenty. Adapted from A.S. Kaufman, C.R. Reynolds and J.E. McLean, 'Age and WAIS-R Intelligence in a National Sample of Adults in the 20–74 Year Age Range', *Intelligence*, **13**, p. 246. Copyright 1989 by Ablex Publishing Corporation. Reprinted by permission of the publisher.

Why does this overall pattern occur? Crystallised intelligence is heavily knowledge-based, and knowledge tends to grow throughout our lifetime. The even brighter side of this change is the acquisition of 'wisdom', a kind of interpretive knowledge (Kekes, 1983; Smith & Baltes, 1990). Most of us learn how the world and people and all sorts of important things work, and we may organise our lives and work accordingly. We become experts in the life-knowledge domain (Smith & Baltes, 1990), and may behave more intelligently as a result. The tragedy for some people is, as a cynic once said, 'By the time we understand how things work, we are too old to really enjoy using that knowledge'.

Performance IQ may diminish early for several reasons (Salthouse, 1985). One is that the whole cognitive apparatus just does not work as well. Like the components of an ageing car, the bits that underly human intelligence work together less harmoniously. Another reason is a major pervasive change that comes over us all, sets in in earnest after age thirty, and leads to many of the declines in specific mental functions. It is the slowing down of thinking with age. This change is general, affecting most mental processes. Many elderly complain that they just cannot think as quickly as they used to. A study by Myerson et al. (1989) found the slowing quite apparent by age forty, and that it could not be eliminated even with extensive practice at various tasks. As tasks get more difficult, the speed differences between young and old get more pronounced. Salthouse (1985) estimates that we lose between 5 and 15 per cent of our speed each decade after age thirty. Thus, a fifty-year-old on average would think at perhaps 90 per cent of his or her speed at age forty. An illustration is with some aged drivers, who typically drive along the road very slowly. It is not that they always have. Rather, their mental processes have slowed down and the world simply moves too fast for them when they travel at normal speeds. They cope by trying to slow everything down. Performance subtests are all timed, and those that show the earliest decline are the ones that best tap mental speed, such as the digit-symbol, in which one must also coordinate a variety of mental functions. The score will decline as the power to coordinate declines.

But all is not so bleak. First, there are wide individual differences in general mental speed at any age. Some people are faster at age seventy than others are at twenty. Second, speed at specific, well practised tasks may stay. If an older person is very well practised at a given domain, he or she may be faster at it than youngsters. An example is chess, where older experts have a lot of automated components and a good idea of what is important and what is not. They often play much faster than less-experienced young people. The young outperform them at the relatively novel tasks like nonverbal Ravens items, where raw speed and fluid ability are what count.

Most tasks require some fluid and some crystallised ability, and performance may be some kind of averaging of both. The proportion of each required may partly determine average peak years. In chess, which requires fluid ability and a lot of knowledge, the typical peak is about age thirty, but players may stay near the top until their sixties or even later. Similarly, such fields as philosophy and history require more knowledge, which may explain the later best work peak.

Declines in Specific Mental Functions

So much for general intelligence. A lot of work has been done on changes in the more specific mental functions over the adult years, although there is much unreliable folklore about these. Older people tend to complain about memory loss, for example, while many companies and nations have compulsory retirement at sixty or sixty-five and may encourage workers to throw in the towel even earlier. In many professions, it is virtually impossible for even the over-forties to find a job. Certain occupations or tasks even require periodic testing to check that a person's efficiency is up to scratch. Pilots are periodically tested (and usually must retire at sixty), and so are older drivers. Here is a brief survey of a few functions that decline.

Senses. Our senses decline in various ways. Vision is the most obvious. The lens gets less flexible with age and less adept at changing shape to focus on near objects. This is why so many people need spectacles to read by age forty. By the sixties depth perception is much worse, one reason why elderly people are more likely to bump into obstacles, and colour perception also may diminish (Kausler, 1982). We get less accurate at identifying various colours, and lose about 25 per cent of our capacity to do so by age seventy. We also tend to lose the ability of our eyes to adapt quickly to the dark.

Hearing also declines. The classic pattern is loss of ability to pick up higher tone frequencies, which need to be much louder for the elderly to hear, and they may appreciate music less than they did in earlier days. There is also evidence for loss of taste sensitivity. Older people may not get as much excitement from their food.

The general picture is a loss of ability to sense the world, at least in some ways. However, many perceptual functions are not affected by ageing, so the pattern is not so bleak.

Attention. Ageing brings with it several changes in this marvellous ability. First, we get less adept at focusing our attention. The elderly tend to be more distractible, which is one reason why they are more likely to complain about noisy neighbours or eyesores such as billboards. The young are better able to gate them out. We also find it harder to switch attention back and forth, as is required on, say, the digit-symbol test of the WAIS. Driving in heavy traffic becomes more difficult since it requires constant shifting of attention to hazards such as other cars, road obstacles, and street signs. We also become less adept at dividing our attention. The elderly get quite flustered if they have to juggle a variety of things at once.

Learning and memory. The older often lament that their memory is just not what it used to be, and there is some evidence that they are right. But not all aspects of memory deteriorate. Memory for actions like typing, skiing, and riding a bicycle stays pretty much intact, though the tasks themselves may be harder to perform because of physical decline. Memory for information learned well many years before also alters little. However, memory for more recently learned information may decline. Some say it is because the older know so much more. Ability to take in information and retrieve it from memory when needed also shows some decline, and there seems to be a decline in working memory; people cannot hold and handle as much information as previously.

7

EDUCATION AND INTELLIGENCE

L ots of people are getting worried about Western education, and although the media whip things up further with scare stories, many commentators agree that schools really are in crisis (Weis et al., 1989). Such headlines as these are common:

SCHOOLS IN CRISIS!
ACHIEVEMENT TEST SCORES CONTINUE TO PLUMMET.
AVERAGE QUALITY OF TEACHER TRAINEES DROPS FURTHER: ENTRANCE SCORE CUT-OFFS FOR TEACHER TRAINING PROGRAMS LOWEST EVER!
INNER CITY SCHOOLS ARE CENTRES OF VIOLENCE AND DRUG TAKING — ARMED GUARDS HIRED TO PATROL CORRIDORS!
STUDENTS TODAY ARE JUST NOT INTERESTED IN LEARNING, SAY TEACHERS.

The major concerns are as follows. The first is the average quality of teachers. While the profession has many fine and outstanding members — and like any profession, also duds — there are too many of the latter. Teachers' pay and status have dropped and many bright, energetic students choose more prestigious and lucrative careers. As

154

a result, many teacher training courses have low entry standards and much classroom teaching is dreary and inefficient (Weis et al., 1989). Training programs themselves may be pretty uninspiring.

A second concern is that the students' basic skills are often woefully inadequate. Academic standards are falling. Employers and universities alike bewail the system's products, and the complaints seem to be more than the usual gripes of one generation about the next. The three Rs are one target. One recent survey found that half of American seventeen-year-olds could not read and understand a newspaper editorial. Many cannot read and write at all, and many more cannot for all practical purposes. Lots of students do not seem bothered by it, having little interest in the printed word, and some pundits even tip the ultimate demise of literature through sheer lack of interest. Basic arithmetic skills are another problem. Many employers say that lots of youngsters cannot do simple computations. I once had a dispute in a shop with a young girl who gave 50 cents change from two dollars for six 30-cent cakes. I could not convince her that $6 \times 3 = 18$ ($1.80) rather than 15 ($1.50). Her inability to multiply must have cost her employer dearly. Some school systems in the United States have responded with minimal competency tests: Students must meet certain standards to move to the next grade or to graduate. The legions of high school graduates unable to read prompted the step, and many American employers now prefer to hire university graduates, not because a job requires a degree but because it ensures that the recruit can read and write and will be motivated to work.

Another complaint is that students know less and less. Professors often say that the current generation of university students know little about the world and have little interest in it. They just want a qualification to earn money and a number of recent surveys show that many students and adults know little. An American survey found that many young adults could not find the U.S.A., England, or the Pacific and Atlantic Oceans on an unlabelled globe. A survey of English adults by Durant et al. (1989) found that only 34 per cent knew that the Earth goes around the Sun and takes a year to do so. Only 31 per cent knew that electrons are smaller than atoms and only 46 per cent knew that the earliest humans did not live at the same time as dinosaurs. Hirsch (1987) gives some anecdotal examples. He could not find a single student at his son's high school who could state the years in which World Wars I and II were fought, what the Alamo was, or where Vietnam was and that America had fought a major war there. He tells of a girl studying Latin who was amazed to discover it to be a dead language not spoken in Latin America!

Not all societies are dissatisfied with their education systems. The Japanese generally seem content with their products, who work hard and know a great deal when they finish. But the system is very trying for those in it. Rote learning is stressed at all levels, and lots of it. Students finish their regular school classes (six days a week) and go to private cram sessions at night. And there are examinations all the way through. The students only rest at university; the institution has to justify its selection and is loath to fail anyone. But although the graduates know a lot, they are often uncreative and unoriginal. Perhaps Japanese society, with its great emphasis on conformity, wants them to be. The system sometimes is offered as a model for other nations, but it probably would not transplant even if anyone else really wanted it.

But why are Western systems apparently failing? Why is the atmosphere one of crisis? One reason may be the decline in average teacher quality. Another may be the students themselves. Anecdotes abound about how different they are from earlier generations. They have grown up with television and a much more stimulating environment in general. Their attention spans are short, some say, because of television. Their minds are tuned to the thirty-second or two-minute grab, with a lot of attention-getting action packed in. Some say that they segment life into five-minute spans, based on the five minutes of program between the ads. Teachers also say that they have little fear of authority and punishments that schools can dish out. They also may have little interest in traditional school-work, often seeing it as irrelevant to their needs and concerns. Some other possible reasons are described later.

One result of this is great strain on teachers (e.g., Otto, 1986). In their initial foray into the classroom student teachers are struck by the disrespect, the failure of students to do what they are told, even the physical threats in some inner-city schools. What most observers in classrooms notice is the noise. Children talk, get up and walk around, and their attention constantly shifts back and forth. If the kids are bored, they are not afraid to show it. If they don't want to do something, often they refuse to. Textbook publishers are also putting out easier and easier texts, for students less willing to strain themselves reading.

A rather horrific illustration of life in classrooms comes from a study by Sizer (1984). He toured American high schools, observing many classrooms in action. The following session by a heroic biology teacher named Martha Schiffe, with a class of eighteen tenth-graders, is frightening and apparently not atypical:

> Schiffe ... [worked] through lists on the blackboard. Phylum chordata ... subphylum tetrapoda ... she went from one to the next pointing out various examples from handsome charts ... The students paid her little attention. Some had swivelled themselves around on their stools and kept watching me, the odd visitor. Others talked among themselves quietly ... Even while the names of living things poured out of Schiffe's lecture, no one was taking any notes. She wanted the students to know these names. They did not want to know them and were not going to learn them. Apparently no kind of outside threat — flunking, for example — affected the students ... Here was a class that was full of disembodied names in which the students had no interest at all. Indeed, they were in total agreement to ignore the substance of the class ... Schiffe could not flunk them all.

Some teachers cope with such treatment by declining to beat their heads repeatedly against the metaphorical brick wall. Sizer describes another teacher who made his history class as easy as possible in what Sizer called a 'conspiracy for the least hassle'. The history teacher made no great demands on students, signalled what the few questions for the exam would be, and 'the students picked up the signal and kept their part of the bargain by being friendly and orderly'. Only two-thirds of the class time observed was devoted to history, and even that was undemanding.

Education has problems and various critics offer various solutions. At one extreme, some say that formal schooling should be junked. Let us do away with schools, classes, courses, exams, paper qualifications, and graduation ceremonies. There is no sense trying to force unwilling people to learn. The whole system creates stress and violence as a result. Others are less radical. They say let us improve average teacher quality by better training and higher salaries. Let us improve the system.

What has all this got to do with intelligence? A great deal. Intelligence is of fundamental importance in education, and some education system problems stem from failure to deal with aspects of it. It is important for two major reasons.

First, intelligence is a major individual difference that has to be coped with effectively. It determines how rapidly a person learns (almost by definition), and what an individual can learn. Most subjects build on themselves, getting harder and harder as one progresses, and most of us reach a sort of barrier in a given field. We may move a bit past it with enormous effort, but the barrier is still there. For the very bright, the barrier is a long way up the educational ladder, but for others is low down. They just cannot do the work in late high school or university. There may even be a limit for the human species, as J. B. S. Haldane's famous quote in Chapter 1 suggests. Quantum physics may already have tested our limits. Virtually everyone has enormous difficulty with the topic because its ideas are so different from our everyday ones. Even physicists have problems. As prominent physicist Richard Feynman put it, 'I think it's safe to say that no one really understands quantum mechanics'.

Education system administrators know about all this, of course. Places in courses get scarcer as one goes up the educational ladder and many administrators use student differences essentially to select out the most intelligent and hard-working students. University undergraduate places are usually rationed, especially in prestigious law and medical schools. Those who run the courses use entrance tests and the education system itself to pick out those best able to understand the material, to do the work, and who are likely to make good practitioners. Without such weeding, the courses would fill up with the incapable. Failure to select this way can be fatal. It was tried in China during the Cultural Revolution in the late 1960s, when ideological soundness became all-important. Students were selected for university on the grounds of party loyalty, the correct peasant ancestry, and the right attitudes. The universities filled up with the unable and the result was a disaster from which Chinese education is still recovering. Effective education systems act like nature, selecting for brightness and willingness to work hard.

Education and intelligence are also related because schools are charged with improving intelligence, not just with coping with what they get. They aim to develop intellect, to train raw general intelligence and more specialised abilities.

Because the topic of intelligence is important, student teachers learn a lot about it in their training courses, and teach themselves even more in the classroom. They learn to quickly pick out the bright and dull, and if possible, tailor instruction to individual students' capacities. Indeed, a study by MacLeod et al. (1989) asked 136 Australian teachers just what their ideas of intelligence were. A few stressed 'the ability to reason' and 'to learn quickly' and used various cues to pick it out; 'the look in their eyes', 'how bright their eyes are', and so on. They coped with ability differences in various ways. Many secondary school teachers tried to teach to the middle-range ability and varied methods a bit for children at the extremes. Primary teachers often preferred to set up separate classes based on ability.

The views administrators take about intelligence profoundly

affect how they organise their schools. In the main, they have believed in one of two ideas. The first belief is in a fixed g, or something like it, that is largely innate as was used when setting up the English eleven-plus system. Belief in g may suggest picking out the talented young, lavishing the best teachers and resources on them, and preparing them for university. Worry less about the others, who don't really have what it takes. Teach them practical things, and prepare them for trade or unskilled occupations. We may not like it, but ability is pretty fixed and that must be faced. Intelligence cannot much be raised. Such a view sometimes prevails even when dealing with the cream of talent. Some universities run 'pass' and 'honours' streams, often dividing students into them in their first or second year of study. The few honours students take special classes, are set additional work, and get much of the professors' attention. The others are treated in a more workmanlike fashion. The talent is selected out early.

The other major view is a rabid environmentalism, as has been traditional in the United States. The view is that all are created more or less equal and that differences in school achievement are due to environment, motivation, or personality. In theory at any rate, ability grouping is to be frowned on. It is 'elitist'. Let us provide equal opportunities at all levels, and try to raise the intelligence of those lower on the distribution. We just have to find the key to doing so. Some education systems officially hold one view but practise another; the Soviet Union, for instance.

At any rate, intelligence enters into educational computations in several ways. Schools are the major consumers of IQ and other ability tests, and teachers, administrators, and parents need to understand the issues involved. This chapter will look at two major issues. The first is one major concern of educators; how to cope with ability differences. The second is the perennial issue of whether educators can actually raise general intelligence.

Coping with Ability Differences

You are a classroom teacher with thirty ten-year-old pupils. You teach them many subjects: mathematics, science, history, English, and art. Some of your children learn just about everything quickly and effortlessly, and sit waiting with an air of boredom while their fellows plod through the same work. Some children have trouble with just about everything. They simply do not catch on, and have completed only part of the set work when most of the others have finished. Most children are in between. The distribution of prowess that the typical teacher has to face is this dramatic. Gettinger and White (1980) tried to measure learning speed range in single classes in the same school and in classes in different schools. In a typical classroom, the range was an astronomical five to one: The fastest child learned at five times the rate of the slowest. Across schools, it went up to nine to one. And the two very extremes, the retarded and highly gifted, have been clipped off from these calculations!

There are also differences in more specific abilities such as verbal, mathematical, spatial relations, and so on. Some students find particular subjects more or less easy because of such talents. Then there are learning disabilities, and different preferred ways of learning, such as cognitive styles. Field-independent children like to work things out for themselves and prefer FI teachers, while field-dependent students are the opposite. These are just the capability differences. There are other differences in motivation, attention-span, activity level, and so on.

What do you do? If you subscribe to Gardner's multiple intelligences theory, as some schools do, then you could assess every child early and profile strengths and weaknesses. The weaknesses could be improved as much as possible by special training and the child may be pushed in the direction of his or her strengths. Not all students will appreciate this, since many may have great talent in something they do not like but mediocre talent in things they love, such as art and music. But most teachers probably subscribe to the g view and follow traditional methods. Let us look at each.

Teaching to the Middle
Many teachers cope by simply pitching their material and methods to the 'average' student. After teaching for a few years, they get a good general idea of their students' capabilities. The very slow may get some special attention and the very fast may get extra work to do while they wait for others to finish, though some may resent it. This strategy is just a survival tactic, and it can leave the gifted so bored and the slow so frustrated that either group may even disrupt the class as a result. Many teachers say that they dislike 'mixed-ability classes' that make them use the strategy. But an advantage is that all students meet peers of all abilities, and the fast can sometimes help the slow.

Adapting Teaching Methods and Pace to Each Individual
A new educationese catchphrase is 'aptitude by treatment interaction'. Simply, it means that children with a certain pattern of abili-

ties learn best from one teaching method, and those with another pattern from a different technique. For example, very intelligent students tend to do better when they can organise material as they please. Less able students learn better when they are given organised material. (Interestingly enough, however, the less able prefer low-organisation teaching such as small-group work or independent study.) Anxiety also has an effect. Very anxious students tend to prefer methods that do not ask for much socialising; the teacher does most of the talking. There are lots of abilities and lots of teaching methods (textbooks, discussions, lectures, programmed learning, and so on).

Researchers are trying to find the optimum mix of abilities and methods, and the list of interactions is growing. But while such information may be useful, it is very difficult to individualise instruction for thirty pupils, at least in traditional schools. However, educational computer programs may solve the problem. They can go at an individual's pace, have branches to clarify what he or she does not understand, and lots of visual stuff for those who lack good imagery. Computers don't get bored or inattentive, and are infinitely patient.

Acceleration and Deceleration

Acceleration is letting a child move ahead at his or her own pace, the logic of which is to let the racehorses speed ahead. Don't keep them back. Children can be accelerated in several ways. They may simply go through the textbook faster, with specially prepared exercises and tests. The teacher may also give additional work. Some schools have 'resource rooms' with special advanced training in some topic of interest. Others run enrichment courses for the gifted after school hours or during summer recesses. Some gifted high-school students may take courses in certain subjects at a local university.

But the most dramatic mode is to push a talented child a grade, or two or three, ahead. Sometimes it may be in all courses, but usually it is just in one of special talent. A few children jump through the grades at an alarming pace. One hears of children finishing high school at age twelve or thirteen, entering a university and gaining a doctorate by nineteen or twenty.

Is the idea sound? There are arguments on each side. Some say it is necessary. Otherwise the children will get bored, lazy, and unchallenged, and may drop out of school as soon as they can. Society's talent must be encouraged. Others counter that the pupils' social and emotional development will lag well behind their intellectual. Putting them in with older, more mature students who will dwarf them in size and social development may do great harm. The eventual result may be a social cripple. The children themselves may have their own preferences, with some wanting to move ahead while others choose to stay with their age mates. Children who have been accelerated often report that they experienced problems but felt that being held back would have been worse. Others say they were happy to stay behind. In New Zealand, students can enter university at the end of their eleventh or twelfth year of study. Many go as soon as possible, while others stay the extra year to keep level with age mates and enjoy being a 'senior'. The research evidence is mixed. Some studies suggest that acceleration may do no great harm.

Deceleration is the mirror image. It can involve special remedial classes, or holding a child back a year because he or she has not mastered the work and cannot cope with next year's. Schools take this step with enormous reluctance, and some do not do so at all, since it may be such a blow to the child's self-esteem. Parents may object and even launch a lawsuit. But a child who cannot handle the work of the next grade may become very frustrated, disruptive, and be beyond the help of remedial classes.

Streaming

Streaming involves dividing students into different groups according to ability. Ability may be measured by IQ tests, or by school grades, teacher's ratings, or perhaps all three. The students are usually divided up in one of two major ways. The first is by sending them to different schools, as in the eleven-plus system. Sometimes it is done very discreetly, so that no one gets upset. Just 1 or 2 per cent are unobtrusively creamed off. Some systems take out the very top in specific areas. New York City runs specialist high schools for the very able in such areas as science; they study regular high school subjects but get lots of advanced instruction in their talent areas from the best teachers around. The High School of Science has turned out some of America's Nobel Prize winners. The High School of Performing Arts has developed much theatrical talent, and was featured in the film *Fame*. At the other extreme, the mentally retarded may also go to special schools.

The second and more usual option is to stream within a school. The groups often have euphemistic names like 'bellbirds' and 'robins' for quite young children, or are just called A, B, C, and so on. American high schools often have 'honors', 'college', and 'general' streams, where the work pace and atmospheres are quite different. Whatever the tags, the students soon figure out what they mean and where they stand. Grouping is sometimes done just by topic. A school might have reading groups and mathematics groups, but teach everything else in unstreamed classes. Though many teachers favour streaming, some oppose it as 'elitist'. United States law favours mainstreaming the retarded, prescribing that they stay in a normal classroom as far as practicable.

The standard argument for streaming is that teachers can pitch lessons to the students' ability. The vast range of prowess is narrowed down to one easily dealt with. The bright will not be lost because the work is too easy or the dull because it is too hard. As a result, students benefit. The bright can move ahead quickly, and the dull will not be frustrated by being consistently outclassed. Why run an ill-matched race?

That is the argument. A lot of research has investigated the reality and most of it points to one sad conclusion: Large-scale streaming generally is a bad idea. It is not so bad if done discreetly on a small scale, clipping off the two extremes, grouping by topic, or providing special enrichment classes. But on a large scale, it can be harmful. The typical finding is that it helps the very bright, but may harm everyone else (Slavin, 1987). The lower stream students suffer from many ills. First, they tend to perform worse. Their grades are lower. They tend to lose motivation to study and get unhappy about school in general. The low-stream classes themselves can be less than happy places. Teachers tend to dislike them and studies of their work show them to be less keen, less organised, and less willing to push the students too hard (Slavin, 1987). At the very bottom stream, the teacher may see him or herself as largely a babysitter, trying to get through the class time without undue pain. The children pick up these expectations that they will do badly and start to believe them. They also miss out on the stimulation of bright kids in class and good academic role models.

Being in the bottom stream can also devastate a child's self-esteem. The child has been officially labelled dull, and has to carry the tag around for life. Many fall into line with the view, losing interest in schoolwork and getting out as soon as possible. When an entire school is a low ability stream, it can become a very unhappy place indeed. The present author spent part of 1965 in a secondary school in England that was a bin for the 80 per cent of students categorised as too dull for grammar school and university. The atmosphere was one of general gloom. The children felt that they had 'failed the eleven-plus', and would not amount to much in life. We even had to carry our dull label on our backs out on the streets. We wore blue uniforms and the bright kids from the local grammar school wore red. The school principal understood the syndrome and gave us frequent pep talks to try to raise morale. He pointed out that we could compete on the job market with the grammar school children, often giving actual examples. But few were convinced.

Another problem with streaming is that there will sometimes be mistakes in placement. Often it is hard to jump from one stream to another. Getting stuck in a low stream because of laziness may mean one is left behind in schoolwork, perhaps fatally.

CAN INTELLIGENCE BE RAISED?

Humanity has a few timeless dreams. There is the fountain of youth, the philosopher's stone to turn base metals into gold, and the stairway to heaven. Some way down the list is the power to make people brighter, to increase general intelligence. Science fiction has explored the theme, and Chapter 4 mentioned Charlie's neuronal transplant in *Flowers for Algernon*. In Robert Heinlein's *Beyond this Horizon*, people get brighter after being 'Renshawed'. They take a special training course which improves memory, reasoning, and a few other faculties.

People want to raise intelligence for several reasons. Parents want to help their children go further in the education system and do well in their occupations. Governments may see it as a national resource, as mentioned in Chapter 6, and want to increase the stock as they would reserves of timber and agricultural land. Large numbers of retarded and borderline retarded cases may burden the economy, and the problem may get worse as society and technology becomes more complex. Children have to cope with an increasingly information-rich world, which takes much ability.

It is interesting to speculate just how far governments would raise the average intelligence level if they could. Every society has a lot of dull, routine, dangerous, and unskilled jobs, and will have them until all unskilled work can be performed by robots. Once people get too bright and educated they start to sneer at such tasks. It happened in West Germany in the 1960s and to a lesser extent in the United States in the 1960s and later. Advanced industrial nations had to import foreign workers to toil in their fields, steel mills, hotel kitchens, and garbage dumps. This theme was explored in depth in *Brainwave*, where just about everyone tired of his or her routine job and society broke down. Anecdotal evidence from Mensa members suggests that the very bright avoid or quickly lose interest in routine tasks that they see as trivial and repetitive. What, then, is the optimum average intelligence level for an advanced industrial nation?

When there is a demand, some enterprising people move in quickly to fill it. Suppliers of products and services try to meet the demand for intelligence-raisers in several ways. Numerous popular books promise to raise intelligence or intellectual skills. They range from the serious based on science (Sternberg, 1986; Whimbey, 1975) to the spurious. The latter sometimes recommend starting the program before the child is even born. There are many programs that promise to make children brighter. Glen Doman runs a sort of institute in the United States which provides courses to stimulate the children. There are a lot of exercises in the program that involve stimulating a child's senses. The fees are hefty and the waiting list is long.

Such promises often raise much media interest, and when one research group in the United States claimed to have a cure for retardation it was widely reported on. However, the claims appear highly exaggerated and some sceptics suspect possible fraud (see Spitz, 1986). The episode is sometimes referred to sarcastically as 'The Miracle in Milwaukee', no real miracle at all. A late 1960s study got massive media attention and is still mentioned in many textbooks. Rosenthal and Jacobsen (1968) thought that teacher's expectations about their students could raise or lower the student's intelligence. In their study, they told some teachers that certain children would be 'late bloomers', evidently inducing the teachers to treat them differently. The students' performance apparently shot up dramatically as a result, and the study was dubbed 'Pygmalian in the classroom'. The results seemed very promising. Perhaps everyone could benefit this way. However, it was fatally flawed. No one can get the same results and most researchers now dismiss the findings. Teachers will often have a good idea of their students' capabilities (though not always), and may use their own judgment instead of what a researcher tells them. However, the effect has almost become a popular myth nowadays.

Can intelligence be raised? The question is complex, and again turns on what one means by the term 'intelligence'. What if we consider it to be g, or intelligence B, or what Spitz (1986) calls 'the pervasive way in which we meet everyday challenges, how quickly we learn, the scope and complexity of material we can understand, and the intricacy of problems we can solve'? Can this broad ability be raised?

On a population-wide basis, yes it could. As we saw in Chapter 6, the average intelligence level has been rising. A society could raise it further by better screening of genetic and environmental factors that lower intelligence, by providing better nutrition, perhaps by increasing funds for Head Start programs, and by restricting immigration. A government could go even further with marginal practices like encouraging selective breeding, or genetic engineering when the technology is available. However, such practices may open a Pandora's box of problems, and a society based on such control is a familiar science fiction nightmare.

On an individual basis, the problem is much trickier, and what can be done is open to dispute. On the one hand, Spitz (1986, 1988) argues that there is no firm evidence that one can improve that sort of intelligence in given individuals. He surveys many programs, including the much-touted 'instrumental enrichment' program of Reuben Feuerstein, and documents many cases of fraud — of programs that really just teach children to do IQ tests better, or compensate for different cultural backgrounds. Ultimately, he argues that educators should worry less about improving intelligence but more about finding good methods to teach the retarded. Some studies suggest that slight intelligence gains can be made with lots of early stimulation, but they are hard to evaluate (Lee et al., 1988).

What about the commercially available programs for normal or above-average children? There is little evidence that they work, and some scientists believe that programs such as Doman's may actually do harm. In fact those offering programs rarely give any evidence that their systems work. Sometimes they speak of testimonials from pleased clients or show off an obviously bright child and say, 'Look at what my program has done for this child'. The problem is that the child might have been just the same without the program, or even better. We simply do not know. Anyone staking such a claim (or claiming a cure for cancer, or a method of doubling lifespan) must give evidence. Many governments fund agencies to test the claims of makers of various products and services and forbid outrageous, unsupported promises (e.g., 'Tasteee toothpaste reduces cavities by 28%'). The claims must be tested by comparing a group using the product with another without it. Such evidence is rarely if ever given by the program designers, and when claims are tested this way, they rarely hold up.

It may be possible to increase this sort of intelligence, but no one has struck on exactly the right method. We have to await further research.

A much more profitable tack is to improve a person's propensity to behave intelligently; crystallised intelligence, largely based on knowledge and skills. A sound knowledge base is essential to intelligent behaviour, be it in voting, conducting one's personal life (avoiding debt traps and bad marriages or self-inflicted health problems), doing a job well, and so on. Chapter 4 mentioned that the performance of retardates, and sometimes the learning disabled, may improve when they acquire and use various strategies. We can make people more intelligent, in a sense, by teaching them things. But this is not everything because, as we also saw, kids today are generally bright but seem to know less and less.

Of course, this not news and it is not particularly profound. All governments know it and spend huge sums on education. Quite often, education is a nation's second or third largest budget item. A developing nation that wants to compete better on the international stage or just improve life at home pours money into schools and universities. Literacy becomes a priority, with the most reluctant of young citizens drawn in by compulsory schooling. The best and brightest are sent overseas to study, and foreign academics are attracted to local universities. The government may try hard to keep children in schools as long as possible, giving incentives and high pay for jobs that require many years of schooling. Governments may also provide and require in-service, update, and refresher courses for teachers, doctors, engineers, and other professionals. Schools try to make people brighter by teaching both facts and strategies for thinking better. Indeed, classical education involved training in Latin and Greek to generally 'strengthen the mind'. The idea was that it would transfer to all other topics, but studies show that in fact it did not.

No one much disputes the general idea. But they dispute what should be taught and how it should be taught. Ideally, there should be a general theory of intelligence and learning from which teachers could derive teaching methods, just as engineers draw from theory provided by physics and doctors and physiotherapists from physiology. It would be pretty disastrous to have such practicalities based on no theory at all, which is one reason why alternative practitioners such as chiropractors are sometimes severely criticised. But this is the situation in education. There is no generally accepted theory of education. There are a number of competing theories, but these rarely clearly prescribe what and how to teach. Trainee teachers get little rationale for their classroom actions, and instead get a hodge-podge of ideas, theories, and rules of thumb that are sometimes junked after a few months in the classroom. Such a theory should come from educational psychology, but has not yet. As

Stones (1984) put it, 'Courses in . . . educational psychology provided ideas [which] wilt quickly . . . come graduation neophyte teachers rapidly forgot such ephemera or complained at their inutility'.

Many educators themselves do not seem unduly worried about this. The educational journals are full of studies of all sorts of side issues that seem unimportant by comparison. Piaget's theory was used for a time but is becoming unfashionable, partly because educational implications don't clearly follow from it. Sometimes a new theory comes in, or a new technique (such as Skinnerian programmed learning), to enormous initial enthusiasm that wanes when expectations are not met. Much the same problem occurs in psychotherapy, with a hodge-podge of theories, techniques, and so on.

However, research on intelligence and in cognitive psychology is giving the outlines of such a theory and a few simple aspects of it are presented below. The general idea is to raise crystallised intelligence by improving the factual knowledge base and by training strategies and other general thinking skills. Let us look at each.

Increasing the Knowledge Base

As we have seen, the more one knows about a domain, the faster the thinking and learning in that domain, and the more intelligently one is likely to behave. Knowledge gives standard solutions to standard problems. Much education simply teaches students how to recognise the typical problems and apply the set solutions. A good example is word problems that need to be solved by applying algebra (e.g., 'If it takes three men two days . . .'). Another is medical diagnosis. A medical student learns symptoms, signs, and how to diagnose. Once a given patient's condition is identified, standard textbook remedies are applied. An architect learns about building types, uses, and things done in the past and may apply these to a given client's problems. Educated people are different from uneducated ones: They can do more and generally act more intelligently because of their knowledge.

Many dispute exactly what knowledge should be taught. There is little controversy for practical courses like medicine and engineering. Most practitioners have a good notion of what the students need to know before they can be loosed upon the world. But disputes may arise at a more general level. Exactly what ought to be taught in schools depends on philosophy and culture. Different societies have quite different ideas. For example, some Islamic school systems spend much time inducing students to memorise large chunks of the Koran. Saudi Arabia has little sex education, while the United States has a lot. Texas requires schools to teach the value of free enterprise but teaches little about basic Marxism. Communist North Korea teaches a lot of Marxism but not much free enterprise. What schools teach depends on many things; values, what the universities that many students will attend want them to know, what employers want, and what countless pressure groups want and do not want. The latter may lobby for or against the teaching, say, of evolution, and school systems sometimes sway with the prevailing winds. Most American high school texts say little about evolution because of such pressure groups.

A decent theory of education will prescribe exactly what should be taught at a narrower level. Imagine that a society decrees that students must learn algebra, Wagnerian opera, Trobriand Island folk-dancing, and quantum physics. What aspects of them ought to be taught, and how? How does one analyse these domains and pick out the essential knowledge in them to teach? Often this is not done well, one result of which is that students may be inundated with facts and facts and facts, which to them seem disconnected. Exams tap such factual knowledge and students learn to learn by rote to pass courses. One result is that many students simply do not understand a great deal of what is taught in classrooms and textbooks.

Many researchers have tried the following approach, based on much work on intelligence. They look at what experts in a given domain know and can do. They look at how their knowledge is organised and used to tackle the domain's problems. Then they devise a curriculum with its goal as explicitly teaching that expert knowledge to students, or at least pushing them along the path to expertise. The entire curriculum can be analysed into separate domains, and each into expert knowledge.

An illustration of this idea is with chess. What should we teach novice chessplayers after they learn the rules? How do we create chess experts? Let us look at what the experts know. In fact they know many things. They have a lot of rote-learned facts. They must memorise many opening-move sequences, which are continually updated in long, encyclopaedic compendia. Many use computer databases to supply the latest variations and what opponents are currently playing. A player who does not keep up with developments may be tripped up by the latest wrinkle in some variation: His opponent just has to apply rote-facts to beat him. A player also must rote-learn a vast number of set endgames and principles, which have standard solutions, and also learn many of the famous games of chess history that provide model solutions to certain kinds of problems. A player must memorise a vast number of configurations of chess pieces. Chess skill is largely pattern-recognition. Even relatively dull persons can become good players by absorbing such knowledge. There are also many basic concepts like *passed pawn, insecure king, bad bishop,* etc., and many practical rules like 'look to see if there are any checks', 'keep your opponent's army under restraint', and 'calculate variations far ahead'. Other domains are organised differently. Research can find out how and try to teach them.

Another line of research to help build a theory of teaching is to figure out exactly what knowledge itself is. This will help analyse a given domain and tell what particularly to look for. There is an old distinction between two types of knowledge; skills and factual. It is the difference between knowing *how* and knowing *that*. Skills pertain to actions, like typing, playing tennis, tying a shoelace, and executing fine dance steps. They can only be learned from practice, by repeating actions again and again. One cannot learn the knowledge needed to ride a bicycle just by reading a book. One must actually get on and ride. Such knowledge is often soon removed from awareness. After learning to use a manual gear shift, for example, we may forget what we are doing, and when teaching someone else we may need to watch exactly how we do it. Skills are hardly ever forgotten. One can pick up a bicycle thirty years after last riding and still traverse smoothly. Factual knowledge is facts like France's capital is Paris, apples are fruits, and that the year has twelve months. We learn facts without having to practise, and forget them easily if not continually using them. Most tasks require a mix of both skills and facts.

Factual knowledge is largely organised around concepts (Howard, 1987), which are the basic units for learning and thinking. As mentioned in Chapter 2, a concept is an idea, a person's information about a category such as dogs, fish, or triangles. (The notion of intelligence itself is a concept.) Every domain's knowledge is largely organised around key basic concepts that constitute the expert's knowledge structure. For example, some key concepts in music are *chord, fugue, symphony, sonata form, note,* and *key*. Some in physics are *force, gravity, pressure, electron,* and *atom*; in mathematics, *set, prime number, fraction, base,* and *group*; in literature, *novel, epic, personification, archetype*. The lists could go on and on. Most domains continually develop new concepts and refine existing ones. For example, some relatively new ones in astronomy are *pulsar, quasar,* and *black hole*. Experts know the concepts well, know how they relate to each other, and know how to use them. A good physicist can use the concept of *gravity* and some of the knowledge in it to calculate spacecraft and astronomical body orbits. A computer programmer uses such concepts as *data structure* and *computer language* to get a computer to do things. Education in each discipline involves determining the fundamental concepts that the experts know and teaching them to students, along with how to use them and some other things, such as those listed in the example of learning to play chess. At least education should involve this. In practice, it often does not.

Here is a simple example, a simple model of education to illustrate the points. There is a domain in which many people behave unintelligently, often making serious errors that may cause them and others much suffering. It is the domain of dating and marriage. Every individual needs a good knowledge base to behave in it intelligently. The base would consist of many facts organised around basic concepts of types of dating partner. One would categorise oneself and any prospective partner to predict who would be suitable, and the likely course of a relationship. Numerous facts can be added to the basic concept framework, and many persons develop such a concept system from their own experiences. But many do not, and they are severely handicapped in the dating game. The solution is to work out what concepts the experts know, and to teach people these and how to use them.

Hoffman (1981) tried to do just this. She wrote a somewhat light-hearted book for women that lists twenty-two types of man as dating partner and how to identify them. Each concept contains many facts about their characteristics and their advantages and drawbacks. Here are three cases:

1. *The Idle Lord.* He is a mesmerist who emanates creativity and nonconformity. He likes strong and independent women. He will not commit himself to anything, contributes little to a relationship, and is likely to become dull and dependent on his partner after a few years.

2. *The Doe Stalker.* He is very male, a loner, and is likely to drink and smoke heavily. He likes small, young, sheltered women (and groupies) and does not want to be a modern man. He is a poor long-term prospect because a woman soon will pass his usual maximum favoured age of twenty-two.

3. *The Amoral Passion-Monger.* He is very dangerous. He will make enormous demands and may pursue someone for years. He is to be avoided at all costs.

Using these categories gives some basis for making intelligent decisions. Many people also work out concepts of their own, and learn
things such as the natural history of most relationships and so on.
Knowing and using them should mean more intelligent actions.

Concepts themselves are organised into forms. Most domains
have strict forms, structures in which things must be done. For
example, music has such forms as the symphony and concerto. A
concerto has three parts called movements, usually two fast ones
with a slow one in the middle. There also are strict rules for gener-
ating note sequences within each. Literature has forms like the
detective story, the Mills and Boon romance, the adventure story,
and so on. The romance usually has a young woman, an older man,
some form of conflict between them, and a reconciliation at the end.
Stories themselves must have such elements as characters, plot,
conflicts, resolutions, and episodes; the elements of the form. Scientific theories also have a set form. A few great people invent a new
form. Dashiell Hammett invented the modern detective story form
and Roger Bacon and Isaac Newton invented many of the forms of
science. However, almost everyone works within forms, producing
minor variations on them. Education should emphasise such forms,
how to use them, and how to work within them. Students therefore
should behave more intelligently in each domain.

The general idea of extending the factual knowledge base by
teaching concepts and so on was recently advanced by Hirsch
(1987). His book had enormous impact in the United States and he
brought the new term 'cultural literacy' into the language. (One can
even buy books now to test one's cultural literacy.) Hirsch reiterates
some points made above. The knowledge base is crucial to intelligent thinking. He further argues that American schools in the last
two decades have neglected teaching facts, focusing instead on
abstract thinking skills. Students know little as a result, and therefore are not 'culturally literate'. They do not have a good store of the
culture's important concepts, and cannot understand fully the
books, newspapers, magazines, and other works of their society.
However, they need such knowledge to converse with others of their
culture. Hirsch goes even further. He actually presents a list of 5,000
concepts that make up the knowledge base needed to be culturally
literate. It was gathered by him and a couple of friends, though he
acknowledges its limitations. Table 7.1 presents some examples of
its concepts. He argues that it should be a bulwark of schooling.
Students should be taught the 5,000 concepts and should know
them when they graduate. One problem, however, is that many such

concepts contain a vast amount of knowledge. One cannot just learn a concept like *life* or *satire* in an instant.

Table 7.1   A Sampling of the 5,000 Concepts That Hirsch Proposes Every American Should Know to be Culturally Literate

Alchemy	Hedonism	Quark
Brainwashing	Mafia	Radar
Crescendo	Marxism	Satire
Galaxy	Nemesis	Typhoid Mary
Iron Curtain	Origin of Species	Zeitgeist

Though acquiring much domain-specific knowledge may improve crystallised intelligence, there will still be differences among people, who acquire knowledge at different rates and differ in speed and skill at applying what they know. Anecdotal evidence also suggests that most people strike a barrier of skill, beyond which they improve little even with prodigious practice. In chess, for instance, most players reach a certain rating ceiling (playing strength being measured by a rating based on wins and losses) that practice and study eventually seem to shift little. Perhaps the barrier is not absolute, if one devoted idiot savante-style efforts to improving, but it still is there. Most persons will never become star physicists or concert pianists.

This sort of factual knowledge is important, but it does not tell the whole story. Intelligence may also be raised by teaching thinking skills.

Improving Thinking Prowess by Teaching Strategies

Every trainee boxer learns the following trick very early. At a bout's start, pull back the right glove as if to punch. The opponent moves to parry the telegraphed right, but is met with a surprise lightning left hook. Military officers of all lands and eras learn a few timeless tricks. An old one is divide and conquer. A large force will usually defeat a much smaller one, all other things being equal. So a larger army is cut in half and each portion is dealt with in turn. Another is to take the high ground and fight from there, be it the hills, airspace, or outer space itself. Chess and fencing bouts consist partly of set manoeuvres adapted to different opponents. Fencers go through their repertoire, parrying the opponent's, and trying to come up with one that scores the point. The winner is the one who knows most manoeuvres, and is faster in choosing and executing them while parrying the opponent's. Large corporations often espouse the virtues of a free market but when sizeable enough try to make life as comfortable as possible by such tricks as destroying the competition or seeking much government protection. Love as well as war has countless tricks. To induce marriage or a steady relationship, one person may try to make another jealous or appear uninterested to make their acquisition seem much more valuable (playing hard to get). To rise rapidly in large organisations, there are many standard manoeuvres like 'get to know the top people', 'adopt the organisation's culture', and 'make your work successes very visible'.

All these are *strategies*. Strategies have been mentioned in earlier chapters. They are plans to solve a problem, to deal with a situation. Almost every domain has set strategies to solve its problems; politics, business, war, soccer, love, and so on. Some strategies only work in one domain while others work in many. For example, divide and conquer works in war, politics, and business. The strategy 'plan and calculate consequences of possible actions' works in just about every domain. Performance improves when we use strategies and generally, the more strategies one knows and can adeptly apply, the more intelligently one is likely to behave. Much practical education teaches set strategies, how to use and adapt them to changing circumstances. For example, management training teaches many quite rigid strategies to deal with common situations (if the market is contracting, reduce production). So, let us make people behave more intelligently by teaching strategies.

This elegant but not terribly profound or original idea is all the rage in educational research at the moment (e.g., McCormick et al., 1989). Students are taught to analyse situations, search out what strategies may work, try them out, and figure out how well they did. Students who do not plan or think much in advance must be taught to 'be strategic' rather than impulsive. There are several published programs, each purporting to teach thinking skills, that are used for the retarded, learning disabled, and others. They teach students how their own memory, thinking, and learning work; what their strengths and weaknesses are; and how to use various strategies in major areas like the following.

Memory. Many books and magazine articles list simple strategies to improve remembering, though nothing works as well as writing things down. Some strategies date from the Ancient Greeks, who got interested in memory strategies when required to give long speeches for which notes were taboo. Many rely on imagery. For example, the method of places dates from Simonides. According to legend, he gave a speech at a banquet and was called outside to speak to a messenger, whereupon the hall collapsed, killing everyone inside. The relatives asked him to identify the remains, and he did so by imagining the hall as it had been that fateful night and where each person was seated. The technique involves visualising some familiar place like a living room, locating items to be remembered around it, and recalling the image later. You then take a mental walk around the image, and each location triggers off memory of the item there. Another memory strategy is to try to understand material being learned. Meaningless material is very hard to recall. The more one understands, often the more one can remember.

Reading. Many people are poor readers (or are nonreaders) because they are not strategic. For example, many do not slow down or speed up according to what they are reading. They read physics or philosophy texts at the same rate as romance novels and comic books. Students also can learn to skim material to speed up, to identify main ideas in passages, to summarise what they are reading, and to monitor their comprehension as they go. Many poor readers get to the end of a page without even realising that they have understood little.

General problem-solving. A lot of problem-solving strategies just apply to one domain. But some are quite general, and useful for complex problems lacking standard solutions. An example is, 'Try to find a counter-example'. If the problem is to decide whether all swans are white, try to find a black one. Another is 'analogical reasoning'. Try to find an analogous problem or situation. An example is deciding how to behave in the presence of a person just met. We may try to think of someone similar, and what worked then. A manager wanting to know whether to expand his company might look at similar companies that expanded or did not expand in similar circumstances, and what happened. A very general strategy is to approach problems in four steps; define exactly what the problem is, generate several possible solutions, try one out, then later evaluate whether it worked.

Edward de Bono (e.g., de Bono, 1976) believes thinking strategies can be taught and has written a series of popular books on the theme. Some of his ideas run as follows. First, he lists common thinking errors to avoid. 'Initial judgment' is deciding quickly if one likes a proposal and then using logic to back up that hasty move, rather than exploring all the issues and problems in depth before deciding. Another is to operate on too short a time scale. For instance, one might do something for an immediate reward, neglecting the long-term. De Bono then gives ways to improve thinking. An example is to train one's attention to things, to be alert to certain sorts of pattern.

Teaching logic. Try the problems below. Read the first two statements in each of the three groups and decide if the conclusion really follows.

1. Some Fosterites wear yellow shoes. No Wallyites are Fosterites as well. Therefore, at least some Wallyites do not wear yellow shoes.
2. If the ship comes in, life will be wonderful. The ship is not coming in. Therefore, life will not be wonderful.
3. Some trees with cones are poisonous. Some trees in the park have cones. Therefore, some of the trees in the park are poisonous.

Many people believe that the conclusions follow, but none of those listed does. Indeed, people often make quite glaring logical errors that can make them act unintelligently.

The errors fall into several clear-cut types (Galotti, 1989). For instance, we have trouble reasoning from a negative premise (no A are B, or some A are not B). Our minds cannot easily wrap around them. It is difficult to infer from a statement such as 'Some smokers are not ever cancer sufferers'. Second, we are likely to change the meaning of premises, perhaps to make them easier to understand. 'All A are B' might be altered to 'All B are A'. The error becomes obvious with a familiar case: 'All apples are fruits' is not 'All fruits are apples'. Third, we are prone to 'confirmation bias'. We tend to look for evidence to support our beliefs and ignore that which contradicts it, even though it is a lot easier to test propositions by hunting for contradictory evidence. It is easier to test 'all swans are white' by hunting for black ones rather than white ones. A good illustration is an old psychology problem. People are given three digits in a certain order and then are allowed to generate other three-digit sets. He or she is told which sets fit a rule, and must discover what the rule is. For example:

346, 379, and 389 fit the rule;
354, 892, and 435 do not.

The subjects happily generate more trios to find out the rule. They think of hypotheses about the rule but typically test these, not by trying to disconfirm them but by producing ones that fit it. (The rule simply is that the digits must increase in the trio.)

Much Western education tries to teach the formal rules of logic, which were partly laid down by Aristotle. They are formulated as abstract rules and permissible inferences. A familiar example is:

If p, then q. p, therefore q.

We do make logical errors, but Western schooling can train us to be more logical. Indeed, some scientists believe that our ability to think logically derives largely from Western schooling, and so does Piaget's final stage of cognitive development. Some evidence that they offer is this very famous conversation from Cole et al. (1971) between a Westerner studying logical thinking and a member of the Kpelle tribe of Liberia.

Experimenter: Flumo and Yakpalo always drink cane juice together. Flumo is drinking cane juice. Is Yakpalo drinking cane juice?

Subject: Flumo and Yakpalo drink cane juice together, but the time Flumo was drinking the first one Yakpalo was not there on that day.

Experimenter: But I told you that Flumo and Yakpalo always drink cane juice together. One day Flumo was drinking cane juice. Was Yakpalo drinking cane juice that day?

Subject: The day Flumo was drinking the cane juice Yakpalo was not there on that day.

Experimenter: What is the reason?

Subject: The reason is that Yakpalo went to his farm on that day . . .

As Neisser (1976) points out, the tribesman was not willing to enter the logic game. Western schooling teaches us to enter that game, to accept some abstract statement detached from reality or from our interest, and to work out its implications as prescribed. We do this in classrooms all the time. Neisser points out that people such as the Kpelle do badly on IQ tests (which often have such logical reasoning problems) because they do not accept the task. Perhaps schooling could teach Westerners even more logic and to avoid logical errors.

Our thinking is susceptible to other sorts of illogicality. We may reason badly when under stress, when we have firmly entrenched beliefs, or under strong emotion (love is blind). Albert Ellis (1977) argues that humanity is biologically predisposed toward irrationality and that a lot of psychiatric and related problems are due to people holding and acting on them. Some examples are 'I must have order or certainty around me to feel comfortable', 'Things must go the way I want them to go', and 'Others must treat everyone in a fair and just manner'. Inevitably these things will not happen. Ellis argues that people will only stop making themselves miserable by recognising such logical thinking errors and no longer acting on them.

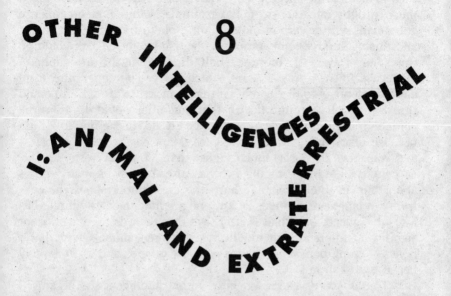

OTHER 8
INTELLIGENCES
1: ANIMAL AND EXTRATERRESTRIAL

And now from human intelligence to other sorts. Animal intelligence has been studied for a long time, both formally and informally. Many a pet owner watches his or her beast and has a few anecdotes about its brightness. The pet seems to 'understand what is going'. A dog alerts its sleeping master to a house fire, saving his life. A lost cat finds its home from 4,000 kilometres away, straggles through the front door, and settles down unceremoniously in front of the fire as if nothing had happened. The formal study of animal intelligence at the turn of the century was largely anecdotal as well. However, Charles Darwin had studied aspects of it more rigorously, looking in detail at animal emotional expression.

Animal intelligence is often studied out of curiosity, and to help us deal better with pets and farm animals, finding how best to feed and house them, and to induce them to breed prolifically. There are even pet psychologists, who may counsel that a 'neurotic' dog needs more exercise or to see more people. But animal intelligence is also studied to help cast more light on our own intelligence. Indeed, we can often understand something much more clearly if we have something else with which to compare it. A good example is our own planet Earth. Space probe studies of other worlds have given much insight into our own. For example, Venus is a greenhouse gone mad, with a carbon dioxide atmosphere trapping heat inside and raising surface temperatures to hellish heights. Earth could go the same way with more carbon dioxide in the atmosphere. Planetwide dust storms on Mars, which induced a temperature drop, alerted scientists to the likelihood that a nuclear war on Earth could throw so much dust into the air that much life would die from the cold and darkness. Volcanoes on Earth do not grow too high because of its moving tectonic plates. Mars has no tectonic plates and volcanoes there rise much higher than Mount Everest.

Studying animal intelligence has already told us many things about human intelligence. Perhaps the most important is the centrality of language. Animals lack it and are fundamentally limited as a result. Indeed, MacPhail (1987) says that there is no evidence for significant differences in intelligence between animals with backbones, except between humans and all others, and then largely because we can talk.

This chapter's excursion into animal intelligence is organised as follows. First is a caution; it is difficult to study and one should know the pitfalls. Then follow some details on the evolution of intelligence, a description of the mental capacities of various animal species, and an effort to peer into the animal mind. The final section considers a closely related topic; the nature of possible extraterrestrial intelligence.

STUDYING ANIMAL INTELLIGENCE

Animals do some very impressive things. Griffin (1984) gives many examples. Some are engineers. The North American beaver alters its territory to suit, chopping down trees, damming a stream, and sometimes changing an entire local landscape. It creates a large pond for winter (up to thirty metres across) and protects itself against preying wolves. Male Australasian bower birds construct intricate bowers of leaves, moss and branches which they decorate elaborately to lure the fickle females. The meadow vole makes covered pathways to guard against predatory birds. Ant species carve out elaborate underground cities. Some ants even cultivate their own plants and animals, as do human farmers, and have slaves to do much of the work. Various animals also appear to show commendable foresight and thrift. Some birds feign injury to draw a predator away from their nests, just keeping out of reach until the danger is well away. Many store food for the winter. Animals also use tools. The Archer fish squirts water to knock down hovering insects. The marine crab *Melia tessellata* takes sea anemones (which have organs that discharge a stinging projectile) and holds them in its front appendages, brandishing them at anything threatening. Some hermit crabs mount the organs on their shells to create a spiked shield.

Animals also communicate with each other extensively. Wolves bare their teeth to warn off rivals and offer their throats to appease superiors. Ants communicate by chemical signals. A bee that has found a food source returns to the hive and dances in various ways to show the food's direction and distance. Whales 'sing', sending messages across hundreds of kilometres of ocean.

Such actions make animals seem very intelligent, since their behaviours fit some of the criteria for display of intelligence. They solve present or future problems such as finding food and mates, surviving the winter, and adroitly fending off predators. But most of the above examples do not signify intelligence at all, at least not in the word's usual senses, since they involve little or no thought. Most of the actions above are hard-wired 'instincts', genetically programmed through natural selection.

The examples illustrate a major pitfall in studying animal intelligence. We often ascribe human thoughts, feelings, emotions, and purposes to animals. We believe that animals perform such feats as dam-building because they can see its purpose, when in fact they do not. The lesson is to look very closely at animal behaviour before using 'intelligence' or other names, to be sceptical. There is a very famous example of what can happen when one does not do this in the case of the ploughhorse Clever Hans. Apparently, Hans could count, understand German, and identify musical intervals. If asked the square root of twenty-five he would tap out five hoof beats, for example. Hans was feted and exhibited, but was just an ordinary horse. Sceptics took a good look at his apparent abilities, and found them nonexistent. Hans could only read expressions and postures well, and used subtle changes in those of his keeper to decide when to start and stop tapping. The same error may occur with anecdotal reports about pet intelligence, and that of whales and dolphins. One must be sceptical and look very closely.

EVOLUTION

Last century, humanity's ideas of who and what we are got a severe shake-up. These metaphorical earthquakes occur very seldom.

Another was Copernicus' dethroning of the Earth as the centre of the universe, and a third (arguably) was Freud's debunking of humanity as rational and in total control of its actions. This nineteenth-century revolution was sparked off by Charles Darwin. He took ideas from others, from his own observations of the results of selective breeding of farm animals, and from his world travels as naturalist on the *Beagle*, to come up with a few simple principles which make sense of the enormous diversity of life on Earth, and explain why many things are as they are. Biology and psychology both rest on evolutionary ideas. Very few scientists dispute their major tenets, because the evidence is just too overwhelming. They only dispute some specifics, like whether evolution occurs through slow, steady changes or very rapidly. The shock waves from Darwin's ideas still reverberate because so many people cannot accept that humanity is descended from animals. The idea that our species is something entirely different is deeply ingrained. Once a couple ran a newspaper birth column notice to praise their new child and say 'Our beautiful daughter is certainly not the descendant of a monkey'. American high-school biology textbooks barely mention evolution at all. Some evolutionary ideas have been mentioned earlier, but here are presented in more detail.

As mentioned earlier, members of a given species vary in various traits. Examples in humans include differences in height, weight, skin lightness, running speed, and so on. These traits are called 'characters'. Darwin pointed out that parents pass such characters on to offspring, though environmental factors like diet also may affect them. Thus, an individual's height is partly determined by genes and partly by such factors as diet. Any species usually produces more offspring than can survive because food is limited and predators abound. There is a high-school calculation that shows flies breed so rapidly that, theoretically, a group of them would soon equal the mass of planet Earth and expand outwards at near the speed of light. It does not happen, of course, because food runs out and predators get many offspring. Darwin said that those of each generation who do survive pass their characters on to offspring and so their traits will become more common. Thus, the environment selects characters that give an advantage for survival and reproduction. Consider skin colour in humans. People who live in tropical climes tend to be dark because it promotes survival — less susceptibility to skin cancer, for example. White skin is more adaptive in cloudy, cold, northern climes with little sun, and so predominates in people who live in them. The giraffe's neck apparently is long because length was selected for over many generations. The longer the neck, the easier it was to reach leaves on treetops. A character such as eyes is so adaptive that it has evolved independently at least forty times. Light carries enormously valuable information about food, predators, and so on, and the ability to use it gives a great survival advantage in most environments. If a given character gives just a tiny selective advantage, eventually every species member will have it, given enough generations.

Species sometimes do acquire evolutionary deadweight; characters no longer useful, at least for a time. The male peacock's tail is a pretty but large burden to drag about, good for nothing except attracting the small, drab, fickle female. (Perhaps a human parallel is an enormously expensive sports car.) As well, two species may even conduct an 'arms race', leaving each burdened with useless characters. For example, a caterpillar species may become dependent on one type of plant, eating its leaves and no other. The plant then may evolve a chemical to poison them, which works for a time until the caterpillars evolve a defence. The plant may then evolve another type of poison and so on. As with the Cold War between the U.S.A. and U.S.S.R., each becomes encumbered with expensive weapons useful only for fighting each other. However, with time, characters that are no longer useful or maladaptive may disappear. For example, some birds that have migrated to islands without predators over many generations may lose the power of flight; preserving it both takes resources and exposes the bird to the risk of being blown out to sea. The Mauritius dodo and New Zealand kiwi are evident examples.

Characters come in several types. One kind is physical ones like wings, arms, tails, height, and so on. Another is behaviours, the specific actions. Just as the environment may select for neck length or eyes, it may also select for certain behaviours that get hard-wired into the genes. One example is the eye-watering reflex to flush out a particle. Another is in the gull species the kittiwake, which nests on tiny rock cliff ledges only centimeters wide. Now, chicks of most gull species, which typically nest on beaches or rocks, are active. They want to see the world and walk about a lot. Not so the kittiwake chicks. They stay relatively immobile before taking their first flight, and it is easy to see why. Immobility was selected for because the more active chicks would tumble over the cliffs. Behaviours that are no longer useful also may be lost. Consider the emergency response to danger. The dodo and whale have or had largely lost it, because they had few or no natural enemies. Whales do little to avoid harpoons as a result.

Much of the behaviour of most animals is largely or entirely hard-wired. It is automatically programmed, just like functions of a dedicated computer such as a calculator or word processor. For many animals, it is best to hard-wire pretty much everything to solve the problems they face. However, hard-wiring has its drawbacks. Programming cannot anticipate everything that might happen, and can leave an individual quite inflexible when confronted with novelty. A good example is a fly stuck against a window. Its reflexes say 'go forward!' and it cannot extract itself from the situation. Another is the sad tale of swallows taken from the Northern Hemisphere to New Zealand. In winter, swallows fly south to warmer climes where food is more abundant, and this migration is hard-wired. But in the Southern Hemisphere, the birds mindlessly flew south toward Antarctica, never to be heard from again. Their hard-wiring meant they could not cope with the new situation. There is a goose species that migrates from Siberia to India in winter. But its yearly exodus begins strangely. The geese walk the first few hundred kilometres and many get killed. They leave before the young can fly because their programming tells them to. Waiting an extra week so that all could fly would be a brighter option, but they cannot resist.

Species cope with the problem of environmental change in one or both of two major ways. One is by breeding rapidly and prolifically. Changes in the environment are handled by survival of those with some tendency to cope. The second way is by exercising intelligence, to which we now turn.

The Evolution of Intelligence

Intelligence is a character, albeit a very complex, varied, and ill-defined one. One aspect of it is learning — varying one's behaviour to cope with changes in the environment. Most species have some basic ability to learn, to partially break out of their hard-wiring. In many species it is only rudimentary, and they are strongly predisposed to learn certain things and not others. So-called 'higher animals' are much less hard-wired, much more flexible. Humans are more like supercomputers than dedicated word processors, able to be programmed for many things, and very flexible in dealing with changes.

Here are some examples of animal learning to illustrate how useful it can be. The honeybee is a fairly intelligent insect, well-shown by its dealings with the unfriendly alfalfa flower, which has a spring-loaded club which deals the bee a hefty blow when it enters. Not surprisingly, bees avoid alfalfa and forage far afield when a hive is placed in the centre of an alfalfa patch. However, to avoid outright starvation, they will learn to deal with it. Some bees learn to distinguish between loaded and unloaded flowers, as we learn to tell poisonous and harmless snakes apart. Other bees chew a hole in the flower's back and secure the precious nectar without venturing inside. Gould and Gould (1982) give an example of bee learning in the laboratory. They trained bees to fly to a food source, which was then progressively moved further and further away. Soon the bees 'caught on' to the trick, anticipating the next location and waiting there for the food source to arrive. There are other examples. Hawks learn to take shells to a great height and dash them on to rocks below to open them up. Crows can be taught to use a stick to push a disc for food. The value of all such learning is clear. It's impossible to hard-wire everything and learning promotes survival. If nothing else, an animal has to learn the layout of its territory, who its relatives and mates are, and so on, which information is very difficult to preprogram, if not impossible.

Exercising intelligence involves varying behaviour, if necessary, to solve a problem. Animals readily do this. Chimpanzees poke sticks into narrow termite holes to get the insects out. The termites reflexively latch onto the stick which the chimp then pulls up to devour them. Dolphins can learn to be 'creative'. Pryor et al., (1969) rewarded dolphins simply for doing something new each day. The creatures soon caught on, continually coming up with new actions. There was even a report of a monkey telling a lie. Two troupes were fighting, and one on the losing side suddenly let out the distress call for 'leopard', even though no leopard was in sight. The other side scattered. Many birds are territorial, staking out some space in the morning and chirping away to warn off others. But some species seem to rise early, check out the situation, and decide if enough nectar is about to make the territory worth defending. If there is not, they do not.

Animals also evolve specific abilities. A good example is human language. Another is in a bird called Clark's Nutcracker that has evolved a super-memory. It accumulates thousands of seeds for the winter and caches them in lots of one to five. Each winter it retrieves the seeds, remembering as many as 2,500 different locations.

Intelligence can be thought of as a kind of general ability that was selected for, or as the sum of a lot of separate abilities that have separately evolved.

SOME CAPABILITIES OF VARIOUS ANIMAL SPECIES

Intelligence has its own natural history. As Darwin pointed out, human intelligence and abilities evolved from those of other animals, which must have included working and long-term memory, selective attention, reasoning, and so on. One approach to studying animal intelligence is to figure which of such capabilities various species possess. However, finding out is a long, painstaking and difficult task.

This section will briefly cover the capacities of a few widely spaced species just to give the flavour of this sort of work. Not much is really known, simply because the topic is so hard to study. As well, it is very difficult to even list such capabilities without implicitly making intelligence comparisons, and the next section looks at the general problem of ranking species along an intelligence scale. We will start very low on the evolutionary scale, but not right at the bottom. It makes little sense to talk of the intelligence of viruses and plants, for which there was no selective pressure. The signs of 'intelligence' that they do show, such as plants turning leaves to catch sunlight or the AIDS virus knocking off the most dangerous immune system cells, are genetically programmed. They do not show intelligence, in this book's sense of the word.

Paramecia

This tiny creature can grow up to about 0.3 mm long, and has almost no intelligence to speak of. Its abilities are minimal. It can sense the world to some extent, responding to touch, light, gravity, and various chemicals. It can move about by flapping thousands of appendages called cilia, and it tends to congregate with its fellows. It takes in organic food particles and bacteria as food, gets rid of waste, and occasionally reproduces. There is speculation that it can learn, although it cannot learn much. It cannot think, of course. Its actions are automatically controlled by its internal machinery.

Ants

Biologists generally believe that ants and other insects are mainly just bundles of automatic reflexes (Roitblat, 1987), though some species seem to be a bit more than this. Ants have been around for at least 100 million years, and live almost everywhere on the planet. Biologists estimate that at least 12,000 different species exist.

Ants are social creatures *par excellence*. All live in frighteningly well-organised Orwellian societies in which each has its own specialised task to do, and is discarded when no longer useful. Ant society is based on a queen, which is little more than an egg-laying machine patiently tended by chambermaids, and on workers and males. There are many subtypes of these, specialised for different tasks, and they do many things. Sudd and Franks (1987) describe ant equivalents of slave-takers, farmers, cuckoos, muggers, claim jumpers, guests, thieves, and parasites. Ants even use deception. Some ants on slave raids spray a nest with an odour that means 'flee' to confuse their enemies and empty it for an attack. But ant society involves no thought. The complex behaviours that ants show are genetically programmed, and sometimes it is a real puzzle to figure out how they did evolve. Thankfully, human society is not so well-organised because it is not programmed. Just how dreadful it would be is shown in Frank Herbert's novel *Hellstrom's Hive*, which describes an appalling human society organised along the terrifying lines of an anthill.

An individual ant cannot do a great deal. It has a very strong body but a small nervous system containing few neurons. Ants can see, but smell, taste, and touch are their important senses. Their antennas are very sensitive, which is useful for groping about in dark underground chambers. They communicate with each other by chemical signals and antenna touches, and recognise nestmates because each nest has its own distinctive smell. Ants have a rudimentary ability to learn, but are basically reflex machines.

Pigeons

Birds are visual creatures in the main, with some exceptions such as the very odd flightless New Zealand kiwi, which gets around at night and lives in a burrow. But vision is the most useful sense of all for a flying creature. Indeed, darkness quietens many species immediately, which is one reason why falconers use hoods to pacify their birds. Pigeons can hear, smell and taste, and navigate by the Earth's magnetic field. An enormous amount of research has looked at pigeon learning, and the reason for this is an historical curiosity. Many psychologists long believed that all animal learning conformed to the same principles, and that as a result one could study even human learning by generalising from pigeon learning. So a lot is known about pigeon learning, just as geneticists know a lot about fruit-fly genetics.

In fact pigeons cannot think very abstractly and they have enormous trouble learning an abstract rule. But they can still do a great deal. They have a working memory and a long-term memory, and can remember things for years. They can 'chunk' items to improve working memory capacity. They can selectively attend to things. They can learn sequences of actions. They can learn concepts like *human being, man-made object, tree, fish*, and *pigeon*. But they have nothing like human language, not even Pidgin English, as the old joke goes.

Some psychologists speculate that pigeons are not very bright birds, but they believe the flightless birds such as the emu and now-extinct Mauritius dodo are or were even duller. The dodos lived on an island with no enemies and stupidly gazed on as newly-arrived humans clubbed them and ultimately exterminated the species. Some recent work has suggested that parrots are quite intelligent, again as birds go. Pepperberg (1990) has studied the capabilities of an African Gray Parrot that may have mastered some basics of human language. It could learn to label shapes and colours and even answer questions like 'What colour?', 'What is same?' and 'How many?'. The parrot even seems to understand its own utterances, says Pepperberg.

Dolphins and Whales

These sea creatures form an order called Ceteceans. Essentially, dolphins are small whales, and though they look like fish, they are warm-blooded mammals, descended from land animals that colonised the sea after the extinction of the dinosaurs. Biologists believe that their ancestor was a small otter-like animal that ate fish.

Dolphins live about twenty-five to thirty-five years, and usually flock in herds of hundreds. They must breathe air, but can submerge for up to twenty minutes. They sleep in snatches of five to six minutes, but then surface. There are reports of sick dolphins being supported above the waterline by their fellows. They are commonly very playful, often following ships at sea, frolicking in the waves, and even surfing. People who work with them say that they have a special affinity with humans, even though an estimated half-million a year are killed in fishing nets. There are cases of dolphins guiding ships through dangerous waters and saving humans lost at sea. They quickly and easily learn a wide range of tricks and are popular marine circus performers. The U.S. Navy has a dolphin regiment, whose members are trained for surveillance and mine detection.

Dolphins usually are thought to be highly intelligent. Certainly, many New Agers think so, and much work suggests that they are. They have a rich social life and, as with people and apes, the young depend on parents for a long time. They have elaborate courtship rituals. They also can learn easily by imitation, sometimes parody-ing their human keepers as children do. Fichtelius and Sjolander (1972) recount a tale of a dolphin clever enough to evict an eel from its hole by pushing a poison fish down it, which rapidly brought out the eel.

What does research say? Much scientific work has tried to figure out dolphins' capabilities, although conclusions are still pretty tentative and indeed are controversial. Dolphins have many abilities but are not geniuses, and are not really all that intelligent compared with people. Herman (1980, 1988) lists some things that they can do. They can readily learn actions by watching others. They can learn and follow simple rules. They can classify things and discover relationships between them. They have an excellent audi-tory memory, since they rely largely on their sonar system, but have poorer visual memory since eyes are not as useful in the sea. While they can communicate with each other, having distress signals and so on, their system appears to be nothing much like a human language. Some studies have tried to teach dolphins simple artificial languages, and they can learn to associate symbols with objects and even string them together (e.g., 'basket toss', said the dolphin), but this is not much like human language, either. They cannot learn to use all that many symbols. Dolphins may only have some of lan-guage's precursors and Herman speculates that they do not even like to talk all that much!

Dolphins are small enough to study in laboratories. However, the study of whales is mostly restricted to watching them frolic in the ocean. There are many species, ranging in size up to the largest animal ever to live on Earth; the blue whale. They typically live in harems consisting of a large male, twenty to thirty females, and the youngsters. They range over very wide expanses of ocean, appar-ently navigating in part with a magnetic sense like that of pigeons.

How intelligent are they? It is open to speculation, but whales do not need to be too bright. Essentially they are grazing animals like cows (Fichtelius & Sjolander, 1972), and have no natural enemies except humans. They have large brains but their nature and size has meant they have faced little pressure to do anything much with them, or to become brighter as a consequence. As the above authors suggest, their behaviour suggests they are not very bright. Humanity has hunted some species almost to extinction, but they do not try to avoid whalers or bear humanity any ill will. There is the occasional report of a whale sinking a ship, but real Moby Dicks are thin in the water. Apparently there was a misanthropic whale in the Mediterranean in AD 500, which sank ships on sight for fifty years, terrorising sailors (Fichtelius & Sjolander, 1972).

The sea is a relatively benign environment for animals the size of dolphins and whales. They never needed to evolve hands, losing the limbs they had on land, and there was little pressure for high intelligence except to conduct their social life.

Apes

This category includes several species, including gorillas, orangutans, chimpanzees, baboons, and many others. Apes look and act a lot like humans, as many tribes living near them have long noted. Indeed, the word 'chimpanzee' itself is Angolan for 'mock man' and the Malay word for orangutan means 'man of the woods' (Mackintosh, 1987). Humanity split from our last common ancestor with other apes several million years ago, but we still are genetically very similar to our nearest relative, the chimpanzee. Like humans, apes depend heavily on vision, are adept with their hands, and are highly social. Perhaps the most strictly controlled simian society is the baboon's. They move about on the dangerous African plain in groups under the charge of a dominant male, with the expendable young males on the outer rim. Gorillas live in groups numbering between two and twenty, under the eye of a large male boss. Chimpanzees have very complex social lives, with multiple social relationships with their fellows. Because they mostly live safely in trees, their groups are fairly loose, with a lot of individual freedom.

Chimpanzees have been studied extensively, both in the wild and in the laboratory. They seem to be very intelligent creatures. They make and use tools. They can reason adeptly. They can learn by watching others, and even pass knowledge on to others. They understand the motives of other chimps in their groups and use long-term strategies to get ahead in chimp society, as people do in their own. They reportedly look at their reflections in pools, and use them as mirrors to inspect body parts that they otherwise could not see. They gaze appreciatively at sunsets. They have even been known to plot and carry out the murders of other chimps. They can count to some extent and can learn to deftly operate a joystick to chase moving targets on a screen (Rumbaugh, 1990).

Chimpanzees have been the leading candidates in efforts to answer an age-old question; is language uniquely human? Can animals learn anything like a human language, associating symbols with meanings and combining these to make new meanings? If only we could 'talk to the animals', as the saying goes. Walt Disney and many others made fortunes with fictional talking beasts, and many a pet-owner swears that his or her animal communicates and understands a lot. But if they could talk, what would animals say to us? It is hard to know. A BBC animated sketch once gave one answer in a brilliant spoof. An interviewer went about the animal cages in a zoo and the inhabitants gave their views on zoo life, as might new residents in a housing estate. Few seemed very happy about it, except the koala. The others looked strained but tried to find something positive about conditions, such as regular food, 'Animals in the wild can go *days* without food'. The jaguar did not like English weather and the lack of *space*. The tortoises wanted to get out more, and took refuge in books. In fact, animals probably would not have much to say to us even if they could talk, as we will see.

A great deal of research on chimpanzees has tried to train them to talk. In early studies, young chimps were raised as children in human homes, and scientists tried to get them to link vocalisations with meanings, but to no avail. Later work used sign language or plastic tokens with more success. Thus a chimp might learn that a certain hand sign or symbol meant 'water'. One chimp called Washoe learned a vocabulary of 132 signs, and could string up to five together (e.g., 'You tickle me'). Another called Sarah learned a vocabulary consisting of plastic token signs and learned to use questions and negatives. A famous example of one chimp's sign-use is referring to a duck with the symbols for 'water' and 'bird' and when put back with other chimps referring to the chimps as 'black bugs'. The chimp Koko was asked which of two trainers she preferred and signed 'Bad question'.

Though early results were impressive, some critics say that the animals are not really learning a human-like language. Whether they can create actual sentences like people is controversial, and they may just be mechanically stringing signs together for rewards. They also are not very willing communicators, unlike people. Humanity is the communicative species. Chimpanzees in general only communicate spontaneously when they want something.

Herman (1988) argues that ape intellectual capabilities are comparable to dolphins', perhaps because each has evolved to cope with complex social life. Understanding others and trying to predict their actions requires many capabilities.

THE NATURAL SCALE

Which is more intelligent — a pigeon or a dolphin? A snail or a rabbit? A pig or a dog? Can we rank all animals along a single scale, as IQ test designers try to do with people? Some scientists believe so. For example, Jensen (1980) writes:

> Single-cell protozoans (e.g., the amoeba) rank at the bottom of the scale, followed in order by the invertebrates, the lower vertebrates, the lower mammals, the primates and man. The vertebrates have been studied more intensively and show fishes at the bottom of the capacity scale, followed by amphibia, reptiles, and birds. Then come the mammals, with rodents at the bottom followed by the ungulates (cow, horse, pig, and elephant, in ascending order), then the carnivores (cats and dogs) and finally the primates, in order; New World monkeys, Old World monkeys, the apes (gibbon, orangutan, gorilla, chimpanzee), and, at the pinnacle, humans.

The idea in fact goes back to Aristotle.

A single scale has a lot of appeal. We intuitively feel that dogs are brighter than snails or ants. They have more capabilities. They can learn a lot more. They can solve more problems. They are much more versatile and their brains are a lot more complicated. No one would dream of looking for complex thinking and deep philosophical ideas in ants and snails. But how exactly should animals be ranked? We cannot use just intuition.

Scientists have tried to find a way; something that gives a clear-cut order. An early effort was an 'encephalisation index', which is a ratio of brain to body size. Humans come out almost on top, second to dolphins, but the problem is that size is not everything. The way in which the brain is organised is more important.

Scientists also tried ranking by 'learning set'. This really is how long it takes an animal to learn to learn. Say an animal is given a simple discrimination problem, with a food reward for success. Perhaps it has to learn that food is under a red jar but not a blue one. When it solves this problem, it would get another, say green versus yellow, which also might take a number of trials to learn. After solving several such problems, animals often get faster at solving each new one. They form a *set* to solve problems. Learning sets have been studied in animals from goldfish to chimpanzees, and species learn them at vastly differing rates. Speed of forming a set is a possible measure of intelligence, which indicates that rhesus monkeys learn faster than squirrel monkeys, who in turn learn faster than cats and rats. A related task sometimes used to rank species is oddity learning. An animal is shown sets of three objects, such as two cubes and a ball, and gets a reward for picking out the odd one.

Though a ranking by such means has intuitive appeal, it is fraught with difficulty. Some say we should abandon the effort, as the question itself is bad. There is no definition of intelligence, so it

is unclear what the creatures really are being ranked on (Mackintosh, 1987). The other major problem is that performance differences on simple tasks like those named are often reversed by
switching from shapes to colours, for instance. All animals in a
sense are equally intelligent for their environments. They have
evolved special abilities and behaviours for their niches that are all
but impossible to compare. There is no animal IQ test for the task,
just as many believe that one cannot use a single IQ test to compare
people in different cultures (or even in the same one).

THE ANIMAL MIND

This section is speculative. We will try to better understand animal
intelligence by peering into the 'animal mind', which is a mystery.
The human mind evolved from animal precursors, but in many ways
animal minds would be very alien. Two questions are examined;
how the world might appear to members of a given animal species,
and whether animals have 'consciousness'.

Animal Senses

You are driving very fast along a highway. Not far down the road, a
couple of birds squat. They barely glance up and, just before your
car is upon them, they lackadaisically amble out of the way. Why
are the birds so unconcerned? We put ourselves in their own place
and imagine how, no doubt, we would feel so fearful that we would
shift much sooner. Why don't the birds? They don't because their
sense of time is different from ours. Birds' time sense is speeded up.
Some scientists argue that they perceive the world at about ten
times the rate we do. So, to the bird, the car would be coming very
slowly (the equivalent of our watching a film running at only one-
tenth usual speed). Some fish have a time sense about twice as fast
as ours.

   Sense of time is one difference in perception. But there are a lot
of others. Many species have much poorer senses than we do. Frog
eyes are basically motion-detectors. They are very adept at picking
up moving objects such as flies, but if the world is still they do not
see a scene as we do. They don't have the brain to process the
information, anyway. Some species have much better vision,
especially birds of prey such as eagles and hawks. One bird of prey
has even evolved a bifocal lens. Bees can see further into the ultra-
violet, and flowers have evolved in a way that attracts them. What
seems a dull and drab flower patch to a human may be full of
bright, exciting colours to a bee; hues that we cannot perceive at all.

Snakes can see into the infra-red. Mosquitoes have a very highly developed temperature detection sense, being able to pick out some unfortunate heat source from afar. Dogs can hear higher noise frequencies than us, hence those 'soundless' whistles that emit a frequency beyond the human ear's limit but that bring the dogs running. Dogs also have a better sense of smell. They perceive many more odours and can make very refined discriminations. The bloodhound can pick up odours that are days old and track the spoor. It is hard even to imagine what kind of an olfactory world the dog senses, because we rely largely on our eyes and ears.

Many species have senses that we do not have at all. A science-fiction novel once tried to give some impression of what such a new sense would be like. The sense was called 'rault', and it greatly expanded perception of the universe, analogous to giving a blind person sight. Some strange animal senses are as follows. Bats emit high-pitched whistles and use the echoes to locate objects. The dolphin has a sonar sense that works much the same way. Some species have electro-detection senses. Sharks can pick up the weak electric fields animals give off when they move muscles. (The shark also has an extremely keen sense of smell.) The duck-billed platypus has a similar electrical sense, which it uses to find underground prey. Rays can detect lines of flux in a magnetic field, using them to determine the size and location of various objects. Pigeons, robins and possibly whales use variations in the Earth's magnetic field as cues to navigation. Some scientists speculate that the occasional mass strandings of whales occur in places where there are anomalies in the Earth's magnetic field, which play havoc with their sense.

What all this means is that many animals live in a sensory world fundamentally different from ours. They sense quite different things. Such data led the philosopher Nagel (1974) to speculate that this means that we could never understand the animal mind completely. In an intriguing article called 'What is it Like to Be a Bat?', he answers that we could never know. The bat's different senses and capacities mean that its mind is simply too alien for us to understand. We could never put ourselves in its place. It is difficult enough to understand people from quite different cultures. Oriental mindsets with a focus on harmony and yin and yang are very difficult for most Westerners to grapple with. Even different generations of the same culture may have trouble communicating with and understanding each other. How about two different species? Rood and Trefil (1981) say that ants at work in a hive have apparent purposes too alien from our own for any commonality or empathy.

So Nagel believes the animal mind to be fundamentally unknow-able.

There is another view, at the opposite extreme. Species in all environments need to evolve certain abilities and other characters because the universe is as it is. All need senses, most need memory, and all need to seek food and avoid noxious things (perhaps this would be a conversation opener). But there still are differences in the kinds of world picture that animals build up, because of different senses and capabilities.

Are Animals Aware?

Consciousness is useful to ponder things, select between alternatives, and to help social life. It allows us to predict which way our fellows may jump, which we often do by gauging their motives and imagining ourselves in their shoes. We also engage consciousness when our old, automatic ways of doing things fail. Consciousness is important, but is not all-important. Gould and Gould (1982) argue that so much human behaviour is automatic that we do not rely on awareness all that much. Artificial intelligence expert Marvin Minsky also says that the importance of consciousness is overrated. Nisbett and Wilson (1977) give many examples of people doing things automatically without being aware of them. A particularly intriguing example is a phenomenon which occurs in a few people blinded because of damage to certain brain areas. If they are set some task that requires indicating if they have seen certain visual signals, they say they can see nothing, even though the signals are still being detected and responded to. They are seeing but are not aware of seeing. Vision and consciousness have been disconnected.

Do animals have consciousness as we do? Are they aware of pain and anxiety. Do they feel fear, anger and joy, along with peculiar animal emotions? Do they have a mental life? For a long time, many thought that the answer is 'no'. The philosopher René Descartes wrote that animals are reflex machines with no souls, like mechanical statues.

However, many scientists now believe differently. On logical grounds one would expect some species to have awareness. It is a useful character and human consciousness must have evolved from animal precursors. Also, there is a lot of anecdotal evidence for awareness in higher animals, although one must be wary of the Clever Hans problem.

Griffin (1984) gives many examples. Dogs and cats seem to dream, and dreaming implies awareness. (Some scientists believe that their dreams may be practice for waking activities. Cats assume hunting postures during sleep, for example.) Chimpanzees seem to know the motives and intentions of other chimps, which again implies awareness. There is a famous story about a subordinate chimp who used such knowledge as follows. He picked up two bits of metal, climbed to a hilltop and ran down it clanging the pieces together. The noise scared his fellows away from food, allowing him to seize it. The story about the lying monkey is another example. Animals also expect various things to happen (e.g., the arrival of food at a certain time) and look 'surprised' when they do not occur. In one experiment, apes were put in a cage with a mirror, and given each a few weeks to get used to their images. Then each was anaesthetised and a red spot was painted on their face, which could only be seen with the mirror. When back in the cage, each ape immediately touched the red spot after looking in the mirror, which implies some idea of self-awareness. However, some monkey species do not touch the spot under the same circumstances. Griffin also cites a Scotland Yard study of the ability of dogs to read intentions. They seem quite adept at this, being social animals and very sensitive to nonverbal cues. A person was unable to shoot them with blanks before they successfully attacked. They seemed to know what the attacker was about to do before he did it. Griffin says this ability is very useful in the wild. Predators such as lions often stampede a herd of prey, noticing subtle distinctions between the animals and picking out the slowest and weakest. He argues that this requires awareness.

The evidence suggests that some animals have consciousness. Several questions then arise. When did consciousness first appear? A paramecia is certainly not aware, but how about a bee or a rat? What would it be like to think without words, and to build up a world picture without language and with strange animal senses? Perhaps, as Nagel says, it is as fundamentally unknowable as the visual world is to a congenitally blind person.

EXTRATERRESTRIAL INTELLIGENCE

Science fiction is replete with examples of extraterrestrial intelligence. Some date back to ancient reports that the moon was covered with cities, houses, and people. They come from planets in this solar system, and from those of nearby stars, different galaxies, and different universes. The aliens come in countless forms. There are sentient stars and planets, giant black clouds hurtling through space, and the bug-eyed monsters of pulp magazines brandishing lasers and trying to carry off beautiful human females. (Why they would be interested was never clear, just as human males would not be attracted by giant female grasshoppers.) There are group minds, bands of creatures linked telepathically so that they constitute a single intelligence like a sort of ant colony. Sometimes the aliens look and think pretty much as humans do, some writers arguing that conditions that produce intelligent life of any kind will produce humanoids. (That seems pretty unlikely, however. The humanoid form resulted from countless evolutionary accidents.) H. G. Wells invented many of the alien forms, and indeed many of science fiction's stock devices. Some authors even claim that there are lots of higher intelligences populating different planes such as the 'astral plane'. However, since there is no evidence for them at all, their exact nature and capabilities are always very, very vague.

In fiction, aliens have done many things to us. They have made war on us ever since H. G. Wells' prototypical invasion from Mars, colonised us, blown up Earth, turned the Sun into a nova, swamped us by melting the polar ice caps, put us in cosmic zoos, turned us into culinary delicacies, made us the equivalents of galley slaves on starships, brought us peace, raised our technological level so that their later destruction of humanity was a more interesting contest, and speeded up our evolution to its next stage.

No one knows for certain if aliens really exist outside the fertile imaginations of science fiction writers. Scientists have discussed the question a great deal, and the usual argument is that the universe is so immense that life must have evolved elsewhere. Indeed, there is evidence that other stars have planets. Some argue that life on Earth arose from spores carried through space that must have seeded other planets as well. Some say that periodic outbreaks of influenza are due to virus seedings from space. A scientist even calculated that there are a possible 12 million life-bearing planets in our galaxy alone, but the assumptions made are pretty tenuous. Making more tenuous assumptions leads to an estimate of up to a thousand other industrial civilisations in the Milky Way.

However, scientists have not yet found evidence for life elsewhere. Space probes of the solar system over the last three decades have shown that the nearby planets are bare of life, at least as we know it. A large scale program called SETI (Search for Extraterrestrial Intelligence) was set up by NASA to probe the heavens for radio transmissions from galactic civilisations, but has turned up nothing so far. A false alarm was rung once. In 1967, astronomers in Cambridge, England, were puzzled by regular radio pulses from a certain spot in the sky that came once every 1.33 seconds. An interstellar beacon? The major milestone in human history discussed for so long? There was talk of little green men for months while the pulses were studied. Soon they found other sources, now known as *pulsars*, collapsed stars orbiting another.

Detecting life from afar is one thing. Having aliens visit us is quite another. The stars are unimaginably distant, and one needs colossal amounts of time and energy to reach them. A few projects exist in planning stages to try to bridge the gap, but they would take generations to reach the nearest star. However, many people believe that aliens are among us already. UFO sightings and cults abound. Some even claim to have been carried off by aliens, spending days being examined in a spacecraft. The U.S. government is supposed to have clear-cut physical evidence. An extraterrestrial craft with bodies inside allegedly crashed in the desert, and the authorities have it under heavy guard.

But when claims are closely investigated, almost all turn to vapour. Only a very tiny percentage of UFO sightings resist explanation as observations of Venus, distant aircraft lights, or meteors. In 1977 U.S. President Jimmy Carter released government files on UFO studies and they revealed no hard evidence of them. Some enthusiasts allege a vast cover-up, that UFO reports are being held back to avoid widespread panic. But would that really happen? Millions already believe in UFOs but don't panic. Most people would probably treat it as a nine-day wonder, and go back to their serious everyday concerns. Governments also are notoriously leak-prone, and so such a momentous secret would surely have come out by now. Extraterrestrial intelligence may exist, but it almost certainly has never visited us.

Why does the fascination with UFOs and extraterrestrial intelligence persist? One reason is the human need to know we are not alone in the universe, a wish arising from our fundamental social nature. Just as we want to contact other people, we wish to contact other species, even if it is not clear if other species would feel the same way. There is also the age-old human archetype of rescue from heaven. A greater power descends from on high to help us deal with earthly problems beyond our own capabilities. This idea occurs not just in religion but extensively in science fiction. The 1951 film *The Day the Earth Stood Still* is a good example of the genre. Earth was on the brink of war, with leaders seemingly unable to cope, before an alien arrived with the solution; a very powerful robot police force to keep the peace.

By using what is known about animal and human intelligence and the constraints that the universe itself imposes on things, we can speculate about what extraterrestrial intelligence would be like. A conference looked at the question (Regis, 1985), and the following discussion borrows some of its ideas and some from Rood and Trefil (1981).

What Would Extraterrestrial Intelligence be Like?

Sometimes a biologist finds a fossil tooth or leg bone of some long-extinct creature and can reconstruct what the animal may have looked like. It is done by using inferences and natural constraints. The tooth will tell if the animal was a plant or meat-eater, because it would be adapted to either sort of food. The tooth's size and shape will give some notion of the jaw shape and the animal's overall size. The jaw has to fit into a skull, and the inferred jaw shape will give some idea of the head shape, and so on. The animal's habitat gives more clues. Did the animal live in the sea, in the desert, in an arctic clime, or in the tropics? The habitat further constrains how the creature would look. If it lived in the sea, it probably moved about and only a few designs to move work. Fins and flippers evolve repeatedly because not much else will do. If the animal lived underground, it may have had claws for digging. There are constraints, and constraints and constraints, which allow inferences and inferences and inferences.

The universe imposes many such constraints on intelligence. Any species that wins the evolutionary struggle on its own planet, which can signal off-world species, or which develops a technological civilisation, is likely to have certain traits. The natural constraints almost guarantee it, and what we know about constraints on animal and human intelligence leads to inferences about what extraterrestrial intelligence would be like. We will assume that the hypothetical extraterrestrial species has not altered itself to suit by selective breeding or genetic engineering.

First, consider physical form, which in fact seems less constrained than intelligence. All life on Earth ultimately derives from the same source; the DNA molecule. Life as we know it is based on carbon, a very versatile element that bonds with many others in countless configurations. Alien intelligence would probably be carbon-based. Biologists speculate about lifeforms based on other chemicals such as silicon, but some discount the possibility. There even could be lifeforms that we do not recognise as such, perhaps even extremely intelligent ones. The problem is that no one really agrees on what life is. We more or less think we know it when we see it, but cannot readily define it. Biologists have long argued about whether a virus is actually alive, for example. Another boundary stretcher is a computer virus, consisting of nothing but lines of code in a machine. It reproduces itself in that machine and may spread to others. It is like a real virus but also different from it. Is it actually alive? Our inability to clearly define life makes it disputable.

There are constraints on the physical form of life, but one can still imagine countless types. Different environments with various evolutionary pressures may create quite varied forms. They certainly have on Earth, when one considers the myriad different forms that life takes. Extraterrestrial cases could be insect-like creatures, giant worms living underground, tendril-like beasts floating in thick atmospheres, giant plants with minute brains, or spineless jellyfish. However, highly intelligent lifeforms that could physically leave the planet or signal others would be likely to have certain forms and not others. A technological civilisation could only arise in certain conditions. It is hard to imagine one arising in an ocean, because many metals corrode in water and there is less pressure to develop technology anyway, which is why dolphins don't have one. An intelligent species also would need some deft appendages to manipulate things, to build radio transmitters or spaceships. Something like the human hand with an opposing thumb would possibly evolve, just as fins and eyes repeatedly do. Few other designs really work. Designers of robots that manipulate objects copy the human hand because it is hard to think of a better multi-purpose device.

The extraterrestrial intelligence would have senses. Every species must take in information about the outside world, else it does not survive. Few senses are possible, because few forms of physical energy are worth using. One would expect vision and hearing to evolve repeatedly, because light and sound convey so much useful information. It is difficult to imagine a nonvisual species building machines. One must be able to see what one is doing, and what other sense could do the trick? Senses such as taste, smell, and touch have evolved repeatedly, and we could expect an extraterrestrial intelligence to have them. Other exotic senses may have evolved, such as electrical field detection, and perhaps in some environments it would be useful to see into other parts of the wavelength spectrum. There may be species with radio detectors, or which communicate via inbuilt radio signals. Perhaps some species have exotic senses like rault or telepathy, if physics allows them, which is doubtful.

By necessity, extraterrestrial intelligence would be able to learn and remember. Otherwise they would not be intelligent. A knowledge base is essential. The principles of learning are much the same in all species on Earth, though affected by biology, simply because of constraints. Several types of learning are so useful that it is hard to imagine an intelligent species without them. Consider the most basic type of learning; habituation, the ability simply to get used to a repeatedly presented stimulus that proves harmless. This ability occurs in most animal species because no natural environment could be so benign that it would not evolve. Another type of learning is to learn to repeat actions that are rewarded and avoid those that produce pain, which is also present in many animal species. How could an intelligent creature not have such an ability? It is a defining trait of intelligence.

Extraterrestrial intelligence would also have such elements of intelligence as selective attention, working and long-term memory. As Minsky (1985) points out, how could intelligence exist without some way to select out what to pay attention to, to remember for long periods, and so on? Consciousness also has its uses, and would probably evolve repeatedly. Extraterrestrial intelligences would also have logical reasoning ability. They need it to construct machines that work, and the universe prescribes that a logic such as ours is all that would work, on the macro-level anyway. Species elsewhere may also evolve cognitive abilities that we do not have, but it is hard to imagine them. Perhaps if they were primarily auditory creatures, say, like dolphins, they would acquire certain kinds of powers. However, perhaps every intelligent species evolves to a point where it can quickly develop technology to amplify its intelligence; computers for better memory and calculation, devices like telescopes to amplify senses, and so on.

And what about other characteristics? Any species intelligent enough to signal or visit us would almost certainly be social. It would be group-oriented like people, not individualistic like cats. Developing technology and building spaceships requires enormous effort and cooperation. The technology in a machine such as the space-shuttle is immensely complex, and draws on decades of work by countless persons. No individual could ever hope to develop even a tiny part of it. If they are technological and social, they must have an excellent communciation system to cooperate with each other and pass on knowledge so that it can accumulate. They must have a language, as nothing else will do the trick (aside, perhaps, from telepathy!).

Such a species also would almost certainly be aggressive and self-interested, as people are (Rood & Trefil, 1981). Science fiction writers often portray species as altruistic and benevolent, crusading about the universe hunting for other species to help. Would they really be that way? Altruism on Earth occurs mainly within species, and then typically just for close relatives (perhaps the occasional dolphin is an exception). It arises when it gives a selective advantage. Sometimes species cooperate by sharing a niche, but again for self-interest. The latter is the evolutionary rule because it gives a selective advantage. Any species that wins the evolutionary struggle on its own planet will be self-interested, fierce and aggressive, just as humans are. We do our best to exterminate pests like viruses and bacteria. Our ancestors probably exterminated competitors like the Neanderthals and various predators. Aggression is selected for. Indeed, for this reason one scientist opposed sending the plaque on the 1977 Pioneer space probe that gave the location of the solar system. We do not know exactly what is out there, but it may be powerful and mean, and advertising our existence may bring it running. (In fact, the chances of that happening are remote, and television and radio signals have been beaming out from the Earth for decades, anyway.) There was a science fiction story on this theme. A supposedly altruistic species arrived on Earth to help us. Later, it invited many humans to its home planet, ostensibly to study its technology. The creatures even had a handbook called *How to Serve Man*. A sceptic visits their world, and returns to Earth with a translation of the handbook. It turns out to be a cookbook! Grim stuff, but the point is clear. Altruism for other species is rarely selected for. If an alien species helps us, it will almost certainly be from self-interest.

What sort of technology and culture might extraterrestrial species develop? Here we get even more speculative, because animal analogies do not help much. We can use imagination and comparisons of different human civilisations to make some guesses. Would they even have arts, sciences, religions, moral systems, and philosophies like ours? Would they separate such things, or link science and religion as Europeans did in the Middle Ages? Minsky (1985) argues that at least some of their science would be like ours. There is only one law of gravity, set of electromagnetic equations, and set of laws of electricity to discover. To build a spaceship or radio transmitter, only one set of laws will do. One cannot develop a useful technology from other principles. Minsky also believes that their mathematics would be much like ours for similar reasons. A species which thought that $2 + 2 = 5$ would never get far. However, some aspects might be different. Blind jellyfish living in a fluid environment could develop quite a different geometry, since ours derives in part from the sort of visual, land-dwelling creature we are. But many aspects would be similar. Concepts such as *point* and *line* seem so fundamental that it is hard to imagine a geometry without them.

However, their interests in science might develop along quite different lines. Different human civilisations have pursued different fields of interest, as would different species. Our interests partly derive from the sorts of creature we are and where we live. A given species in a relatively benign environment might be totally uninterested in physics but very interested in psychology and social sciences. Astronomy is a major human interest, but blind jellyfish living under a permanent cloud cover might have no interest in it at all.

Science is constrained, but philosophy, religion and art are much less so. Ours derive partly from the kind of creature we are. For example, music and art enable us to express thoughts and feelings, to entertain, and they help hold groups together. A species very different from us might not have such needs to the same extent, or have none of them. Their own needs, based on what kind of creatures they are, might be totally alien, and so strange that we could not understand them. Much the same can occur with different human mindsets. Oriental philosophies are difficult for Westerners to grasp. Even those who have lived in the Orient for many years may say they never understood the ideas there. What about different species?

In summary, there would be some similarities but also many differences. That brings us to the interesting question of communication with an alien species. Most people assume that aliens would be eager to contact us and to discuss everything under our respective suns. That is possible, since they would also be a social species, but only if there was a lot of similarity. Would we want to converse long with a cockroach or something else so alien and unpleasant that people want to kill them? Perhaps the conversation would not go on long. Another problem is what to talk about. There might be few common areas of concern. Many people already avoid other people very different from themselves. With widely varying concepts and concerns, what would we discuss? We saw the same problem with conversing with animals, if they could talk. Still, the effort would be of great interest. It may happen some day.

9

OTHER INTELLIGENCES II: ARTIFICIAL

What things are alive? Ask a very young child and he or she may say that people, dogs and other large animals are, but that fish, insects and birds are not. An older child may list all of these but not plants. The border between life and nonlife gets pushed further back as a child grows older. But exactly where it should stop is unclear. Biologists themselves disagree about whether viruses are alive, and the universe could have countless extraterrestrial creatures that are tricky to pigeonhole, as discussed in Chapter 8.

The computer age has made the life/nonlife boundary even harder to draw. Several artificial 'lifeforms' have been spawned already: computers themselves, which some say already live (Simons, 1983); computer viruses; and electronic animals. Scientists all over the world are busy creating computer ants, bacteria, and biological chemicals. Many of these creatures 'live', in a sense, within the machines, just as computer jets fly in them, computer thunderstorms rage, and computer economies balance supply and demand. Some such inventions even reproduce themselves, like real animals. Other creatures already walk the Earth. Scientists at MIT have built some tiny artificial creatures that stalk prey and dodge predators. In the early 1960s the famous robot the Johns Hopkins Beast used to roam corridors at that university looking for power points to plug itself into, an energy-seeking behaviour like a wolf hunting deer or a cow searching for grass.

Arguably, artificial life of a kind has already been created. How about artificial intelligence? Can synthetic intelligence be constructed from the ground up, so to speak? How would scientists go about the task, and would the result be much like the natural intelligences so far examined in this book? Could it equal or surpass human intelligence, using a suggested bootstrap method? It has been argued that we can build a machine slightly brighter than humans, which in turn could build a machine slightly brighter than itself, and so on.

The idea of artificial intelligence has been around for a long time, and as a science fiction staple it has been explored in great depth. Example from films include HAL, the highly intelligent computer in *2001: A Space Odyssey*. HAL could easily converse with people, could delicately discuss personal difficulties with them, and readily beat them at chess. In *Demon Seed*, an intelligent computer goes wild and eventually impregnates the wife of its designer. The machine then somehow implants its artificial mind in the resulting child, and is clever enough to have the child look like the couple's dead daughter. They take it in as birds take in cuckoo eggs. Isaac Asimov wrote many stories about intelligent robots with 'positronic' brains. They must act according to the 'Three Laws of Robots', one being to not harm a human being, and story themes revolve around conflicts between these laws. Roger Zelazny's story 'For a Breath I Tarry' features an artificial being called Frost. Frost is intelligent and curious but has no real emotions, is very detached, and spends ages pondering problems. He eventually is made into a human being, with emotions and feelings of pain. The 1960s television series *Lost in Space* had an intelligent robot.

Many of the creations are very human-like, often having human emotions. For example, C3PO in *Star Wars* is fearful, self-pitying, and prone to depression. Some even have severe emotional problems. Marvin, the paranoid android in the *Hitchhiker's Guide to the Galaxy* series, is chronically negative and depressed. In Robert Silverberg's short story 'Going Down Smooth' a psychiatric computer handles several cases at a time, giving therapy and dispensing drugs. But, after a time, the machine starts to go crazy itself from continually dealing with disturbed people, just as folklore claims some human psychiatrists do. It hallucinates giant telescopes rising out of the sea, continuously dishes out dreadful verbal obscenities, and frightens patients into catatonia with its 'nightmare therapy'. Frederick Pohl's *Gateway* series has a quite rational psychiatric computer which projects an on-screen image that resembles Sigmund Freud.

All such creations were just science fiction until the dawn of the computer era in the 1940s. The breathtaking advances in hardware and software since then have raised the real possibility of creating artificial intelligence, or 'AI'. Efforts to do so began in earnest at a conference at Dartmouth College in the United States in 1956, where the term AI was coined by John McCarthy. Today, AI is a distinct discipline, usually seen as a subfield of computer science which borders on psychology, philosophy and other fields. Many people belong to the AI field, and they are concentrated at several major universities; notably MIT, Carnegie-Mellon, and Stanford. Some have even set up private companies to develop AI programs, as it became big business in the 1970s.

AI's early workers were very optimistic. A founder and a later Nobel Prize winner, Herbert Simon, made the following claims in 1957: In ten years' time (i.e. by 1967) a digital computer will be the world's chess champion, will discover and prove an important new mathematical theorem, and will write music that critics will accept as having great aesthetic value. Events proved him over-optimistic. Even today none of these goals has been reached and only the first even looks within sight. Indeed, some critics say that the whole approach has been vastly oversold, and will never really succeed.

The aim of this chapter is to give a brief snapshot of the AI field. It is moving too fast to do more. The following section looks at the goals of AI researchers, which in fact are quite diverse. The section after that examines how one would go about creating a synthetic intelligence, and some results to date. Then we look at the criticisms of AI and conclude by speculating about the future of it and the natural intelligences that some AI enthusiasts say will be replaced.

SOME MAJOR AI GOALS

AI researchers are a pretty diverse group, with differing aims. Some of their major goals are as follows, from Haugheland (1985) and Barr and Feigenbaum (1986). In practice, the goals overlap, and achieving one can help achieve the others.

Understanding Human Intelligence Better

Many AI workers are not latter-day Frankensteins trying to create an artificial being. Some are mainly interested in human (or animal) intelligence and how it operates, and use AI programs as tools to study it. Some examples have been given in earlier chapters; the ANALOGY program, and the computer idiot savante. Another is research by Holyoak et al. (1989), who tried to work out the rules underlying a simple form of learning called classical conditioning. They proposed some rules, wrote a program that implemented them, and saw if it behaved as biological intelligence does. Computer simulation is an oft-used method in psychology. Journal articles abound with computer rats, pigeons, and humans who learn mazes, detect signals, abstract out simple rules, and interact with other creatures.

Psychologists have taken the lead from other scientists who use computer simulation extensively. There are computer models of the atmosphere to predict weather, of the forces inside an atom, and of economies. The stealth bomber was designed and flown inside computers and the prototype took to the skies without ever being tested in a wind tunnel. Some scientists even speculate that experiments will eventually become obsolete, and all theories will be tested by computer simulation. That seems very doubtful.

Amplifying and Aiding Human Intelligence

A lot of AI research turns out programs to amplify our own abilities. Traditional computers augment our ability to think with their fantastic, flawless memories and number-crunching powers. A neat computer database can replace cabinets and cabinets of files and legions of clerks. Indeed, their power to calculate has made it possible to solve scientific problems that otherwise were just too complicated. Particle physicists used to hire numerous humans to scan photographs of particle collisions, a tedious job that often took months. Now a computer does it quickly. Only a few decades ago, institutions such as banks employed countless people to handle routine tasks such as accounts, which are now dealt with infinitely more quickly and accurately by computers.

Traditional computer programs are fine for many such routine tasks, but are not up to tasks that need sophisticated knowledge juggling. AI techniques try to fill the gap. Here are some examples. Expert system programs help human experts make decisions in a variety of areas, from medicine to mineral prospecting, and in some narrow domains can replace a human expert entirely. Mobile AI devices (robots) can perform dangerous or unpleasant tasks in factories and can help explore space. Some AI systems have taken over much of the drudgery of security work. They scan video screens for certain kinds of intruders, and can tell the dangerous human ones from harmless ones like cats and dogs. An AI robot called SENTRY moves about a building at 4–5 km/hr, detects intruders and then radios back to human guards. McDonalds has a robot system to cut potatoes and fry chips (French fries). The military uses many AI systems for routine tasks. Some interpret radar and sonar signals, being able to cope with a lot of information at once and respond appropriately. Cruise missiles have AI systems that scan the landscape below and thread the correct path to the target. The Star Wars anti-missile system would rely on AI devices because people are too slow and limited to handle the information that must be juggled. (Using nonhuman intelligence in warfare is not new, of course. Horses and elephants have long been used. In World War II, the Russians strapped bombs to dogs and trained them to run under enemy tanks. In the early 1950s, psychologist B. F. Skinner trained pigeons to guide a missile to its target by pecking different discs.) Gray (1987) argues that AI methods are very useful for some dull tasks that are beyond traditional computing techniques. Currently, the jobs need well-trained people who know a lot, but get bored and usually could make more money elsewhere. He gives examples including answering British Rail ticketing inquiries and diagnosing faults in washing machines. A lot of knowledge is needed to perform them but the work is routine.

A good example of such AI research is the fabled Japanese 'Fifth Generation' project, mentioned earlier. It was launched with great fanfare in 1981, and for a time was a bogeyman held up by Westerners to alert others to the 'Japanese technological threat'. With a roar of metaphorical trumpets and clash of cymbals, a consortium of corporations announced a plan to create user-friendly, highly intelligent computers. These would understand conversational English, and so could obey instructions without needing complex and difficult programming. The programs would solve complex problems using AI methods, recognise and analyse scenes, and continually update their data and adapt them to new circumstances. They could rearrange such data to suit users, and would be very fast and adept at reasoning quickly with vast amounts of information. They would be reliable and cheap. The machines were to be based on AI software and on hardware that used massive parallel processing. A traditional computer works by doing each specified step in sequence (one after the next). Even if the machine operates very quickly, it is fundamentally limited by the necessity to act in sequence. Parallel processors work like the human brain, which gets round its speed limit partly by performing many tasks at once. Imagine a car factory that made each car component in sequence and then assembled them. It would be tediously slow. It is better to make all the components simultaneously in different places, and then bring them together for assembly. The project was dubbed the 'Fifth Generation' by counting back to the 'first' — the primitive vacuum-tube behemoths of the 1940s that are now easily outdone by $10 pocket calculators. The 'fourth' it was to supersede was the current traditional serial computer.

By 1990 some goals were met, but expectations had been far too high. Some problems proved too difficult to solve and the project was scaled back. As well, researchers in England and the United States had outpaced some Fifth-Generation researchers and the 'Sixth Generation' of neurocomputers started creeping up from nowhere. Some believe that the future belongs to neurocomputers, loosely based on the human brain. These programs can learn and do various impressive feats, as described later.

Creating an Ultra-Intelligent Machine

Some AI enthusiasts have much more ambitious goals than those listed above. They want to create the equal or superior of human intelligence. They want to build what Jack Good dubbed the 'UIM': the Ultra-Intelligent Machine. To be sure, work on the UIM draws from the more modest goal-directed work described above. The next section looks at how they might succeed.

BUILDING A SYNTHETIC INTELLIGENCE

There is an old theme in literature, which dates back to Greek mythology, about a creation which ultimately turns on its creator. A good example of its use is in Mary Shelley's novel *Frankenstein*. Dr Frankenstein builds a monster by assembling human parts pirated from graveyards and brings it to life with a bolt of lightning. The monster eventually goes on the rampage, relentlessly pursuing its maker like an avenging fury. The parable is one of science fiction's staples, and its most overworked version is the computer gone wild.

Let us imagine a group of latter-day Dr Frankensteins who plan to create an artificial intelligence (but one that will not turn on them) in a basement laboratory. They will not use biological materials, so how do they go about it? AI designers faced this problem in building a UIM, and tried to solve it pretty much as engineers sometimes try to solve other difficult practical problems. When engineers are stuck or need inspiration they often look to nature for ideas about a design that will work. Nature experiments a great deal with different forms, and comes up time and time again with clever designs that do some task. For example, the special curved shape of an aircraft wing is copied from birds, as are sloping wings for greater manoeuvrability. Dolphin skin is specially streamlined for easy passage through water, and submarine builders are trying to copy it. The great strength of spider webs is a model for very strong, lightweight fabrics. Nature has been experimenting for millions of years with intelligence, and the universe's constraints mean that only a few major sorts of design survive. So, AI researchers looked to nature. An artificial intelligence can differ from a natural one because it does not have to dodge predators and hunt food; it can just be fed electrically and is not subject to at least some physical constraints on natural intelligence. It can be much larger or smaller and one can greatly expand or contract various functions. But natural — and especially human — intelligence has been the major model for AI designers.

The general approach is to try to simulate the major functions of human intelligence. One that an artificial intelligence needs is senses. It has to be able to take in information about the outside world, which involves taking advantage of the few useful forms of physical energy about. It also should be able to learn and remember, to solve problems, to create new works, to understand and speak natural language, and possibly to move about and manipulate an object. These and other elements of intelligence are simulated and built into a machine. Some of these functions are extremely complex, however, so the task is not easy. But there is an interaction between UIM designers and workers with other goals. Trying to simulate a function like vision or natural language has many practical applications, as described below.

How will we know when true artificial intelligence has been built? When will we know if the creation is truly intelligent? It is hard to say, because the border here again is murky. Simons (1983) argues that it has already been achieved; computers are an evolving lifeform. Soon we must think about a bill of rights for them, instead of treating them like slaves.

Others are less optimistic. Some say that it never will be achieved. However, there is a famous, oft-used test proposed by a founder of computing; Alan Turing. His 'Turing test' works as follows. Say that you are communciating down a teletype line, typing in messages and getting typed replies. At the wire's other end is a person or a machine. The computer would have the equivalent of human intelligence if you could not tell whether a machine or person was communicating. The test is a useful way to think about AI, but has its flaws. Artificial intelligence might have great thinking powers but still be readily discriminable from human intelligence. Something like this occurs in chess already. Existing programs can beat almost all human players but it's usually easy to tell that a computer is playing a given game. Computer play has a strange quality, impossible to define but easy to identify.

Turing's test inspired a hoax that backfired badly, and the story is still an AI favourite. In 1966, Joseph Weizenbaum wrote a program called ELIZA that simulates a Rogerian psychotherapist. Rogerian therapy sometimes is facetiously called 'Uh hum' treatment, because the therapist does little more than generally approve of the client and reflect back his or her words (e.g., 'Today I am feeling happy' . . . 'So, today you are happy', etc.). ELIZA takes a person's words through a keyboard, applies some set rules to the input, and gives back a Rogerian-like answer: It reflects back one's words and when stuck gives a stereotyped answer such as 'Tell me more about X'. ELIZA is entirely mindless. It has no empathy or understanding or consciousness, but is cleverly constructed to be mistaken for a person. Here is a sample conversation:

Client:	Men are all alike.
ELIZA:	In what way?
Client:	They're always bugging us about something or other.
ELIZA:	Can you think of a specific example?
Client:	Well, my boyfriend made me come here.
ELIZA:	Your boyfriend made you come here?
Client:	He says I'm depressed much of the time.
ELIZA:	I am sorry to hear you are depressed.
Client:	It's true. I am unhappy.
ELIZA:	Do you think coming here will help you not to be unhappy?
Client:	I need some help, that much seems certain.
ELIZA:	What would it mean to you if you got some help?
Client:	Perhaps I could learn to get along with my mother.
ELIZA:	Tell me more about your family.

ELIZA really is saying nothing. It is just mechanically applying rules to the input. But one must look closely to tell. The story then gets fascinating. Weizenbaum put ELIZA on the MIT computer system and soon users began to tune into it in droves, having deep meaningful conversations. He knew that the joke had really gone wrong when his own secretary asked him to leave the room because she was having a private discussion with ELIZA. Even today, the program is available for personal computers and some psycho-therapists actually prescribe it for their clients. Rogerian therapy given by a human is quite rare nowadays, however.

Parenthetically, psychiatric programs have become more sophisticated. An American company called Interactive Health Systems has a program that uses a menu. Patients select one of several alternatives, which then determines a new set of alternatives. For example, one question is; 'Is what's causing your stress your family life/work life/academic life?' If the patient selects 'family life', the computer asks 'Is the problem that you have too many arguments/you are losing control of your children?', and so on. Eventually, the patient gets a summary of what might be wrong and what to do about it. It is hard to imagine a machine ever actually replacing a human therapist, but the system is still on trial and it will be interesting to see how well it does. People open up to machines, often more than they do to other people.

Human intelligence is made up of many functions, some of them very complex and ill-defined, and AI workers have come only some distance in simulating some of these. The rest of this section briefly surveys some major functions, progress to date, and the work's applications. The hypothetical UIM will have all these func-tions and more. Just trying to simulate them has not just had prac-tical spinoffs but also has revealed much about human intelligence, especially how complicated it all is. The best place to start is with senses.

Senses

As mentioned in Chapter 2, the seat of human intelligence is sealed off from the outside world. Our sense organs gather up information and relay it along chains of neurons to the brain. At way stations, the data are analysed and transformed and then relayed further. A UIM needs sensory systems. Vision and hearing are likely to be the most useful, but it could also have taste, smell, a radar detection sense, and even an electro-detection sense like the shark's. Most AI work has concentrated on vision, often for practical applications.

Vision is very complex and is not fully understood in humans.

Much of the human brain is devoted to it and AI designers trying to simulate vision have used the human visual system as a model. The latter works in stages. First, light is picked up, focused onto the retina in the back of the eye, where it causes biochemical changes which are turned into nerve impulses and are sent to the brain. The second phase is classification of the image; the objects in it go into various categories (a person, a car, a block). Then follows comprehension, trying to understand the scene. This is very difficult because it requires a large knowledge base. Consider a picture of a three-ring circus. To understand the image, one must know a great deal about entertainment, its purposes, the acts portrayed, and so on.

Existing programs generally operate by breaking the task into four major stages (e.g., Frenzel, 1987), not unlike the human system's operation. The first phase is acquiring the image, usually by a video camera. The image is then transformed into binary form, which corresponds to the biochemical change in the human retina. The usual computer technique is to code areas of light and shade in the image using units called *pixels* (short for picture elements). Newswire photos consist of dot patterns of light and shade that our eye interprets as an image. When the image is so coded, image analysis programs go to work on it. They may hunt for features such as edges, places of contrast, and so on. Finally, the image is 'comprehended'. A program works out from the features what the objects in the scene are and how they relate to each other. One technique for comprehension is template-matching, the same system used to identify symbols on bank cheques. The computer's memory is full of knowledge of certain objects, and compares the analysed one in a scene to each stored template to find a match.

Research into computer vision has a long way to go but has had some successes. Some early programs lived and moved in worlds consisting of artificial blocks. They could sense and identify various types of block, where each was located, and move them about according to command. But there is nothing anywhere near as good as human vision, which rests on much processing and an enormous knowledge base. The systems that are in use are usually limited to a specific type of vision, not a general system. Several systems give limited vision to industrial robots, to make them more versatile and mobile. A good example is quality control on an assembly line. Computer eyes survey products rolling down the line and identify those with certain kinds of defect. They can replace humans performing a routine job. Some robots have systems that allow navigation around well-known areas or to perform complex tasks in factories that need some vision. Another major application is automatic image recognition. A Japanese system studies stomach X-rays and brain tomographs and can recognise certain disease conditions.

There are other AI sensory systems. Some hearing systems are up and running, and have such applications as voice recognition. Touch has been implemented in a limited way. Some systems have pressure-detection senses, useful for industrial applications like gently handling certain objects.

Natural Language

If only we could talk to the computers. Traditional computers are very poor communicators. Sometimes a computer will know things that you want to know, but it is almost impossible to discover the needed data. Telling a machine what to do is often even harder than extracting information from it, and programming is often painstaking, tedious work. The machine only understands special formal languages, of which only some are much like human language. The computer must be told every single step and a tiny error like a misplaced semi-colon may induce chaos: The computer interprets it in a certain way and sends a stream of error messages through an otherwise perfect program. Nothing else so impresses the programmer that the machine has no idea what is going on. It does not 'understand' a program. A UIM should be able to easily converse with humans in a language like English.

Lots of AI work tries to implement natural language, which would have many practical uses; it would make computers more user-friendly, as in the Fifth-Generation project, and simply reduce the work of programmers. In fact, much human effort aims to make less future work, and programmers have been trying to make their tasks easier for as long as computers have been around. The first computers were told what to do by inputting binary digits. Then came machine language, assembly language, and the early higher level languages such as FORTRAN. Even English-like ones such as PASCAL have strict rules and are difficult to learn and use.

Why is creating a computer with natural language ability so difficult? The reason is that natural language itself is incredibly complex. An AI system has to do many complicated things. First, the speech signal (spoken words) itself is complex. Different people pronounce the same word differently and the same person may do so on different occasions. There are different tones and accents that many people have trouble deciphering. As well, natural speech is continuous, as anyone hearing a foreign language speaker can attest.

Just breaking up speech into word segments is very difficult. Some speech recognition systems have been developed, but they have trouble, and most natural language AI programs make do with keyboard input.

Second, the rules and word meanings are complex. A native language is the most complicated thing that most people ever learn, but as mentioned in Chapter 6 the human brain seems to be wired up to make the task easy. AI programs have trouble because words may have many meanings and the meanings can vary with context. Consider the word 'form', with such meanings as shape, a printed sheet, the current performance level of a competitor, and so on. A sentence can have two or more meanings, as in Noam Chomsky's examples: Visiting relatives can be boring; Flying planes can be dangerous. Then there are metaphorical uses of words; 'She is the apple of my eye', 'Bangkok is the Venice of the East'. How does an AI program cope with the countless metaphorical meanings of words and of proverbs like 'Strike while the iron is hot'? Natural language is full of such metaphors. Computers are very literal-minded and have trouble dealing with the simplest of them. Then there are the numerous grammatical rules of English and the numerous exceptions. One begins to see why the fifth-generation project foundered on this reef.

The problems were well shown by the early machine foreign language translation programs of the 1960s. The really primitive ones were little more than dictionaries that gave equivalents of words in another language (e.g., 'horse' in English would be replaced by 'caballo' in Spanish). They did not work and the results were often very amusing when one translated a sentence from English to another language and then back to English. 'The spirit was willing but the flesh was weak' (original) could return as gibberish: 'The alcohol was wanting but the meat is not strong'. Word-for-word translation did not work, and machine language translation research eventually halted for years. Human translators could have told them why their approach would fail. They have enormous difficulty translating material that they do not understand, such as technical works. So do computers.

A third reason for difficulty became apparent with more research on human intelligence. Understanding even a simple sentence or two takes an enormous knowledge base. Consider this example: 'Sally entered the building. She picked up a menu.' One must know the individual word meanings, how they change with context, the rules of grammar, and a lot of additional knowledge to read between the lines and connect up the sentences. One must infer that 'she' refers to Sally, the building is likely to be a restaurant, what restaurants are, what people do in them, and so on.

Despite such problems, some natural language AI programs are in use. However, typically they are very limited and just work in fairly narrow domains. There is nothing like a HAL, and probably will not be for some time, if ever. Frenzel (1987) describes a few programs. Most existing ones are for specific practical purposes, such as making a computer more user-friendly. One such major application is 'front end' use. Everyday computer users often do not want to trouble to learn countless set commands for a given system, and AI programs simplify the task of dealing with the computer. One example is with a data base, such as one used in corporations or research libraries. An AI program allows a user to type in 'Give me a list of all our suppliers who allow more than 30 days credit' or 'List all articles on animal hypnotism published in 1990'. Another such use is abstracting. Many individuals, such as scientists, are flooded with so much information from many sources that they lack the time or inclination to sort through countless sources for the few bits they really want. AI programs process data such as news reports and summarise them, or just select out certain specified items of interest. A related use is foreign language translation. The problems mentioned above have not really been solved and many small programs used by foreign tourists are little more than automated dictionaries and phrase books. However, computer languages are more logical than human ones and some AI programs translate from one to another. A final use is automatic reading. An Israeli computer about the size of a microwave oven reads any text out loud — newspaper, book, magazine. It's a great aid for the blind (and perhaps the lazy).

The natural language problem ultimately may be solved with neural nets. For example, a British Telecom system was taught to recognise spoken words, to translate simple phrases from English to French, and to determine if a given sentence was grammatical. Neurocomputers may succeed where traditional AI techniques have largely failed.

Problem Solving and Reasoning (Expert Systems)
In 1970 a fellow high-school student and I battled a chess-playing computer that was a continent away at MIT. Though we were the scourges of our local chess club, we were not particularly strong players. Yet the computer was even weaker and we despatched it with little strain. The program ran on a large mainframe and was

one of the world's best of the day, but it did not behave very intelligently on the chessboard. Few then thought that chess-playing computers would ever amount to much. In the 1960s Scottish master David Levy even bet a large sum that no computer would beat him within the next ten years. He kept raising the sum and the time frame. Like chess players in general, he was unimpressed with what programmers had come up with.

Today, opinion has changed radically. Computers have improved dramatically and are big business. A small micro called Mephisto Porterose, which sells for a few thousand dollars, can beat all but the top few thousand human players and is especially formidable in very fast games (say five minutes a side). It won the West German Lightning Chess title in 1990 by a very wide margin. In 1990, the strongest computer is Deep Thought, which runs on a system at Carnegie-Mellon University and has several grandmaster scalps hanging from its mainframe. It was considered good enough to contest a match with the human world champion, Garry Kasparov, at Harvard University in late 1989. The champ won both games but pronounced the machine good, though lacking in imagination and a sense of when it was in trouble. He added that it should be taught when to give up, as it had struggled on for a long time in a hopelessly lost game. David Levy finally lost his bet in December 1989. He was trounced by Deep Thought in a four-game match, losing every one.

Chess-playing computers are among the most successful examples of *expert systems*, themselves the most successful of commercial AI programs. An expert system has expertise in a very specific knowledge domain, such as chess, bacterial infections, mineral prospecting, and chemical analysis. What they can do is reason and solve problems in a narrow domain, problems such as winning a chess game, finding a promising site to look for mineral ore, diagnosing a disease, or helping a manager deal with a problematic business situation. Solving such problems is a major function of human intelligence. The ability rests partly on knowledge and partly on reasoning prowess. Humans are good general problem-solvers, able to tackle difficulties in many domains. Expert systems are specific solvers, adept only at problems within a narrow domain. They are the computer equivalents of idiots savantes. In principle at least, one could construct a UIM with good reasoning and problem-solving by specifying all the domains a typical human knows and writing expert system programs for each. In practice, the difficulties are formidable. There are too many domains, and many cannot be reduced to the rules on which an expert system runs.

Newspapers are full of reports about expert systems. They have been developed in many areas and some private companies have been set up to develop more. They have several uses. Some replace human experts. A chess player can buy a chess system and need no longer seek human opposition, except for variety or a weaker opponent. Many systems also can be set up to solve chess problems. Most expert systems, however, help human experts (or administrators) make decisions. They advise. They propose a solution or series of possible solutions to a problem, and the user then makes his or her own judgment with the advice.

This section surveys some major expert systems, briefly describes how they work, and then considers their prospects.

MYCIN. This 1970s system is one of many medical diagnosis programs. Medical diagnosis is a good domain for expert systems because it is relatively small and the disease entities can be easily defined and categorised. MYCIN helps diagnose bacterial infections and prescribes antibiotics (and the correct dosage) for a given case. The system user enters such patient data as age, symptoms, history, laboratory test results, and any other relevant information. MYCIN goes to work and suggests the probable disorder. It works quite well, in fact diagnosing better than many human doctors.

DENDRAL. Much of a chemist's work involves analysing compounds to see what atoms they are made of and how the molecule itself is structured. Such analysis often is painstaking, lengthy work. DENDRAL can simplify it. It takes data about the compound, gathered by a mass spectrograph and nuclear resonance imaging, gives an analysis, and generates the likely structure of the molecule. It has successfully analysed many substances, such as new antibiotics and insect sex hormones. Several spin-off programs perform other analytical tasks. In some cases, its analytic ability is better than that of human experts.

FOLIO. Investors with money to spread about cover many breeds. They have different sums of cash, goals, time frames for results (e.g., depending on age and patience), and tolerance for risk. As well, the markets are constantly changing, and human experts have trouble keeping track of all relevant information. FOLIO helps deal with such investment problems. It takes data about a given client and suggests an investment portfolio.

Legal systems. Lawyers are among the most highly paid of all professionals. They use a large amount of somewhat amorphous knowledge; specific laws, landmark cases, and rules of thumb. Most of this information is stored in a legal library rather than in the lawyer's head, and sometimes it is hard to retrieve or combine the relevant data for a given case. A variety of expert systems help lawyers make decisions. JUDITH helps lawyers reason about civil cases. Another system automates the drawing-up of difficult, lengthy legal documents such as contracts. SARA helps determine which factors are relevant to a particular case decision. TAXMAN helps a person investigate tax consequence of specific supportive decisions, thereby helping companies legally minimise taxes. LDA takes in information about product liability and calculates defendant liability, equitable settlement sums, and case worth.

Maintenance programs. Most mechanical objects are notoriously prone to breakdowns, as everyone eventually realises, and repairs are often expensive and difficult. Mechanics frequently miss what is wrong with a car, for instance, and replace particular parts unnecessarily. Training good expert diagnosers is a lengthy process. So system designers took their cue from expert systems designed to diagnose faults in devices such as human bodies and developed programs to promote better maintenance. As with humans, the symptoms and other relevant data (e.g., age of vehicle) are fed in and a probable diagnosis is made. Various systems help diagnose problems in cars, diesel engines, industrial plants, and one is being developed to help maintain the space-shuttle.

PROSPECTOR. This early system is an explorer, in a sense, anyway. It helps geologists find ore deposits. The user inserts data about a given geographical area; such data as terrain features and distributions of various rock and soil types (which humans gathered, of course). PROSPECTOR may suggest further data collection and eventually indicates how favourable a given site is for exploration. Its greatest success was in detecting a previously unknown molybdenum deposit in Washington, which it followed up later by finding another in Canada. Like some other AI systems, its feats have surprised its creators.

Game-playing systems. Intellectual games are good candidates for the writing of expert system programs to play them because the domains are very narrow and easy to define. Self-conscious early AI workers also tried to build them partly because, in folklore, skill at chess or bridge is a sign of intelligence. Chess, for instance, is the intellectual game *par excellence* and expertise in it is often featured in films and books to denote a highly intelligent person. What could be better evidence of true AI than a good chess-playing program? Nowadays, they are big business. Several companies such as Scisystems and Mephisto sell a number of models of chess computer. No human ever need be stuck for an opponent. The machines don't get tired or bored or impatient with slow or weak play, and they don't blow cigarette smoke across the board. As well as chess, there are programs that play bridge, poker, and backgammon. An AI milestone was reached in 1979, when an AI system beat the world champion backgammon player in an exhibition match. As mentioned in Chapter 1, a computer is indisputable world champion in the intellectual game Othello.

Chess-playing systems do not operate much like human chess players or, indeed, like other expert systems. They use a variety of techniques, the most important being search. A given chess position might have a number of legal moves (say twenty-five) of which only two or three might be sound. A human expert unconsciously ignores most of the bad moves and focuses on the few plausible ones. That kind of positional sense is very hard to implement in a machine. Most systems look at all possible moves, and examine each resulting position. They weigh such factors as material advantage, king safety, and so on. Each is rated, the opponent's replies are then considered, and further resulting positions are evaluated. A good move is then selected. This look-ahead has a fundamental limitation, however. The number of possible variations only three or four moves deep soon becomes astronomical. Some algorithms reduce the number of possibilities to look at, while newer programs use more human-like reasoning, but they still rely largely on look-ahead. Computers have improved partly because they have become so much faster: They can look much faster, and thus consider more possibilities. Computers also are programmed with a lot of automatic responses, as people are. They are taught standard opening sequences and endgames.

Look-ahead has other flaws. Machines do not understand what is going on and sometimes come up with very strange, poor moves that show it. They lack human chess intuition, the sense of what is important, and games between two computers often have an odd mechanical quality. Perhaps partly it is because they lack personality which colours every human player's game, and which makes a human opponent more interesting.

How expert systems work. Typically, expert systems have two major parts; a knowledge base and an 'inference engine'. The knowledge base usually consists of a very large number of rules of thumb, which may lead to the correct answer (e.g., a diagnosis) but do not guarantee it. Examples might include 'Getting a good job requires getting a good education' and 'Try to think of a similar problem in the past'. The rules are often formulated as if/then ones. If a given condition is met, then a certain action should be performed: If it is raining, carry an umbrella; If organism X is present, then the diagnosis is Y.

Some systems use different formats of rules, but the if/then ones are easiest to write and implement, and the easiest to change when more knowledge needs to be added to the base. Many knowledge domains can be reduced to such rules. Indeed, a human expert about to retire became very depressed to realise that his lifetime's occupational knowledge largely boiled down to a few hundred such rules.

The knowledge itself comes from textbooks, journals, and human experts, although it is not always easy to extract information from the latter. A new profession called 'knowledge engineering' involves transferring knowledge from human expert heads, coding it into rules, and implementing it in an expert system. The engineer spends many hours doing so, trying to get the expert to make his or her knowledge explicit, probing here and there, and summarising. Some expert systems can learn themselves, updating their knowledge to some extent.

The inference engine manipulates the knowledge base to come up with conclusions and decisions. It takes in data (e.g., symptoms, results of spectrograph analyses) and matches it up against its rules. Say the input says that conditions a, b, and c are met. The program looks up each rule, infers the consequences, and then may make a series of inferences from them. The engine typically uses one of two major techniques to make inferences, which are two sides of one coin. The first is called *forward chaining*. Say that the input says that conditions a and b are met. The knowledge base says that if a is met, then x follows, and if b is met, then y follows. If x and y are met, then z follows (e.g., the disease is shingles). The chain goes forward. *Backward chaining* works in reverse. The engine forms an hypothesis and tests it against the input and rules in its knowledge base. (If the disease is shingles, then conditions x and y should hold, and these can be checked, and so on.) Inference engines are complex, and take a lot of time to write. Programmers have partially got around this problem by writing 'shell programs', which are engines that can be used for different knowledge domains. One pours the knowledge gleaned from experts into an existing program, rather than having to start from scratch.

Expert systems often have additional features. Some not only give a conclusion, but tell how they arrived at it. The human expert can check the reasoning and see how well the conclusions follow. Such programs also are good teaching aids for creating human experts like doctors. Another feature is that expert systems are more adaptable than traditional computer programs. The latter will not run unless they get all the right data in exactly the specified way. Expert systems can cope with missing data, just as human experts can.

Limitations. Expert systems have a lot of practical applications, but have not replaced human experts by any stretch of the imagination. They have some fundamental limitations, the first being that they only work in very narrow domains which can be easily reduced to set rules. A lot of domains cannot be readily specified. What are the rules underlying scientific research or writing novels? It is hard to reduce such domains to a series of if-then rules. Somerset Maugham once was asked how one writes a novel, and he replied: 'There are three rules. But no one knows what they are'. Once the knowledge base widens, the performance of expert systems deteriorates rapidly, just as with a human idiot savante. Frenzel (1987) lists some other limits. Current systems often need very powerful computers to operate, and are not 100 per cent reliable; they are very expensive and difficult to develop, even with shell programs; and many hours of programmer, knowledge engineer, and human expert time are needed.

Finally, expert systems lack the generality and versatility of human intelligence, which often operates in a different way. They cannot readily update their knowledge to cope with a variety of changing circumstances. A different approach to complex domains is needed.

Learning
The ability to learn is a crucial aspect of intelligence, and as mentioned in Chapter 8, the ability to acquire new knowledge and skills is a major sign of evolutionary development. Higher animals can learn more and are thus more flexible. A UIM would learn.

Creating an educable AI program is not easy, and indeed has not been a major concern in AI until recently (Haugeland, 1985). Researchers adopted the easier task of figuring out what knowledge is and how it is put together, rather than how machines can acquire it themselves. But a computer that can learn could be a great boon. One would not have to feed in all the knowledge one wanted it to have, which is a laborious task. As well, many tasks that require knowledge are extremely hard to program because the rules underlying performance are complex, numerous, and very hard to specify, as with expert systems above. Finally, there is the dream of automatic programming. Programmers would like just to have to briefly describe what they wanted and a computer would then write its own instructions.

Computers can learn in one sense. They can acquire knowledge which is directly fed into them. One adds some more rules to an expert system, for example. It is learning of a sort, but it is not really gathering and abstracting information by the program itself. Some AI programs have a rudimentary learning ability. For example, some chess computers learn from their mistakes. If a machine consistently loses in a certain variation, it will learn to avoid it. Some expert systems retain inferences that they have worked out as new rules. A more sophisticated AI learning program works out the rules of a given sport by 'observing' it being played. A variety of AI programs that learn concepts are operating. Winston (1970) wrote a program which operates in a world consisting of blocks. It could learn simple concepts such as *arch* from examples and nonexamples, and could subsequently identify further examples. Another such program is HACKER, which lives in a synthetic blocks world. It plans the actions of a one-armed robot, which moves blocks about. The blocks are scattered about, some alone and some in piles, and HACKER makes plans to move them and simulates their manipulation. It learns from its actions, correcting movement errors and looking to see if subgoals are enough alike to combine into one movement step.

Neural networks. AI programs can learn in the above ways. However, they remain fundamentally limited if one sticks just to those methods of building in learning. In knowledge domains that cannot be readily reduced to rules, humans operate by 'intuition' or 'gut feeling', just seeming to arrive at the right decisions or categorisations without being able to say how. Intuition is responsible for many wonderful creations in science and the arts and lots of intelligent behaviour in everyday life. A UIM should have it too, or it will be too dumb.

How does one program the kind of learning that builds up such intuitive knowledge? AI researchers did what engineers in other fields sometimes do when stuck — they looked to nature. The basis of human intuition is the neuron, which alters its connections as a result of experience. Nature has not come up with anything better to underly intuition, and nor have AI designers. Who would ever think up an idea like connected neurons without nature's model to copy? Who would ever imagine what such a system would be capable of?

Neural networks are computer systems that try to copy the

human brain. They cannot copy all aspects of it, as no one is sure exactly how real neurons work (Minsky, 1988). However, they model some essentials. They simulate neurons and the changing strength (and existence of) connections between them. A neural net consists of a number of individual units, corresponding to neurons, and of links between them. Some units are not linked with others, and some are. The system also can create or destroy existing connections. The links that do exist vary greatly in strength, from very weak to very strong. Consider an individual unit as being like a person. A given individual has links (relationships) with many other people. Some links are very strong, as with a spouse or children. Others are weaker, as with a friend, and some are very weak (as with a distant acquaintance). Information is represented in the network as a pattern of unit interconnections and strengths. For example, knowledge of what a human face looks like would be represented as units x, y, and z (and a lot more) being interconnected with certain strengths of link. The link strength would mean that a given unit would or would not fire given certain stimulation by other units. Just how to represent such knowledge is something the unit system itself figures out from the experience that people give to it. Information can be added or altered by manipulating the connections. Knowledge is distributed to different parts of the network as such patterns (Johnson & Brown, 1988). The whole system works by doing many things at once, as does the human brain.

Neural networks learn quite well, often surprising their designers. They can acquire a sort of intuitive knowledge, which allows 'gut feeling' decisions. They can be shown examples and nonexamples of some concept, abstract out the concept themselves, and accurately categorise more cases. And they can do this with very intuitive concepts that cannot be readily reduced to rules. Consider walking through an art gallery and noting many artistic styles. One eventually usually notes that most fall into distinct styles; surrealist, impressionist, and so on. Even a given artist has definite style. Similarly, the music of an individual composer usually conforms to a certain style. We know it when we encounter it, but it is almost impossible to say what makes a work a case of that style. Somehow our own system of interconnected neurons figures it out.

Here are some things that various neural net programs have learned. A program called NESTORWRITER takes in samples of a person's handwriting. A lot of cases are fed in and eventually it gives a pretty fair imitation of that handwriting. A Finnish program can take dictation in Japanese and in Finnish with an accuracy of about 90 per cent. This task is beyond traditional AI programs. The system learned by being fed spoken words and by learning to match these up to the correct written words. Other programs can learn to recognise objects by similar means. Some practical programs are already in use. One may try neural networks in domains that expert systems cannot handle because no one knows the exact rules. An example is assessing loan applications. Banks need to tell good risks from bad ones. How to decide? There are rules, but not a complete set. A lot must be considered; the individual's apparent capacity to repay, riskiness of his or her purpose for the cash, and so on. The program is fed details of all the bank's past loans, both successful and unsuccessful, and learns to distinguish cases. The loan manager can then feed in details of a given applicant and the system can pigeonhole him or her.

Neural networks are creating a lot of excitement in the computer world. Their future looks promising, and several companies have sprung up to develop more commercial ones. They are a programmer's dream in that they teach themselves what they need to know. They do have limitations, however. For some applications that can be reduced to set rules, expert systems are preferable. Another is the vast extent of hardware that they need. Only in the last decade or so has hardware developed that really allows interesting neural nets to run.

Neural nets have another major application. They are being used extensively in psychology to try to solve some long-standing scientific problems. A net gives a model of how the brain does things and allows them to be tested. There are 'connectionist' neural net models of memory, learning, and various other phenomena. All kinds of interesting things emerge when one tries to simulate mental functions this way. For example, a net when run may come up with a sort of model of reality if run long enough, as the human brain does. There is much excitement that such age-old problems as the mind-body problem may actually be solved with the technique.

Creativity.

There is an ancient saying that dates from early in the computer era: 'You can only get out of a computer what you put into it'. This implies that computers can never be creative, that is, come up with new ideas or recombine elements into new wholes. Some say that true creativity only comes from natural intelligence. Computers will never be intelligent because they cannot be 'creative'.

Many AI enthusiasts find this argument unconvincing. They first point out that requiring an AI program to be creative to show true intelligence is too stringent a criterion. Most humans are not very creative. Most people learn rules and archetypes early on and apply these, often avoiding situations and persons that their knowledge does not cover. Relatively few humans come up with a major scientific discovery or work of art, music, or literature. Humanity lives off its few very creative persons.

AI enthusiasts have a second reason for being unconvinced. AI programs already are showing creativity, of a sort at any rate, and they may show more so with further development. Consider chess-playing. Existing AI systems work by applying rules but often come up with quite creative moves, according to their opponents' judgments. The present author has often been impressed with moves and plans that computers find, ones that I miss myself. Chess players now routinely use computers to help analyse their own games (if playing by correspondence, for example) and to solve problems. Computers are also extending chess knowledge itself, which constitutes a kind of scientific research. One program found two new solutions to a famous chess problem thought to have just one. The best computers play more creatively than most skilled humans, whose play is often very stereotyped. The products of other expert systems such as PROSPECTOR also are creative. There also are cases of creative (but not terribly creative) computer art, music, and literature.

But perhaps the most impressive demonstration comes from some famous AI programs that may be the forerunners of systems that will replace human scientists. What could be more creative than scientific research, the extension of the boundaries of knowledge? Let us look at some examples. A famous case is Douglas Lenat's (1976) program AM, short for Automated Mathematician. AM was given a knowledge base of many basic mathematical concepts and a lot of rules of thumb for manipulating them. One novel rule assessed how 'interesting' a particular line of analysis was. AM was set running, and came up with many concepts. Some were quite well-known to mathematics, including *prime number* and *multiplication*. AM also by itself discovered the important 'unique factors theorem'. The performance is impressive, though Lenat later conceded that the computer language used may partially be responsible for AM's success. Relatively few humans would abstract out such concepts. Later Lenat built an updated version of AM called EURISKO, which can cross into domains outside mathematics to discover new things. It is creative. It actually designed an electric circuit; a three-dimensional AND/OR gate which won a patent. Few humans hold patents and doing so is a mark of creativity, since they are only granted for new inventions. EURISKO is the first AI system to get one.

There are more examples of AI creativity (Langley & Zythow, 1989). AI programs have made scientific discoveries. The most famous case is BACON, which performs a major task of human scientists; looking for regularities in data to try to abstract out laws of nature. Consider Newton's law of gravity, which states that the gravitational attraction between two bodies decreases as distance between them increases. BACON abstracts out such laws from masses of observational data. It was fed in facts about planetary motions and induced Kepler's law of planetary motion. From other sets of data, it came up with Columb's law, the ideal gas law, and Black's law of specific heat. Pretty good. It can even define new concepts, as can AM.

Human scientists can do much more than current AI programs, of course. AI systems cannot yet do really creative things such as constructing theories, and finding what problems need solving, which Einstein said is most creative. Eventually they may.

Ability to Move and to Manipulate Objects: Robots

All animals can move. Indeed, the ability to do so is a defining feature of animals. Mature plants, with no intelligence at all, are limited to simple motions like turning leaves toward the sun. They cannot uproot themselves and go walking to avoid predators or to hunt for more fertile soil, like the triffids in John Wyndham's novel *Day of the Triffids*. A few carnivorous plants have more sophisticated powers of motion, like the steel-trap type clamp of the Venus flytrap. Mobility is a very useful ability. Beyond mere power to move is the ability to manipulate objects. Animals use beaks, claws, paws, and flippers to alter objects, but nature has come up with nothing much better than the human hand. It has allowed us to build an enormous array of complicated machines. Dolphins, as mentioned in Chapter 8, cannot develop such technology because they lack our appendages, even if they had the intelligence. The ability to move and manipulate takes a lot of programming. Much of the human brain is devoted to supporting it and the features needed to make it work, such as feedback, balance, coordination, and so on.

For the UIM, the power to move and manipulate is an optional extra. Though not essential, it would be useful to give it such power. Rather than being confined to a mainframe, it could move about and perhaps even construct its own technological devices.

AI systems that move and manipulate things are called robots, from a Czech word. Robots are built for practical reasons as well as theoretical ones. There is an age-old dream of creating an all-purpose household robot that will cook, clean, sew, serve food and drinks, care for the animals, and entertain the children. Another aim is to free people from dull, dangerous jobs. Robots on the assembly line do not need holidays, incentives, unions, or coffee breaks and are easy to retrain. A related application is space exploration. Robot vehicles do not need return tickets, food, or oxygen. Military vehicles are being developed to enter enemy territory and relay back information.

How can an intelligent robot be built? What functions does it need? It needs senses to take in information, so it can avoid obstacles and perform set tasks. Vision is the most popular one used, and is usually based on a front-mounted television camera. A touch gripper on an arm's end can provide a pressure sense, and some robots have temperature and humidity detection senses. It needs devices to actually move and manipulate objects. Wheels often are used, but are not much use on uneven terrain. Nature has come up with nothing better than legs for such purposes (aside from wings), and many robots have legs. The U.S. Army is experimenting with robots and even robot vehicles with spindly legs that allow them to cover rough country that even tanks find difficult. Such legs look much like those of the Empire's attack vehicles in the 1980 film *The Empire Strikes Back*. Some robots have retractable legs that allow them to climb stairs, albeit very slowly. Robot arms come in many shapes and sizes. Many have artificial hands like a human one, with fingers and an opposing thumb. One robot has an appendage based on the elephant's trunk, with analogous muscle structure and great flexibility. Like its model, it has great strength in the right places and can twist about dexterously. Robots also need a lot of programming to make these senses and appendages work. Getting limbs to work effectively takes a great deal of artificial intelligence, with synchronised feedback and command signals.

Many working robots exist already and new models are continually coming on the market. The most primitive ones have little intelligence (they can do little) and are just a few steps beyond toys or assembly line machines. The Japanese operate many single-task robots that carry out set steps to build a house, spray-paint cars, or weld parts together. They are little more than remotely controlled devices, however. Other systems are more sophisticated. A British consortium is building a robot that looks like a spider, which can scurry up the sides of buildings. It will do dangerous tasks like window cleaning and outside repairs from many stories up. Another group has built a robot butcher, which cuts up the carcases of sheep, cows, and pigs. It has a visual system that surveys each carcase and relays the image to its computer. The computer has a notion of an ideal carcase, just as a human mind would, compares the ideal with the actual, and decides where to cut. The French have a prototype robot called MAGALI that has two arms, a visual system, and which replaces twelve human fruitpickers. It can pick about 65 per cent of the apples on a tree. The rest are too much for its limited intelligence. The British have a prototype system of a robot-piloted ship whose sensors collect data about helm settings, draft, present courses, and speed, which it uses to navigate. Perhaps someday automatic ships will ply the world's oceans, just as some factories now are completely automated. There will be no more merchant sailors, sailors' bars, sea stories, and girls in every port. A recent report funded by the British Department of Trade and Industry speculates that a home robot eventually will be built. It will arise as an integrated version of all the single-task industrial robots.

There are some more sophisticated robots about already. A Japanese robot called CUBOT has hands, a good AI system, and can solve Rubic's cube in less than four minutes. Another Japanese robot, called WABOT, with a vaguely human form and a box-shaped head, actually reads music and plays with a symphony orchestra. It plays the organ, by sitting on a bench and pressing the keys with its metal fingers. WABOT renders a quite passable interpretation of various Bach pieces. However, it may be a long time before robots can give new, original interpretations of classical pieces, with all the emotional expression of the best human musicians. No one knows what underlies such performances, although perhaps a very advanced neural network will be able to. Finally, the wave of the future may be indicated by the opening of the world's first robot-operated shop in the United States in 1989. It dispenses, sells, and plays compact discs for customers. There is no human attendant at all.

SOME DIFFERENCES BETWEEN HUMAN INTELLIGENCE AND CURRENT AI SYSTEMS

There are a number. In some ways AI systems are much more proficient than humans, and in others they are much less so. They never forget anything, and what they do remember is exactly as it was acquired. Humans, in contrast, are prone to forgetting what we do not constantly use. We also may alter what we do remember. For example, most of us have experienced re-encountering a house lived in during childhood, only to find it very different from the memory. Our forgetting and memory-altering were once seen as weaknesses, but now are viewed as strengths. It is better to forget what is not needed. Computers have better number-crunching power. They can do computations in microseconds that would take humans years. Computers also are tireless. They do not get bored or fatigued, which can greatly affect the exercise of human intelligence. Our intelligence is also greatly affected by our motivations and emotions, which guide and colour our thinking. A deeply depressed person, for example, thinks differently from an elated one. Some work is being done on computer analogues of emotions, but it is a very difficult problem. Computers might never understand or deal with some human ideas (like love and poetry), but these are tied up with the kind of species we are (see Chapter 8). To borrow from Nagel, we might never understand what it is like to be a computer, just as computers may never understand what it's like to be a human.

With the exception of neural networks, AI systems are based on rules specified by algorithms. They simply follow set recipes like the recipes in cookbooks. Human intelligence is based more on rules of thumb, which makes it far more flexible and able to cope with a diverse, changing world. Here is a good illustration of the difference. A robot system had an arm that fetched an object and placed it elsewhere in a room. But it was tricked by having to lift an object heavier than its strength allowed. The robot was caught in a loop, and tried to lift, failed, went through the motion of depositing the object, went back to the pile, and tried to lift again. Endlessly. (There are human analogues in obsessive-compulsive neurosis.) The robot was defeated by circumstances that its programming could not cope with. Human intelligence can usually get around such problems, but it is extremely difficult to program an AI system to be generally flexible.

AI systems, also with the partial exception of neural nets, lack intuition. They lack human commonsense, human horse sense, which makes us practical, intuitive, and able to make good judgments. We have seen the value of commonsense repeatedly in this book; for example, in the ability of the expert chess player to focus on a position's few good moves, or in an expert scientist's ability to focus rapidly on what is important in a set of data. It is not clear how much this powerful human faculty can be simulated by neural networks. AI systems lack 'consciousness'. They lack 'understanding'. Much criticism of AI rests on this difference, to which we turn in the next section.

ARTIFICIAL INTELLIGENCE?

Creating a UIM, or even a system with some intelligence, is a fiendishly complex task. As mentioned in Chapter 1, AI designers trying to simulate such functions have had a 'sense of awe in the face of the ordinary'. How successful have they really been so far? How much further progress can be expected?

There are two extreme views about AI, with many others in between. The debate between the extremes has been going on a long time. It may only be resolved when an indisputable UIM is created, although even then some may say it is not true AI. Indeed, the critics have become progressively more stringent about the criteria for true AI. As Hoftstadter (1979) put it, true intelligence is whatever computers have not yet done. Once it was to play chess well, then to solve certain kinds of problems, and after that to learn and create. Now it is to be intuitive and conscious.

At one extreme are enthusiasts such as Simons (1983, 1984), who say that computers already are intelligent. They do not just mimic human thought; they are evolving lifeforms whose intelligence already exceeds that of low-level lifeforms like the paramecium. They are alive. They sense the environment, think, move, process information, and create. They can reproduce in a limited way (e.g., by building computer parts). Ultimately, they may design the next robot generation. Simons says that we have to acknowledge all this, and think about a code of ethics for them. Perhaps there may eventually be a Computer Liberation Society, for persons who see them as mistreated slaves (could computers join the society, too?). One enthusiast sets the year 2012 as the likely year in which human intelligence is equalled. They see the problems as very difficult, but ultimately soluble. They see no difference in principle between silicon- and carbon-based intelligence.

An extreme of this extreme is Hans Moravec, a professor of computer science at Carnegie-Mellon University. Moravec (1988) argues that the human mind could ultimately run on hardware other than neurons. The mind is a program, just as an artificial mind in a computer is. We may eventually become immortal by implementing our own minds on silicon hardware. Moravec even describes how it could be done. The human mind could be slowly peeled away on its own hardware and slowly built up on another set. It is not at all clear that this would ever be possible, however.

At the opposing extreme are a number of dissenters. Some say that the entire AI enterprise has been greatly oversold. AI researchers have made exaggerated, inflated claims, which they have continuously failed to meet. Some say that AI achievements to date are mostly illusion, done with smoke and mirrors. Many expert systems perform abysmally, and relatively few really are useful. Social critic Theodore Roszak put it even more savagely: 'AI is . . . still repeating the same unfounded claims, working with many of the same discredited assumptions after failing again and again to perform as advertised. AI's record of barefaced public deception is unparalleled in the annals of academic study'. By this view, not only does AI not live up to its claims, but there is little evidence that it ever will.

Some other severe critics are Dreyfus and Dreyfus (1986). They attack the AI hyperbole, claim that many systems do not live up to the hype, and charge that many AI workers are motivated to keep making claims by the vast sums of funding that they attract. AI only does well in very restricted domains that can be reduced to rules, such as disease diagnosis. The programs lack judgment and commonsense. AI systems only do what they are programmed to do. The theoretical physicist Roger Penrose (1989) takes up much the same cudgels. He argues that the human mind will never be superseded by a computer because the rules by which it operates will never be specified. There is much more to human intelligence than computers can ever simulate.

And there is a final major criticism of AI made by Penrose, by the philosopher John Searle (1980), and by others. They charge that AI systems may produce something that looks like intelligence but is not the real thing, just as a computer can simulate a rainstorm but not produce one. No one gets wet in a computer storm. Searle says that computers lack consciousness and understanding, which are key aspects of human intelligence. AI systems just manipulate symbols according to specified rules, and do not know what they are doing. Searle illustrates his argument with his oft-quoted 'Chinese room' scenario. Imagine a person, who cannot speak Chinese, in a room that has two windows. He has a set of rules for manipulating Chinese characters. Through one window are passed documents writen in Chinese characters. The person manipulates the symbols according to rules and passes the results out through the second window. He does not understand what the symbols mean, because he does not speak Chinese, but may appear to do so. Similarly, a chess-playing computer does not understand a position or what it is doing, but may appear to if its rules are good enough. Computers will never have this understanding.

Who is right? It is still hard to say. It's not really clear how sound Searle's much debated argument really is. As Marvin Minsky has pointed out, consciousness is overrated. A great deal of human intelligence is automated, done without awareness. As for the rest, it may simply be due to the great difficulty of the task of creating artificial intelligence. With hardware and programming advances and development of neural nets, machines may get progressively more intelligent. It may well be that artificial intelligence is fundamentally limited, that it cannot do some tasks, but that is an empirical question. Let us see if a UIM can be built. Some AI accomplishments to date are impressive, especially chess-playing systems. They may not understand what they are doing or be conscious, but some of them play awfully well. Does it really matter if they do not understand?

THE FUTURE

Let us speculate that AI advances very rapidly, that its major problems are overcome. Let us say that a computer eventually becomes the world chess champion, and AI systems take over most intellectual tasks now undertaken by humans. Machines then improve themselves further by bootstrap methods described earlier, building in new senses and perhaps abilities that we have not even thought of. It is hard to say what AI might accomplish in fifty or one hundred years, and what systems then may do. As some enthusiasts like to say, the distance from the Wright brothers' plane at Kitty Hawk to the Boeing 747 and the space-shuttle is only a few decades. The Wright brothers could not have imagined present-day aviation, just as we may not be able to imagine what technology is to come. It may be that fundamental limits on artificial intelligence soon become apparent, but on the other hand, technology has a way of outstripping our expectations.

The long-term development of AI raises several concerns. Some date from the beginnings of other technology that replaced humans. Among the first to complain were the Luddites of England, who destroyed textile machines that did their work. Already, robots and other AI systems are replacing people. There are automatic factories, a shop, and so on. What if there are automatic ships, household robots, travel agents, doctors, teachers, architects, and lawyers? What are people going to do as human occupations disappear?

Some say that there is nothing to fear. Such worries are centuries old, but never really cause undue trouble. Increasing automation merely creates new jobs for those it makes redundant. A few

hundred years ago, most people in the West were farmers, but few
are now. A few decades ago, many worked in manufacturing, but
they have now shifted to service industries as these became automated. AI systems will create occupations that today we cannot
even dream of. Could a Spanish farmer of the year 1700 imagine a
knowledge engineer or a television producer? However, this process
may someday end. At some point there may be no further worth-
while jobs to create, and massive unemployment may follow. Only a
few people will need to work. All our major mental and physical
tasks will be done by machines. The government will have to provide bread and circuses or make-work jobs, as in the Great Depression. Many look on this scenario with dread, but it may be a
problem only if attitudes stay the same. Experience in England in
World War II showed how few people really are needed to keep a
modern nation going. Many existing jobs are already quite
unnecessary, and many people dislike what they have to do for
seven or eight hours a day. Hunter-gatherer societies living in a rich
land usually devote only a few hours a day to the necessities of life.
We may achieve a society devoted to leisure, art, music, and self-
improvement rather than one in which most waking hours are
devoted to work or preparation for it. Automation may truly free us.

Another concern is the blow to human self-esteem that may
arise when confronted by a vastly superior synthetic intelligence,
even one that we created. How would humans feel if continually
outclassed? Would human scientific research grind to a halt? Would
science soon get beyond our capacity to understand it, so that we
benefit from the resulting technology but have no idea how it works,
like an African tribesman driving a car? Would we have AI social
planners, judges, lawyers, and counsellors who know much more
than us? Would humans lose interest in intellectual games? Perhaps
yes. A possible forerunner to what may come is a typical reaction of
human players to losing to a computer in a chess tournament. Many
get angry, and demand that machines be banned from human com-
petitions. Chess magazines increasingly feature letters with such
arguments; 'Would a Ferrari be allowed to enter a marathon event?'
A society is even being formed to try to ban computers forever. Yet
not all players feel that way. And some humans can still beat them.
Perhaps some humans would quit but others would not.

Forsyth and Naylor (1985) believe that the above unhappy
scenario may come to pass and that it will be like a modern mining
company descending suddenly on a stone-age village. What happens to primitive peoples suddenly confronted with space-age technology and products that they cannot understand or hope to

surpass? Their culture and technology seems irrelevant and hopelessly outclassed. Their skills such as hunting, face-painting, and root gathering seem irrelevant. Some social thinkers try to get us to understand life for such displaced persons as the Australian Aborigine or some North and South American tribes by imagining that a vastly superior extraterrestrial culture takes over Earth. It would be dreadful. Members of such tribes sometimes become fringe dwellers. They live on welfare, take menial jobs, and often have serious alcohol problems. Perhaps humans will become the equivalents of the Australian Aborigines of the next century, with AI systems being like the colonising Europeans.

Perhaps this will happen, but perhaps it will not. However, if it does, it would be ironic that the last major exercise of human intelligence was to make itself redundant.

REFERENCES

Albert, R. S. (1975). Toward a behavioral definition of genius. *American Psychologist, 30,* 140–151.

Albert, R. S. (1983). The concept of genius. In R. S. Albert (Ed.), *Genius and eminence*. New York: Pergamon.

Anastasi, A. (1988). *Psychological testing*. New York: Macmillan.

Anderson, J. R. (1990). *Cognitive psychology and its implications*. San Francisco: Freeman.

Ashman, A. F. (1990). Intellectual disability. In A. F. Ashman & J. Elkins (Eds.), *Educating children with special needs*. Sydney: Prentice-Hall.

Ayllon, T., & Kelly, K. (1972). Effects of reinforcement on standardised test performance. *Journal of Applied Behaviour Analysis, 5*, 477–483.

Baron, J., Badgio, P. C., & Gaskins, I. W. (1986). Cognitive style and its improvement. In R. J. Sternberg (Ed.), *Advances in the psychology of human intelligence*. Hillsdale, NJ: Erlbaum.

Barr, A., & Feigenbaum, E. A. (1986). *The handbook of artificial intelligence*. Reading, MA: Addison-Wesley.

Benbow, C. P. (1988). Sex differences in mathematical reasoning ability in intellectually talented preadolescents. *The Behavioural and Brain Sciences, 11*, 169–232.

Berry, P. (1989). Mental handicap. In P. Langford (Ed.), *Educational psychology*. Melbourne: Longman-Cheshire.

Bierce, A. (1906). *The devil's dictionary*. New York: Doubleday.

Bloom, B. (1982). Master teachers. *Phi Delta Kappan, 63*, 664–668.

Campione, J. C., Brown, A. L., & Ferrara, R. A. (1982). Mental retardation and intelligence. In R. J. Sternberg (Ed.), *Handbook of human intelligence*. New York: Cambridge University Press.

Caplan, R. M. (1985). The controversy related to the use of psychological tests. In B. B. Wolman (Ed.), *Handbook of intelligence*. San Diego: Academic Press.

Cattell, R. B. (1937). Some further relations between intelligence, fertility, and socio-economic factors. *Eugenics Review, 29,* 171–179.

Cattell, R. B. (1987). *Intelligence: Its structure, growth and action.* Amsterdam: Elsevier.

Ceci, S. J., & Liker, J. (1986). Academic and nonacademic intelligence: An experimental separation. In R. J. Sternberg & W. K. Wagner (Eds.), *Practical intelligence.* Hillsdale, NJ: Erlbaum.

Chi, M. T. H., & Koeske, R. D. (1983). Network representation of a child's dinosaur knowledge. *Developmental Psychology, 19,* 29–39.

Cole, M., Gay, J., Glick, J. A., & Sharp, D. W. (1971). *The cultural context of learning and thinking.* New York: Basic Books.

Cox, C. M. (1926). The early mental traits of three hundred geniuses. In L. M. Terman (Ed.), *Genetic studies of genius: Volume 2.* Stanford, CA: Stanford University Press.

Cronbach, L. J. (1957). The two disciplines of scientific psychology. *American Psychologist, 12,* 671–684.

De Bono, E. (1976). *Teaching thinking.* London: Temple Smith.

DeFries, J. C., & Decker, S. N. (1981). Cognitive ability profiles in family of reading-disabled children. *Developmental Medicine 23,* 217–227.

Drew, C. J., Logan, D. R., & Harman, M. L. (1984). *Mental retardation: A life cycle approach.* St Louis: Times-Mirror.

Dreyfus, H. J., & Dreyfus, S. E. (1986). *Mind over machine.* New York: The Free Press.

Durant, J. R., Evans, G. A., & Thomas, G. P. (1989). The public understanding of science. *Nature, 340,* 11–14.

Ellis, H. (1904). *A study of British genius.* London: Hurst and Blackett.

Ellis, A. (1977). The basic clinical theory of rational-emotive therapy. In A. Ellis & R. Grieger (Ed.), *Handbook of rational-emotive therapy.* New York: Springer.

Evans, B., & Waites, B. (1981). *IQ and mental testing.* New York: Macmillan.

Eysenck, H. J. (1979). *The structure and measurement of intelligence.* Berlin: Springer-Verlag.

Eysenck, H. J. (1988). The concept of 'intelligence': Useful or useless? *Intelligence, 12,* 1–17.

Fagan, J. F. (1984). Infant memory. In M. Moscovitch (Ed.), *Infant memory.* New York: Plenum.

Feldman, D. (1979). The mysterious case of extreme giftedness. In H. Passow (Ed.), *The gifted and talented.* Chicago: University of Chicago Press.

Fichtelius, K.E., & Sjolander, S. (1972), *Smarter than man? Intelligence in whales, dolphins and humans.* New York: Pantheon.

Flynn, J. R. (1984). The mean IQ of Americans: Massive gains 1932–1978. *Psychological Bulletin, 95,* 29–51.

Flynn, J. R. (1987). Massive IQ gains in 14 nations: What IQ tests really measure. *Psychological Bulletin, 101,* 171–191.

Forsyth, R., & Naylor, C. (1985). *The hitchhiker's guide to artificial intelligence.* London: Chapman and Hall.

Frederiksen, N. (1986). Toward a broader conception of human intelligence. In R. J. Sternberg and W. K. Wagner (Eds.), *Practical intelligence.* Hillsdale, NJ: Erlbaum.

Frensch, P.A., & Sternberg, R. J. (1989). Expertise and intelligent thinking. In R. J. Sternberg (Ed.), *Advances in the study of intelligence.* Hillsdale, NJ: Erlbaum.

Frenzel, L. E. (1987). *Crash course in artificial intelligence and expert systems.* Indianapolis: Sams.

Galanter, E. (1962). Contemporary psychophysics. In E. Galanter (Ed.), *New directions in psychology.* New York: Holt, Rinehart and Winston.

Galotti, K. (1989). Approaches to studying formal and everyday reasoning. *Psychological Bulletin, 105,* 331–351.

Gardner, H. (1983). *Frames of mind: The theory of multiple intelligences.* New York: Basic Books.

Gettinger, M., & White, M. A. (1980). Evaluating curriculum fit with class ability. *Journal of Educational Psychology, 72,* 338–344.

Gould, J. L., & Gould, C. G. (1982). The insect mind: Physics or metaphysics? In D. R. Griffin (Ed.), *Animal mind–human mind.* New York: Springer-Verlag.

Gould, S. J. (1981). *The mismeasure of man.* New York: Norton.

Gray, M. (1987). Understanding AI, understanding ourselves. In S. Nash (Ed.), *Science and intelligence*. Northwood, U.K.: Science Reviews.

Griffin, D. R. (1984). *Animal thinking*. Cambridge MA: Harvard University Press.

Haugeland, J. (1985). *Artificial intelligence: The very idea*. Cambridge, MA: MIT Press.

Herman, L. M. (1980). Cognitive characteristics of dolphins. In L. M. Herman (Ed.), *Cetacean behavior*. New York: Wiley.

Herman, L.M. (1988). The language of animal language research. *Psychological Record, 38,* 349–362.

Herrnstein, R. J. (1973). *IQ in the meritocracy*. Boston: Little, Brown.

Hirsch, E. D. (1987). *Cultural literacy*. Boston: Houghton-Mifflin.

Hoffman, S. M. (1981). *The classified man*. London: Sphere.

Hofstadter, D. (1979). *Godel, Escher, Bach: An eternal golden braid*. London: Harvester.

Hollingworth, L. (1942). *Children above 180 IQ*. New York: World Book.

Holyoak, K. J., Koh, K., & Nisbett, R. E. (1989). A theory of conditioning: Inductive learning within rule-based default hierarchies. *Psychological Review, 96,* 315–340.

Horn, J. L., & Cattell, R. B. (1966). Refinement and test of the theory of fluid and crystallised intelligence. *Journal of Educational Psychology, 57,* 253–270.

Howard, R. W. (1987). *Concepts and schemata: An introduction*. London: Cassell.

Howe, M. J. A. (1988a). Intelligence as an explanation. *British Journal of Psychology, 79,* 349–360.

Howe, M. J. A. (1988 b, December 31). Perspiration beats inspiration. *New Scientist. 120,* 58–60.

Howe, M. J. A. (1989). Separate skills or general intelligence: The autonomy of human abilities. *British Journal of Educational Psychology, 59,* 351–360.

Humphrey, L. G. (1988). Trends in levels of academic achievement of blacks and other minorities. *Intelligence, 12,* 231–240.

Hunt, E. (1978). The mechanics of verbal ability. *Psychological Review, 85,* 109–130.

Jensen, A. R. (1969). How much can we boost IQ and scholastic achievement? *Harvard Educational Review, 33,* 1–123.

Jensen, A. R. (1980). *Bias in mental testing*. London: Methuen.

Jensen, A. R. (1981). *Straight talk about mental tests*. New York: The Free Press.

Jensen, A. R. (1988). Psychometric g as a focus for concerted research effort. *Intelligence, 11,* 193–198.

Johnson, R. C., & Brown, C. (1988). *Cognisers*. New York: Wiley.

Kail, R., & Pellegrino, J. W. (1985). *Human intelligence*. San Francisco: Freeman.

Kamin, L. J. (1974). *The science and politics of IQ*. Hillsdale, NJ: Erlbaum.

Kaufman, A. S., Reynolds, C. R., & McLean J. E. (1989). Age and WAIS-R intelligence in a national sample of adults in the 20–74 year age range. *Intelligence, 13,* 235–253.

Kausler, D. F. (1982). *Experimental psychology and human aging*. New York: Wiley.

Kekes, J. (1983). Wisdom. *American Philosophical Quarterly, 20,* 277–286.

Kemp, G. O., & McClelland, D. C. (1986). What characterises intelligent functioning among senior managers? In R. J. Sternberg & W. K. Wagner (Eds.), *Practical intelligence*. Hillsdale, NJ: Erlbaum.

Khan, R. F. (1985). Mental retardation and paternalist control. In R. S. Laura & A. F. Ashman (Eds.), *Moral issues in retardation*. Dover, NH: Croom-Helm.

Kirk, S. A., & Gallagher, J. J. (1986). *Educating exceptional children*. Boston: Houghton-Mifflin.

Kosslyn, S. M. O. (1980). *Image and mind*. Cambridge, MA: Harvard University Press.

Kuhn, T. S. (1970). *The structure of scientific revolutions*. Chicago: University of Chicago Press.

Labouvier-Vief, G. (1985). Intelligence and cognition. In J. E. Birren & K. W. Schaie (Eds.), *Handbook of the psychology of aging*. New York: Van Nostrand Reinhold.

Langley, P., & Zytkow, J. M. (1989). Data driven approaches to empirical discovery, *Artificial Intelligence, 40,* 283–312.

Lee, V. E., Brooks-Gunn, J., & Schnur, E. (1988). Does head start work? *Developmental Psychology, 24,* 210–222.

Lenat, D. (1976). *AM*. Unpublished doctoral dissertation, Stanford University.

Lohman, D. F. (1988). Spatial abilities as traits, processes and knowledge. In R. J. Sternberg (Ed.), *Advances in the psychology of human intelligence*. Hillsdale, NJ: Erlbaum.

Lohman, D. F. (1989). Human intelligence: An introduction to advances in theory and research. *Review of Educational Research, 59,* 333–373.

Luria, A. R. (1968). *The mind of a mnemonist.* New York: Basic Books.

Lynn, R. (1979). The social ecology of intelligence in the British Isles. *British Journal of Social and Clinical Psychology, 18,* 1–12.

Lynn, R. (1982). IQ in Japan and the United States shows a growing disparity. *Nature, 306,* 222–223.

Lynn, R. (1989). A nutrition theory of the secular increases in intelligence: Positive correlations between height, head size and IQ. *British Journal of Educational Psychology, 59,* 72–77.

Lynn, R., & Hampson, S. (1986). The rise of national intelligence: Evidence from Britain, Japan and the United States. *Personality and Individual Differences, 7,* 23–32.

MacKinnnon, D. W. (1962). The personality correlates of creativity. In C. W. Taylor (Ed.), *The second research conference on the identification of creative scientific talent.* Salt Lake City, UT: University of Utah Press.

Mackintosh, N. J. (1987). A natural history of intelligence in man and other animals. In S. Nash (Ed.), *Science and intelligence.* Northwood, U.K.: Science Reviews.

MacLeod, G., Rankin, M., & Wright, B. (1989). An analysis of experienced and student teachers' definition of the concept of intelligence. *Unicorn, 15,* 157–162.

MacPhail, E. M. (1987). The comparative psychology of intelligence. *The Behavioral and Brain Sciences, 10,* 645–695.

Maurer, D., & Maurer, C. (1988). *The world of the newborn.* New York: Basic Books.

McCormick, C. B., Miller, G. E., & Pressley, M. (1989). *Cognitive strategy research.* New York: Springer-Verlag.

Minsky, M. (1985). Why intelligent aliens will be intelligible. In E. Regis (Ed.), *Extraterrestrials: Science and alien intelligence.* New York: Cambridge University Press.

Minsky, M. (1988). Connectionist models and their prospects. In D. Waltz and J. A. Feldman (Eds.), *Connectionist models and their implications.* Norwood, NJ: Ablex.

Moravec, H. (1988). *Mind children.* Cambridge, MA: Harvard University Press.

Murphy, K. R., & Davidshofer, C.O. (1988). *Psychological testing.* Englewood Cliffs, NJ: Prentice-Hall.

Myerson, J., Hale, S., Hirschman, R., Hansen, C., & Christiansen, B. (1989). Global increase in response latencies by early middle age: Complexity effects in individual performances. *Journal of the Experimental Analysis of Behaviour, 52,* 353–362.

Nagel, T. (1974). What is it like to be a bat? *Philosophical Review, 83,* 435–450.

Neisser, U. (1976). General, academic and artificial intelligence. In L. B. Resnick (Ed.), *The nature of intelligence.* Hillsdale, NJ: Erlbaum.

Nisbett, R. E., & Wilson, T. O. (1977). Telling more than we can know: Verbal reports on mental processes. *Psychological Review, 84,* 231–259

Norman, D. A. (1988). *The psychology of everyday things.* New York: Basic Books.

Norris, D. (1990). How to build a connectionist idiot (savant). *Cognition, 35,* 277–291.

Olson, G. M., & Strauss, M. S. (1984). The development of infant memory. In N. Moscovitch (Ed.), *Infant memory.* New York: Plenum.

Otto, R. (1986). *Teachers under stress.* Melbourne: Hill of Content.

Penrose, R. (1989). *The emperor's new mind.* Oxford: Oxford University Press.

Pepperberg, I. M. (1990). Cognition in an African Gray parrot. *Journal of Comparative Psychology, 104,* 41–52.

Plomin, R. (1989). Environment and genes: Determinants of behaviour. *American Psychologist, 44,* 105–111.

Pryor, K. W., Haag, R., & O'Reilly, J. (1969). The creative porpoise. *Journal of the Experimental Analysis of Behaviour, 12,* 653–661.

Regis, E. (1985). *Extraterrestrials: Science and alien intelligence.* New York: Cambridge University Press.

Retherford, R. D., & Sewell, W. H. (1989). How intelligence affects fertility. *Intelligence, 13,* 169–185.

Reuning, H. (1988). Testing bushmen in the central Kalahari. In S. H. Irvine & J. W. Berry (Eds.), *Human abilities in cultural context.* New York: Cambridge University Press.

Roitblat, H. L. (1987). *Introduction to comparative cognition*. New York: Freeman.

Rood, R. T., & Trefil, J. S. (1981). *Are we alone?* New York: Scribners.

Rosenthal, R., & Jacobsen, C. (1968). *Pygmalian in the classroom*. New York: Holt, Rinehart and Winston.

Rumbaugh, D. M. (1990). Comparative psychology and the great apes: Their competence in learning, language and numbers. *Psychological Record, 40*, 15–39.

Rushton, J. P. (1988). Race differences in behaviour: A review and evolutionary analysis. *Personality and Individual Differences, 9*, 1009–1024.

Rybash, J. M., Hoyer, W. J., & Roodin, P. A. (1986). *Adult cognition and aging*. New York: Pergamon.

Salthouse, T. A. (1985). *A theory of cognitive aging*. Amsterdam: North Holland.

Schaie, K. W. (1983). The Seattle longitudinal study: A twenty-one year investigation of psychometric intelligence. In K. W. Schaie (Ed.), *Longitudinal studies of adult psychological development*. New York: Guilford Press.

Schaie, K. W., & Strother, C. R. (1968). A cross-sequential study of age changes in cognitive behaviour. *Psychological Bulletin, 70*, 671–680.

Schneider, W., Korkel, J., & Weinert, F. E. (1989). Domain-specific knowledge and memory performance. *Journal of Educational Psychology, 81*, 306–312.

Scriber, S. (1986). Thinking in action. In R. J. Sternberg & W. K. Wagner (Eds.), *Practical intelligence*. Hillsdale, NJ: Erlbaum.

Searle, J. (1980). Minds, brains and programs. *Behavioural and Brain Sciences, 3*, 417–457.

Serebriakoff, V. (1965). *IQ: A Mensa analysis and history*. London: Hutchinson.

Siegler, R. S. (1986). *Children's thinking*. Englewood Cliffs, NJ: Prentice-Hall.

Simons, G. L. (1983). *Are computers alive?* Brighton: Harvester.

Simons, G. L. (1984). *Introducing artificial intelligence*. Manchester: NCC Publications.

Simonton, D. K. (1988). *Scientific genius*. New York: Cambridge University Press.

Sizer, T. R. (1984). *Horace's compromise*. Boston: Houghton Mifflin.

Skemp, R. R. (1979). *Intelligence, learning and action*. Chichester, U.K.: Wiley.

Slavin, R. E. (1987). Grouping for instruction in the elementary school. *Educational Psychology, 22*, 109–127.

Smith, J., & Baltes, P. B. (1990). Wisdom-related knowledge: Age/cohort differences in response to life-planning problems. *Developmental Psychology, 26*, 494–505.

Snell, M. E., & Renzaglia, A. M. (1986). Moderate, severe and profound handicaps. In N. G. Haring & L. McCormick (Eds), *Exceptional children and youth*. Columbus, OH: Merrill.

Snyderman, M., & Herrnstein, R. J. (1983). Intelligence tests and the immigration act of 1924. *American Psychologist, 38*, 986–995.

Spearman, C. (1904). General intelligence objectively determined and measured. *American Journal of Psychology, 15*, 201–293.

Spearman, C. (1927). *The abilities of man*. New York: Macmillan.

Spitz, H. H. (1986). *The raising of intelligence*. Hillsdale, NJ: Erlbaum.

Spitz, H. H. (1988). Mental retardation as a thinking disorder. *International Review of Research in Mental Retardation, 15*, 1–32.

Sternberg, R. J. (1977). *Intelligence, information processing, and analogical reasoning*. Hillsdale, NJ: Erlbaum.

Sternberg, R. J. (1985). *Beyond IQ*. New York: Cambridge University Press.

Sternberg, R. J. (1986). *Intelligence applied*. San Diego: Harcourt, Brace, Jovanovich.

Sternberg, R. J., Conway, B. E., Ketron, J. L., & Bernstein, M. (1981). People's conceptions of intelligence. *Journal of Personality and Social Psychology, 41*, 37–55.

Sternberg, R. J., & Detterman, D. K. (1986). *What is intelligence?* Norwood, NJ: Ablex.

Sternberg, R. J., & Wagner, R. K. (1986). *Practical intelligence*. New York: Cambridge University Press.

Stones, E. (1984). *Psychology of education*. London: Methuen.

Sudd, J. H., & Franks, N. R. (1987). *The behavioural ecology of ants*. London: Blackie.

Tannenbaum, A. J. (1986). Giftedness: A psychosocial perspective. In R. J. Sternberg & J. E. Davidson (Eds), *Conceptions of giftedness*. New York: Cambridge University Press.

Teasdale, T. W., & Owen, D. R. (1989). Continuing secular increases in intelligence and a stable prevalence of high intelligence levels. *Intelligence, 13*, 255–262.

Teasdale, T. W., Owen, D. R., & Sorensen, T. I. A. (1988). Regional differences in intelligence and educational level in Denmark. *British Journal of Educational Psychology, 58*, 307–314.

Treffert, D. A. (1989). *Extraordinary people.* New York: Bantam.

Vandenburg, S. G., & Vogler, G. P. (1985). Genetic determinants of intelligence. In B.B. Wolman (Ed.), *Handbook of intelligence.* New York: Wiley.

Vernon, P. E. (1969). *Intelligence and cultural environment.* London: Methuen.

Wallach, M. A. (1976). Tests tell us little about talent. *American Scientist, 64*, 57–63.

Wechsler, D. (1952). *The range of human capacities.* New York: Hafner.

Weinberg, R. A. (1989). Intelligence and IQ. *American Psychologist, 44*, 98–104.

Weis, L., Altbach, P. G., Kelly, G. P., Petrie, H. G., & Slaughter, S. (1989). *Crisis in teaching.* New York: State University of New York Press.

Whimbey, A. (1975). *Intelligence can be taught.* New York: Dutton.

Willerman, L. (1979). *The psychology of individual and group differences.* San Francisco: Freeman.

Williams, R. L. (1974). Scientific racism and IQ: The silent mugging of the black community. *Psychology Today, 7*, 32–41.

Winston, P. H. (1970). *Learning structural descriptions from examples.* Unpublished doctoral dissertation, Massachusetts Institute of Technology.

Zigler, E., & Seitz, V. (1982). Social policy and intelligence. In R. J. Sternberg (Ed.), *Handbook of human intelligence.* New York: Cambridge University Press.

INDEX